RELIGION WITHOUT GOD

LONGMANS, GREEN AND CO.

55 FIFTH AVENUE, NEW YORK
221 EAST 20TH STREET, CHICAGO
TREMONT TEMPLE, BOSTON
210 VICTORIA STREET, TORONTO

LONGMANS, GREEN AND CO. LTD.

39 PATERNOSTER ROW, E C 4, LONDON
53 NICOL ROAD, BOMBAY
6 OLD COURT HOUSE STREET, CALCUTTA
167 MOUNT ROAD, MADRAS

RELIGION WITHOUT GOD

BY

FULTON J. SHEEN
Ph.D., S.T.D.

AGRÈGE EN PHILOSOPHIE DE L'UNIVERSITÉ DE LOUVAIN
MEMBER OF THE FACULTY OF THEOLOGY, THE CATHOLIC UNIVERSITY OF AMERICA

LONGMANS, GREEN AND CO.
NEW YORK · LONDON · TORONTO
1928

SHEEN
RELIGION WITHOUT GOD

Nihil Obstat: ARTHUR J. SCANLAN, S.T.D., *Censor Librorum*

Imprimatur: ✠ PATRICK CARDINAL HAYES, *Archbishop, New York*

New York, May 21, 1928

8175

COPYRIGHT · 1928
BY LONGMANS, GREEN AND COMPANY

FIRST EDITION

MADE IN THE UNITED STATES OF AMERICA

IMMUNI LABE VIRGINI

ORDINIS NOVI PRIMITIIS BEATÆ

A PATRE ELECTÆ QUÆ SPIRITU FECUNDA VERBO

NATURAM HUMANAM TRADENS DIVINÆ PLANE SUBMISSAM

NASCENTIS INDE RELIGIONIS FIERET MATER

EXIGUUM DICAT OPUSCULUM SUPPLEX

SIBI OPEM ALMÆ ROGANS PATRONÆ

PREFACE

PRESENT–DAY religion is not in evolution, but in revolution. Evolution implies growth from a germ, revolution a rupture with a principle; evolution has antecedents, revolution knows not its parentage. When we say that there is revolution in religion, we mean not merely a break with the past, but an abandonment as well of much that is best in the culture and heritage of tradition.

Until a generation ago religion was generally understood in terms of man's attitude toward a Supreme and Perfect Being; today, it is understood in terms of man's friendliness to the universe or as " faith in the conservation of human values." The term " God " is still retained by some thinkers, but it is emptied of all content and dissolved to fit every volatile idea and fleeting fancy. God has been dethroned, the heavens emptied and man has been exalted to His place in fulfillment of an evil prophecy that some day he would be like unto God. Problems which once centered about God now revolve about man, and those which were concerned with man are now fused with the universe. Theism is reduced to humanism and psychology to cos-

mology, for there is no longer a distinction made
between man and matter. God is humanized and
man is naturalized. The science of physics and
not the "flower in the crannied wall" has come
to tell us what God and man are.

No longer do men look to the past as to their
Golden Age; no longer do they have a memory of
a Garden wherein man walked with God in the
cool breezes of evening. The Golden Age is now
placed in the future, but not one wherein man re-
finds at the foot of a Tree the gifts he once lost
there, thanks to a God-Man unfurled on it like a
banner of salvation, but rather a future in which,
due to a cosmic evolutionary urge, man not only
makes but becomes God. Man in the supernatural
state, it is said, needs no Redeemer as in the natural state he needs no God. As a result of this
philosophy of self-sufficiency we have the queer
modern phenomenon of a religion without God and
a Christianity without Christ.

In these new terms religion remains the great
concern of the modern mind. Never before has
an irreligious world taken so much interest in religion. It is the one subject anyone may talk
about, though scientists alone may speak of science
and geographers alone of geography. The press is
teeming with it and university professors are lec-
turing about it even when they lecture against it.
But while it is true that there has never before
been so much *talking* about religion, it is equally
true that never before has there been so little *walk-*

ing in it. Religion today is only doctrinal, not practical — a concern of the Pure but not the Practical Reason. Its purpose seems to be to offer a consoling salve to erring consciences. Men first live and a doctrine is made to fit their living; bad thinking is flatteringly adjusted to bad living and thus phoenix-like a religion rises out of the ashes of irreligion.

Because of this new and revolutionary change in religion, the exponents of the traditional concept have lost the ear of the changing world. The terms " God " and " Religion " are still used, but they mean different things. It is easier for a Frenchman to understand an Englishman, than for a believer in a Perfect God to understand the God of Professor Alexander, " who in the strictest sense of the term is not a Creator but a creature." The two schools are talking a different language and revolving about different poles of thought: the older school is proceeding from God to religion while the new proceeds from religion to God.

The task before the philosopher of religion whose reason commits him to a belief in God, the Alpha and Omega of all things, is not to state contradictory theses which have no common denominator nor multiple with those of his flesh and blood contemporaries. Rather his task is to analyze the assumptions behind the modern view to determine whether or not they are justified. It is the things that are taken for granted in their position that must be challenged, for it may well be that philosophical assumptions are mere lyrical gratuities and their philosophy but free-verse poetry.

It is to this labor of a calm and rational study of the assumptions behind the contemporary idea of religion that we have committed ourselves in writing this book. The method is threefold: expository, historical, and critical. First, we have aimed to give an unprejudiced outline of the modern position both in its negative and positive aspects, refraining from all criticism; secondly, to trace out its historical origins, not so much through persons, as Jacques Maritain has admirably done in his " Les Trois Reformateurs," to which we acknowledge indebtedness, but rather through philosophical principles and their evolution; thirdly, to analyze the assumptions underlying the contemporary philosophy of religion and to present in a constructive way the rational ground for all religion from the natural point of view.

God in relation to the anti-intellectual tendencies of the present day was examined in our previous work " God and Intelligence," of which this present volume is a continuation. The two are destined to be a complete philosophy of religion from both its formal and material angles.

In conclusion we wish to thank Dr. Leon Canon Noel of the University of Louvain and Dr. Gerald B. Phelan of the University of Toronto for their scholarly inspiration and valued assistance. Deepest thanks too are offered to Rt. Rev. Msgr. Edward A. Pace, Ph.D. and Rt. Rev. Msgr. James

H. Ryan, Ph.D. of The Catholic University of
America for their learned and characteristically
kind help, and to Professor A. J. McMullen of
Harvard University for reading the book in manu-
script and offering many valuable suggestions to
make it more readable. For the tedious task of
making the Index we are grateful to our friend,
Rev. Henry J. Gebhard, M.A.

CONTENTS

PART I

Contemporary Philosophy of Religion

PART II

The Historical Origins of the Contemporary Idea of Religion

PART III

Critical Appreciation of the Contemporary Idea of Religion in the Light of the Philosophy of St. Thomas Aquinas

PART I
Contemporary Philosophy
of Religion

RELIGION WITHOUT GOD

PART I

Contemporary Philosophy
of Religion

CHAPTER I

MODERN RELIGION IN ITS NEGATIVE ASPECT

THE scientific study of religion has under-
gone tremendous changes during the last
four centuries, changes due in part to the
modern mode of approaching problems, and in
part to the universal adoption of the experimental
method. This changed attitude towards the problems of religion has been marked with each
succeeding century. The sixteenth century asked
for a "new Church," the eighteenth for a "new
Christ," the nineteenth for a "new God," and
the twentieth asks for a "new religion." In
response to these appeals and in the name of
"progress," "science" and "liberty," the Church
became a sect, Christ but a moral teacher, God the
symbol for the ideal tendency in things, and religion an attitude of friendliness to the universe.

The new conception of religion is quite different from the old; it is different because it has as

its heritage a vast array of negations and as its promise rich hopes for the glorification of man and not God. All these have contributed their share to usher in the new idea of religion: new scientific formulas which ever seek to overflow into theology, an increasing impatience with the traditional and the dogmatic, a growing demand for a system flattering to new ways of living, and finally a desire to reduce everything to a single category. Professor H. W. Carr declares that science is the most important of these influences. "It is the progress of science," he writes, "which has required philosophy from time to time to revise the concept of God. The great metaphysical task which confronts us today is to reform the notion of God which the mathematical philosophers of the seventeenth century have bequeathed to us, in order to bring it into accord with the new concepts of biological science."[1]

And what is this new idea of religion? It is briefly a religion without God, that is, God as traditionally understood. Religion, according to the twentieth century philosophers and theologians, centres not about God but man. "It is man first and not God," says one of the exponents of the new notion; "it is as much God only as man may seem to suggest or prove. Above all, it is God revealed by man and not man by God. Our revelation today is from earth to heaven, from clod to

[1] H. W. Carr, "Changing Backgrounds in Religion and Ethics," 1927, p. 74.

God — not vice versa as in the old days."[2] "The scientific interpretation of natural phenomena," says another, "has made the interest in God more remote, God's existence more problematical, and even the idea of God unnecessary. Mathematics and physics are making it increasingly difficult to assign a place for God in our co-ordinations and constructions of the universe; and the necessity of positing a first cause or of conceiving a designer, a necessity which seemed *prima facie* obvious to a pre-scientific generation, does not exist for us."[3] The word "God" may still be retained in this new idea of religion, but that word takes on an entirely new meaning; it may even reach such a volatile state as to become identified with almost anything from a psychical complex to an ideal. It may even be ignored altogether as it is, for example, by one for whom "new religion will be an outcome of the wants, the hopes and the aspirations of these our times and the near future."[4]

When we speak of the "modern" or the "contemporary" idea of religion we do not mean "modern" in the strict chronological sense of a definite period of time. Rather, we mean a "spirit" — a spirit which is so peculiar to contemporary ways of thinking and so different from the past that in contrast, the new outlook may be

[2] John Haynes Holmes, *The New Basis of Religion* in "Essays towards Truth," 1924, p. 218.

[3] H. W. Carr, "Changing Backgrounds in Religion and Ethics," 1927, p. 74.

[4] C. A. F. Rhys Davids, "Old Creeds and New Needs," 1923, p. 178.

called "modern." The new attitude toward religion is different both in degree and kind from anything which might be called either traditional or
orthodox. It is quite true that there are many notions of religion which do not fit in with the synthesis we are about to present. These notions and
systems may be modern in the sense that they are
presented in our own day but they are not modern
in the sense that they represent the "progressive
and liberating spirit" of contemporary philosophers and theologians.

It is with this new idea of religion that this book
is concerned;[5] special consideration should be
given it for certainly there could be no question of
greater importance or more fundamental than that
of the relationship between God and man. Man
is said to be "incurably religious," and as nothing
human was foreign to Terence so nothing religious
can be foreign to man.

It is only fair to the protagonists of the new
doctrines that they present their own case. For
that reason we propose to divide the work into
three sections. The first section presents the new
idea of religion sympathetically and uncritically;
the second section traces out its historical origins;
and the third examines it critically in the light of
the philosophy of St. Thomas Aquinas.

Every science has a double object: a *material*

---

[5] The modern idea of God is treated expressly and in detail in
"God and Intelligence," Fulton J. Sheen, London, 1925.

object which is the thing studied, for example, matter in physics; a *formal* object, which is the peculiar aspect or "angle" of the study, for example, in physics, matter again, inasmuch as it is in movement. A thorough-going study of modern religion will have to take account of both these objects. Not only that, it will also be obliged to consider the older and the more traditional ideas of religion, for every philosophical and theological movement is either a reaction or a departure from something which preceded it. This means that the modern idea of religion will have to be treated under both its negative and positive aspects; its negative aspect will be the criticism of the old notions it hopes to supplant, and its positive will be the expression of the new tenets it hopes to implant.

Although the following synthesis and summary of the contemporary idea of religion appears at the beginning of this study, *in ordine inventionis* it came only at the end. It has been extracted from the contemporaries themselves and is no *a priori* construction. It is not an architect's plan of something which is to be constructed; rather it is an artist's sketch of a reality already existing — an after-thought rather than an inspiration.

The Modern Idea of Religion

MATERIAL OBJECT	FORMAL OBJECT
Negative — no God (as traditionally understood). Positive — Values.	Negative — anti-intellectual. Positive — Religious Experience.

This book shall concern itself only with the material object of religion, the formal aspect having been already treated in *God and Intelligence*.[6]

The Material Object of Modern Religion Negatively Considered

God as the Supreme and Perfect Being is not the necessary object of religion. This statement represents the negative side of the modern idea of religion and its reaction to the traditional notion. This does not mean that the term God is no longer used in religion by our contemporaries. As a matter of fact, it is used, and used very often. But it is never taken to mean the Supreme Being of traditional thought. God may mean anything from a "harmonization of epochal occasions" to a "projected libido." Here we are not asserting the logical superiority of the traditional over the contemporary idea; we are just asserting a *fact* — viz., God as traditionally understood is no longer accepted as the object of religion. And what is the traditional conception of God? It is that of a Supreme and Perfect Being, the Alpha and the Omega of all things: the Alpha, for without Him there would never be things to progress or evolve; the Omega, for without Him there would never be a reason for their evolving. Perfect He is with the plentitude of Being with its transcendental proprieties of Unity, Truth and Goodness; not static, because Life itself;

[6] The negative aspect, pp. 9–31; pp. 62–141. The positive aspect, pp. 31–47, 141–218.

not dynamic, because Perfect; not evolving, because the Intelligibility of Evolution. Because He
is and because everything else *is not* but *has being,*
there is a dependence of all that is not Him on Him,
and this dependence is the foundation of all religion.

The reasons urged by contemporaries against
the traditional concept of God may be reduced to
three: the *philosophical,* the *psychological* and the
sociological.

Philosophical Negations of the Traditional Object of Religion

Though William James no longer exerts a personal influence in the world of philosophy, it is
nevertheless true that his works carry on the task
which he left unfulfilled. Pragmatism as a method
may be dead, but Pragmatism as a spirit is alive
and palpitating. Professor Julius S. Bixler of
Smith College, in his excellent presentation of " Religion in the Philosophy of William James " has
stressed this point. " Pragmatism," he writes,
" will appeal to the coming generation because of
its creative faith. . . . And James' believing,
achieving, creative individual will find a scope for
his powers and an application for his ideals un-
paralleled in history." [7]   Out of that vast array of
philosophical material he left behind there is only
a small but yet very important part of it which
interests us, namely, his idea of religion. The influ-

[7] 1926, p. 218.

ences which worked for his particular theory of religion were varied and complex. His Swedenborgian father and his empirical training in physiology and medicine equipped him to look upon physical results empirically. The anti-intellectualism of Bergson (the publication of whose "Creative Evolution" James regarded as one of the world's most important events, because it "killed intellectualism absolutely dead"), the pluralism of Renouvier, the utilitarianism of Mill, the reaction to the absolutists of Oxford, all conspired to make him the author of a religion which might be called the religion of a romantic utilitarian.[8]

Did James believe in a Perfect and Supreme Being as the object of religion? The answer is clearly in the negative. The best definition of religion he leaves us is to be found in his "Varieties of Religious Experience," where he says: "Religion, therefore, as I now ask you arbitrarily to take it, shall mean *for us the feelings, acts and experiences of individual men in their solitude, so far as they apprehend themselves to stand in relation to whatever they consider the divine.*"[9] Quite naturally, the meaning of the word "divine" must be the key to this notion, and we must go on to inquire what he means by it. Never is he clear in defining just what it is. "The word 'divine,'" he writes later on in the same work, "as employed therein, shall mean for us not merely the primal and the enveloping and real. . . . The divine shall

---

[8] René Berthelot, "Un Romantisme Utilitaire," 1922, Vol. 3.
[9] P. 31.

mean for us only such a primal reality as the individual feels impelled to respond to solemnly and gravely, and neither by a curse nor a jest." [10] The divine can mean no single quality, it must mean a group of qualities, by being champions of which in alternation, different men may all find worthy missions. "So a 'god of battles' must be allowed to be a god for one kind of person, a 'god of peace and heaven and home' for another." [11] This power which is beyond us and from whom saving experiences come need not be infinite. "All that the facts require is that the power should be both other and larger than our conscious selves. Anything larger will do, if only it be large enough to trust for the next step. It need not be infinite; it need only be solitary." [12]

In this work quite evidently God needs only to be a power, conscious like ourselves, but certainly not perfect. At one point James is logical with his pluralism and entertains the possibility of polytheism, in the sense of a union of these god-like selves.

But in order to make more clear the object of religion as understood by James, it is well to ask if the Absolute will do for religion, and then if the Scholastic notion of God will do. The Absolute can be dismissed at once. It has no religious values, being fit only to give us a " moral holiday." [13] He scandalized his hearers at Oxford by telling them: " Let the Absolute bury the Absolute." While he did not go so far as to believe that all Hegelians were prigs,

[10] *Ibid.*, p. 38.
[11] *Ibid.*, p. 487.
[12] *Ibid.*, p. 525.
[13] " Pragmatism," p. 72.

he did say that he somehow felt, that "all prigs ought to end, if developed, by becoming Hegelians."[14] But if the Absolute will not serve as the object of religion, will not God as conceived by the Scholastics do? James would not admit this either. First of all, the existence of God cannot be proved, and here, strange to say, James offers no other argument than the argument of authority: "that all idealists since Kant have felt entitled either to scout or neglect them (proofs) shows that they are not solid enough to serve as religion's all-sufficient foundation. . . . Causation is indeed too obscure a principle to bear the weight of the whole structure of theology."[15] Secondly, the attributes of God, as conceived by Scholastics are too barren and meaningless for this life; they are only the "shuffling and matching of pedantic dictionary adjectives, aloof from morals, aloof from human needs, something that might be worked out from the mere word 'God' by one of these logical machines of wood and brass which recent ingenuity has contrived as well as by a man of flesh and blood."[16]

What then will the object of religion be, and what will be the meaning of the word "divine"? In his latest work James declares himself in favor of the finite God. "I believe that the only God worthy of the name must be finite."[17] "And He is

[14] "Essays in Radical Empiricism," p. 276, ff. "Pluralistic Universe," pp. 115–116, pp. 47–48.
[15] "Varieties of Religious Experience," p. 437.
[16] Ibid., pp. 446–447.
[17] "Pluralistic Universe," pp. 124, 125.

finite either in power or in knowledge or in both." [18]
Ultimately, however, and to be logical with his
Pragmatism, James would have to admit that any
God which you could use would be the object of
your religion, and if you could not use one in your
religion then for you he would not exist. "If the
hypothesis of God works satisfactorily in the widest sense of the term, it is true." [19] If He does exist,
He is to be conceived more as a co-worker than a
sovereign. "He works in an external environment,
has limits and has enemies." [20] We can even help
Him "to be more effectively faithful to his own
greater tasks." [21] "God Himself in short may draw
vital strength and increase of very being from our
fidelity." [22]

While it is not so much to our point to decide
definitely just what kind of God James did believe
in, it suffices to know that religion for him de-
manded no perfect Supreme Being. God as traditionally understood certainly is not the God-concept
of William James, for whom God was "more
a powerful ally of ideals" rather than a "real existent Being." [23] A God who is "only the ideal tendency in things" [24] is a God already in a state of

[18] *Ibid.*, p. 311. Among other philosophers holding to the finite
God may be mentioned: F. C. S. Schiller, "Riddles of the Sphinx";
James Ward, "Realm of Ends"; H. G. Wells, "God the Invisible
King," and J. C. McTaggart, R. H. Rashdall, R. H. Dotterer, and
G. H. Howison.

[19] "Pragmatism," p. 299.

[20] "Pluralistic Universe," p. 124.

[21] "Varieties of Religious Experience," p. 517.

[22] "The Will to Believe," p. 61.

[23] "Letters," Vol. 2, pp. 213–214.

[24] "Pluralistic Universe," p. 124.

philosophical decomposition. Here is the suggestion of what becomes clearer in more recent philosophers; namely, religion which brings man into more increasing prominence. From a notion of a finite God whom we help in His tasks, or an "ideal tendency in things" to the notion of a God whom we not only help in tasks, but help to create is only a step. Huxley described the religion of Comte as "Catholicism without Christianity," and M. Berthelot continues the figure by saying that the "religion of William James is a Protestantism without Christianity."[25] In a certain sense it may be justly described as a religion without God, for God to him means only what each individual takes as the divine. It is a great departure from the traditional notion and a bold assertion of what was implied in the philosophy of Mill. With James' successors *it takes on a physical or a mathematical* turn but always retains the aseity of the individual in the face of a Perfect and Supreme Being whom thinkers of a different school looked upon as the source and foundation of all religion.

Religion according to Professor Alexander

This distinguished professor of Manchester University has given to the modern world a notion of religion which is quite unlike that of many of his contemporaries and yet has something in common with them; namely, its rejection of a Perfect and Supreme Being as the object of religion.

[25] *Op. cit.*, Vol. 3, p. 8.

His notion of religion can only be understood in relation to his whole philosophy of Space-Time. The stuff of which this universe is made and the matrix whence all things come, is spatio-temporal. This means that the universe is essentially a universe of motion, and of continuous redistribution of instants of Time among points of Space.

Characteristic of the universe of Space-Time is its constant differentiation into higher and higher complexes, a tendency constituting a nisus towards deity, for deity is the upward urge of evolution. Within the all-embracing stuff of Space-Time the universe exhibits, in its emergence in time, successive levels of finite existence, each with its own characteristic empirical quality. At one end of the scale it is undifferentiated Space-Time; at the other end progressive value. Among the three principal qualities, the highest known to us at present is mind or consciousness. Now, deity is always the next higher empirical quality to the one presently evolved. This is true throughout all the levels of existence. When, therefore, the "growing world" was nothing more than empirical configurations of Space-Time, Deity, which by definition is the next quality to the one presently evolved, was matter. When the growing world reached the level matter, deity was at the stage of life. When the world evolved to life, deity was at mind. We are now at the mind stage, and deity is the stage above us, always marching ahead of us very tantalizingly. When we evolve to the stage where deity is now, that stage will be the stage of angels and deity will move up a peg. Deity is therefore "a variable quality, and as the world grows in time, deity changes with it." [26] In brief, "God as actually possessing deity does not exist, but is an ideal, tending toward deity which does exist. . . . As an actual existent, God is the infinite world with its nisus towards deity." [27]

What is religion according to such a notion? Religion is communion with this future quality of deity. It is "the sense of outgoing to the whole universe in its process towards the quality of deity." [28] But, it may be asked, how can this future quality of deity affect us and be an object of religion? Professor Alexander recognizes the difficulty and attempts to answer it by saying that what acts upon us is what brings forth deity, namely the actual world. It contains deity in germ inasmuch as the actual is the seed of the future, and the future

[26] "It is clear that, while for us men deity is the next higher empirical quality to mind, the description of deity is perfectly general. For any level of existence, deity is the next higher empirical quality. It is therefore a variable quality, and as the world grows in time, deity changes with it. On each level a new quality looms ahead, awfully, which plays to it the part of deity. For us who live upon the level of mind deity is, we can but say, deity. To creatures upon the level of life deity is still the quality in front, but to us who come later this quality has been revealed as mind. For creatures who possessed only the primary qualities — mere empirical configurations of space-time — deity was afterwards what appeared as materiality, and their God was matter, for I am supposing that there is no level of existence nearer to the spatio-temporal than matter. On each level of finite creatures deity is for them some 'unknown' (though not 'unexperienced') quality in front, the real nature of which is enjoyed by the creatures of the next level." "Space, Time and Deity," 1922, Vol. 2, p. 348.

[27] *Ibid.*, p. 353.

[28] *Ibid.*, p. 402.

is previsible in so far as we can forecast it in spatio-temporal terms. Just as clairvoyants may see the future, so too, he says, " we may suppose that in religious experience the vague future quality of deity is felt, not in its quality, for that cannot be known, but as giving flavor to the experience of the whole world which it does not possess as merely an object of sense or thought." [29]

There is no further elaboration needed to show that the centre of religion, as understood by this philosopher, is not the God of a Leibnitz nor an Aquinas, but an entirely new concept born of a new science and a new physics. The difference is not merely that his notion of God is one in pursuit of deity, while the traditional notion of God is one who does not pursue but possesses; there is the added difference of our relation to God. Here it is that Professor Alexander separates his notion of religion most widely from all notions which may be classed as traditional. God, according to his opinion, is sustained and helped by us. "We also help," he writes, "to maintain and sustain the nature of God and are not merely his subjects. . . . God himself is involved in our acts and their issues, or as it was put above, not only does he matter to us, but we matter to him," [30] because he is " *in the strictest sense not a creator but a creature*." [31] Quite naturally, if we are not God-made but God-makers, then in virtue of this new relation religion will have an entirely different meaning. Religion will not

[29] *Ibid.*, p. 379. [30] *Ibid.*, p. 388. [31] *Ibid.*, p. 399, *italics ours.*

be something which "commands us to perform our
duties with the consciousness that they are the commands of God." Rather "it is religion to do our
duty with the consciousness of helping to create his
deity." Once it is allowed that "deity owes its being to pre-existing finites with their empirical qualities, and is their outcome,"[32] then religion will become co-operation with God instead of service of
God. It will be something adventurous, something
in which man takes a hand, and man instead of being just a puppet dependent on a Perfect Being will
have as his sublime vocation the duty of contribut-
ing to the deity of God, by his life and actions.
Such an idea of religion, Professor Alexander believes, makes "our human position more serious,
but frees it from the reproach of subjection to arbitrary providence."[33]

Professor Alexander leaves no doubt in the minds
of his readers that he has little sympathy for the theistic view of the world as commonly understood.
His statement that religion means a "consciousness
of helping God to create his deity" is not so important for our present concern as his repudiation
of a God Who possesses Deity in its plentitude,
and Whose Deity is not distinct from His Godhead.
Even the most magnificent gesture of reverence of
such a philosopher to the God of Augustine and
Aquinas and the thought of which they are its
noblest representatives, could not blind a reader
to the obvious fact that Professor Alexander is

[32] "Space, Time and Deity," 1922, Vol. 2, p. 39.   [33] *Ibid.*, p. 400.

through with God, who is not an evolving God. Whatever religion may be positively in his mind, certainly in its negative aspect it has no place in the Theism of the *philosophia perennis*.

Religion according to Professor A. N. Whitehead

Every one naturally approaches with respect any work by Professor Whitehead whose thinking in the field of mathematics, physics, and the philosophy of nature has been marked by profound originality and depth. Encouraged by success in these fields this distinguished scientist has branched out into the field of theology in his " Religion in the Making," which, despite its obtuse terminology and phraseology, has already gone into several editions. He has been described as " one of the worst living expositors of philosophy, though he could be one of the best." It would not do Professor Whitehead justice merely to state his theory of religion without giving his philosophy of the universe which lies behind it. No less than Spencer, Comte, James, he has inaugurated a new outlook on religion, this time based not on biology, or sociology or psychology but on physics and mathematics.

The Philosophy of the Universe

Contemporary philosophical thinking is breaking with the Cartesian tradition which has held sway the last three centuries. Philosophers no longer question the solutions of their immediate predecessors, or swing with the speculative pendulum from

one extreme of the dualist position to the other.
They are challenging the fountain head of their
whole tradition and sounding the depths of their
new philosophical edifice. The question no longer
is: which solution is right — the empirical or the
transcendental? but rather: is the problem we are
attempting to solve a legitimate one?

The challenge against the whole tradition of modern thought has been hurled by no one more boldly
than by Professor Alfred N. Whitehead in his
" Science and the Modern World." [34] Though it is
the Cartesian succession which is attacked, one
cannot help but wonder at the similar role he plays
to Descartes. In both there are the same protests
and the same reforms. Descartes protested against
the old physics of his time such as that of Telesius
with his two principles of heat and cold. Professor
Whitehead protests against the Newtonian physics
of matter and mass in space and time, which has
been serving us for two centuries. Descartes repudiated the decadent Scholasticism he learned at
Fleche, believing there was a conflict between it
and the new science of his time. Dr. Whitehead, in
his turn, repudiates the dualistic philosophy of
either matter or mind as substances, believing it
to be in conflict with the new physics. Both wished
to reform philosophy in the light of mathematical
and physical sciences, Descartes ending in a mathematical philosophy of clear ideas and Professor
Whitehead in a mathematical philosophy of relativity.

[34] 1926.

These are broad lines of similarity which we trace and not essential to the problem at hand. What is important is that the issue of the present philosophical parturition will probably be a new tradition of thought distinct and separate from that which at the present day is called modern. "Men can be provincial in time as well as in place," writes Professor Whitehead. "We may ask ourselves whether the scientific mentality of the modern world in the immediate past is not a successful example of such provincial limitation." [35] He asks the philosophers to examine their conscience and pleads with them in the words of Cromwell: "My brethren, by the bowels of Christ I beseech you, bethink you that you may be mistaken."

Modern philosophy, he argues, has been built on a false science — that of the seventeenth century — and the abandonment of that science must entail the abandonment of the philosophy and even the religion built upon it. The so-called solid foundations of science on which the last century built its anti-religion may after all be no more trustworthy than a house of cards. "The stable foundations of physics have broken up; also for the first time physiology is asserting itself as an effective body of knowledge, as distinct from a scrap-heap. The old foundations of scientific thought are becoming unintelligible. Time, space, matter, material, ether, electricity, mechanism, organism, configuration, structure, pattern, function, all require reinterpretation." [36]

[35] " Science and the Modern World," Chap. 1.   [36] *Ibid.*, p. 24.

That great changes are taking place in the scientific conception of the universe is indisputable. Whether the new notions are true or false has yet to be decided; the fact is, they do jar with the old physics. The curvature of space, for example, when compared with our " old " idea that two parallel lines travelling in the same direction will never meet is like a square peg to a round hole. The new quantum theory of physics upsets the lay notion that we never reach a limit in the unit of electricity. The theory of relativity comes as a surprise to the old scientists who looked upon things as essentially in space and accidentally in time, and rather baffles the untrained mind in its attempt to understand that space and time are relative not to the " simple location " of matter, but to the position and location of the observer. So too we are scandalized to learn that much of the physics and chemistry and geometry we studied in school is now to be scrapped like armaments. The point, we are told, is no longer considered an ultimate in mathematics, but merely a limit of a converging series of lines which cannot be understood apart from that series. Modern physics no longer considers the atom as ultimate but only as a centre of electro-magnetic influence. Geometry is no longer interested in solid bodies but only in their spatial relations. Meaningless in themselves, these relations are intelligible only in reference to the place which they occupy within the system, and the system is the spatio-temporal continuum. No so-called ultimate constituent is intelligible except in relation to the whole system within which it acts. In the words of Professor Ralph Barton Perry: " The physical world is no longer made up of reality behind the scenes which is known only by inference from the phenomenal appearances, but as a system of those appearances — which are no longer appearances in the old sense of the term, but the very substance and tissue of nature." [37]

The whole tradition of modern philosophy has been built on Newtonian physics, so the new school tells us. It may have a head of gold, but its feet are clay and the rock of the new physics hewn from the mountain of Einstein and relativity will sooner or later smash it to pieces. The time has arrived for a new philosophy of the universe.

There is a vast difference between them. The old philosophy was a philosophy of " substance," of " matter," of " nature." Old science from the Ionians up to our own day asked the question: " What is nature made of? The answer was couched in terms of stuff or matter or material — the particular name chosen is indifferent — which has the property of simple location in space and time, or, if you adopt the more modern ideas, in space-time. What I mean by matter, or material is anything which has this property of *simple location*." [38]

Such conceptions of nature, Professor Whitehead considers as mechanical and lifeless. In their place he prefers to carry over into physics the biological

---

[37] " Philosophy of the Recent Past," 1925.
[38] " Science and the Modern World," p. 72.

idea of the organism. The universe is not made up of stones, it is made up of organisms. *Substances are not the units of things and events are not their motion, but events are the units of things* and *what is described as a material object is just a feature of events*. There are no substances — there are only " events." Descartes willed three substances to philosophy — matter, mind and God. Hobbes dropped mind and God from his scheme of nature, but retained matter; Berkeley dropped matter and retained God and mind; the absolutists dropped matter and mind but retained God. Professor Whitehead drops all three. Substances belonging to the " old physics of simple location " are antiquated and guilty of the " Fallacy of Misplaced Concreteness."

If substances do not exist, then what does exist? Professor Whitehead answers: " events, moments, epochal occasions." [39] What we call creatures, or things, or substances are in reality only " epochal occasions." The motion or the event is not an accident of a substance, rather, to put it in the old terminology, it is the substance which is the " accident of the event." The ground or the basis of all things is space-time, and " space-time is nothing else than a system of pulling together of assemblages into unities. But the word ' event ' means one of these spatio-temporal unities." [40] There is complete interdependence of each and every part of the universe, beginning with space, of which every volume

[39] " Religion in the Making," 1927, p. 91.
[40] " Science and the Modern World," p. 106.

mirrors in itself every other volume, and time, of which every moment has reference both to the past and the future. "Everything is everywhere at all times." [41] Each event has a past and a future and is bound up with both.

In other words, the principle at work in this spatio-temporal universe, which links one thing to another and makes all things interdependent is " the principle of concretion." In its simplest form this principle was expressed by Tennyson in his lines about the little flower in the crannied wall: " If I knew you, root and all in all, I should know what God and man is." The principle of concretion means that everything that exists, involves in some way the totality of all being. Everything which is, has some share in the flower, the sun, the moon, the stars, the soil, the air; not only that, even the past events are "organic" in some way with it, such as the disturbances of the earth, laws of evolution and growth and even armies or warriors who passed over that very soil on which the flower grows. Everything that is or ever has been or ever will be is organic in that flower in concentric circles of influence. The flower "prehends" all being; the universe is " concreted" in the flower. [42] The flower is the "unification of the universe, whereby its various elements are combined into aspects of

[41] *Ibid.*, p. 133.
[42] " Things are separated by space, and are separated by time; but they are also together in space and together in time, even if they be not contemporaneous. I will call these characters the ' *separative* ' and the ' *prehensive* ' character of space-time." " Science and the Modern World," p. 94.

each other." It might also be called an "epochal occasion" for an "epochal occasion" is a microcosm inclusive of the whole universe.[43] The flower mirrors the universe.

The flower, is "concrete" and the concrete means the unification of the many in the one, e.g., the color, the earth, the moisture, the sunlight, etc. But there is something important to be added. Not only do other things enter into a particular thing, but *something else* enters in which is more important, and that something else is "form" or possibility or universal. Everything in the world which is "concreted" existed as a form before it came into being in this spatio-temporal universe. A Scholastic might say that all things in the world were made according to the archetypal ideas in the mind of God. Everything was once a form before it had existence, or when it existed in the realm of the possibles. Now these forms enter into things to make them what they are. Not only that, new forms enter into concrete things in the process of the evolution or the unfolding of the universe.[44]

In summary, everything in this universe, or every creature, or even better "every epochal occasion" ("epochal occasions are the creatures") has two sides. On one side it "concretes" or brings together

---

[43] "Religion in the Making," p. 100.

[44] "In the concretion the creatures are qualified by the ideal forms, and conversely ideal forms are qualified by the creatures. Thus the epochal occasion which is the emergent, has in its own nature the other creatures under the aspect of these forms, and analogously it includes the forms under the aspect of these creatures. It is thus a definite limited creature, emergent in consequence of the limitations thus mentally imposed on each other by the elements." *Ibid.*, p. 93.

actual elements of the universe; on the other side, viz., its creative or formative side, it is made up of ideal forms which enter into the actual epochal occasion during the creative process or the unfolding of the universe. "But these are not two actual entities, the creature and creativity. There is only one entity which is the self-creating creature." [45]

Now a question arises which has great consequences for religion. What effects the union of the two sides of the epochal occasion? What introduces the new form into the present concrete thing? What gave the giraffe a long neck, supposing that at one time he was a mere "epochal occasion" with a short neck? The forms are not actual; being only possibilities they have need of some determination. There must be something to decide when the time is ripe for the extra hump on the camel, or when matter is to blossom into life.

The boundless wealth of possibility in the realm of abstract form would leave each creative phase still indeterminate, unable to synthesize under determinate conditions the creatures from which it springs. The definite determination which imposes ordered balance on the world requires an actual entity imposing its own unchanged consistency of character on every phase.[46]

This something is God.

And what is God? Is God, in the answer of the catechism, "the Creator of heaven and earth"?

[45] "Thus the epochal occasion has two sides. On one side it is a mode of creativity bringing together the universe. This side is the occasion as the cause of itself, its own creative act. . . . On the other side, the occasion is the creature. This creature is that one emergent fact." *Ibid.*, p. 101.

[46] *Ibid.*, p. 94.

No, God is the "Principle of Concretion."[47]   And
what is the Principle of Concretion?   It is the system of organization which makes all abstract forms
and all things have a share in the constitution of
every other thing in the universe.   It is God who
determines the universe and admits certain forms
into the creative process when that process is ripe
for them.

On first glance it might seem that Professor
Whitehead holds to the common-sense conception
of God.   There does seem to be a Providential
ordering of the universe in his system; all things do
seem to have been made according to patterns in the
mind of God; God does seem to be beyond this universe and identified with it — but this is only seeming.   The God of Professor Whitehead is the God
of Professor Whitehead, and not the living God of
traditional thought.

First of all, God, according to Professor Whitehead, is not a transcendent being.   If He were, he
argues, it would be impossible to know Him, for
the reason that any proof which commences with
considerations drawn from the actual world can
never rise above the actuality of that world.   If
God is beyond this universe of space and time, independent of both these physical qualities, He would
be non-existent as far as we are concerned for "we
know nothing beyond this temporal world."[48]

[47] "Science and the Modern World," p. 250.
[48] An analysis of the world "cannot discover anything not included
in the totality of the actual fact and yet explanatory of it."   "Religion
in the Making," pp. 71, 90.

This one difference between the new and old
conception of God is fundamental; the old philosophy which Professor Whitehead spurns believed
in a Being Who was independent of the actual world,
transcendent to it, and yet knowable through the
visible things of the world. But there are yet other
reasons why the new God of Professor Whitehead
is quite a different species from that represented to
us, for example, in the philosophy of St. Thomas,
and it is this : if God is not beyond this actual spatio-
temporal universe He must in some way be bound
up with it. And such is the case. The inherent
nature of the spatio-temporal universe is God. God
Himself is not concrete like the flower in the crannied wall, but He is the principle which constitutes
the concreteness of things. As the "Principle of
Concretion " He is the order of the universe, and
since the order is immanent in the universe it can
be truly said that God is immanent in the universe.
"The actual world is the outcome of the æsthetic
order, and the æsthetic order is derived from
the immanence of God." [49] God enters into each
"epochal occasion" along with the concrete element and the formal element, the "creatures and
the creativity." [50] Each new "epochal occasion introduces God into the world." The actual world is
the base for which He provides the ideal form. "He
adds himself to the actual ground from which every

[49] *Ibid.*, p. 105. For the author the order of this universe is not
conceptual or moral, but æsthetic. It is the æsthetic sense which makes
us aware of the concrete fulness of things.

[50] *Ibid.*. p. 90.

creative act takes its rise." He is the great Ideal, and the power by which He sustains the world is that of Himself as this idea. Although omniscient, He is limited and finite in some respect. Evil fights against Him. He may also be described as a "fusion," for it is He Who fuses together all the possibilities of the world in an harmonious way. "Apart from Him there would be no actual world with its creativity, and apart from the actual world with its creativity there would be no rational explanation of the ideal vision which constitutes God." [51]

God then is not outside the universe as a Power, nor immanent in it by His causality, nor is He the end toward which all creation moves. God is not even a substance — nothing is, for there are only "nows" and "thens." What we call things are combinations of something very much like energy which he calls "creativity," something very much like abstract archetypal ideas which he calls "forms," and something unlike anything a pre-Einsteinian philosopher or theologian has ever dreamed of, which he calls "God."

This is not the place to discuss the merits of such an outlook on the universe, and whatever be its merits it has already established itself in the good graces of philosophers who are already tired of biological and psychological and sociological interpretations of religion. It answers the craving for novelty; it does more: it is in apparent keeping with

[51] "Religion in the Making," pp. 153, 156, 157.

the new physics and the new science. It breaks with
the past; it ushers in a new religion in which the
traditional concept of God is banished to the
scrap-heap of Ionian physics and Cartesian substances.

Religion according to Professor Otto

Religion, since a long time, has been confused
with many things which are not religion, such as
ethics, æsthetics, art and science. In certain quar-
ters there has been growing a dissatisfaction with
such all-inclusive religion and an attempt has been
made to analyze its essential elements. The best
work in this field has been done by the German philosophers, first of whom, we might mention Professor Troeltsch who along with Professor Otto has developed the doctrine of the religious *a priori*. This
a priori is to be understood in a wider sense than
used by Kant. " In the ethical, the religious and
the teleologico-æsthetic reason " writes Troeltsch,
" Kant recognizes an *a priori*, which in that
case naturally signifies, not the synthetic unifying function of scientific comprehension, but the
way of judging and regarding the actual under
ethical, religious and teleologico-æsthetic points of
view, which is a necessity for reason and proceeds
in accordance with its own laws." [52] Behind psychical experiences of all kinds there is the *a priori*
which enables us to discover values in the realm
of facts, and to distil out of our impressions and our

[52] " Gesammelte Schriften," 1913, Band 2, p. 758.

sense knowledge, those finer things which enter into religion strictly so called.

Professor Otto [53] has striven to define more accurately the nature of the religious *a priori*. Over and above ethical and moral categories there is another category in us which is bound up with our nature and inseparable from it. This category, or principle of interpretation and valuation is not moral or ethical, neither can it be translated into rational concepts. It is the category of the "numinous" or the "holy."

Since it is primitive it cannot be defined, but can be communicated only by suggestion and analogy.[54] Every human being possesses it, though not everyone realizes it or uses it; some never call it into being. "Most men have only the 'predisposition' in the sense of a receptiveness and susceptibility to religion and a capacity for freely recognizing and judging religious truth at first hand."[55] All men, for example, have a sense of the beautiful but not everyone calls it into action or develops that sense. So it is with this religious *a priori*. It is there rich in promise, if we would but make use of it.

The religious *a priori* is something deeper than Kant's practical reason though it bears many analogies with it. It is essentially non-rational in character, though Professor Otto is not always clear as to what he means by the non-rational. Sometimes

---

[53] Das Heilige," English translation by John W. Harvey, 1923.
[54] *Ibid.*, p. 7.
[55] *Ibid.*, p. 181.

it seems that it is the non-definable,[56] at other times
it is that which produces in us an emotion and not
a concept.[57] This non-rational activity, this power
of " divination," this category of the " holy," is to
be referred to something still deeper than reason,
namely to that which Mysticism has named the
"fundus animæ " — the *Seelengrund*. It is not
constituted by a rational reflection on things any
more than is the Kantian Practical Reason, but it is
occasioned by things; it does not *arise out* of sense
impressions like the idea in Scholastic thought, but
only by *their means*. " They are the incitement, the
stimulus and the ' occasion ' for the numinous experience to become astir, and, in so doing, to begin
— at first with a naïve immediacy of reaction — to
be interfused and interwoven with the present world
of sense experience, until, ~~ dually, it disengages
itself from this and takes its stand in absolute contrast."[58] In the numinous experience the *a priori*
cognitive elements are not so much perceptions as
they are interpretations and valuations of experience. "The facts of the numinous consciousness
point therefore — as likewise do also the ' pure concepts of the understanding ' of Kant and the ideas
and value-judgments of ethics and æsthetics — to
a hidden substantive source, from which the religious ideas and feelings are formed, which lies in the
mind independently of sense-experience; a ' pure
reason ' in the profoundest sense which, because of
the surpassingness of its content, must be distin-

[56] *Ibid.*, pp. 1, 5, 60–61.   [58] *Ibid.*, p. 117.
[57] *Ibid.*, pp. 8–10, 140.

guished from both the pure theoretical and the pure practical reason of Kant, as something yet higher or deeper than they." [59]

So much in general for the category of the Holy or the numinous — it is primitive, it is non-rational. But what elements are contained in it, when it is subjected to an analysis. Professor Otto enumerates five: (1) *The element of awefulness,* which in its primitive form is nameless fear, and in its developed form survives in the quality of exaltedness or sublimity attributed to the Deity in such cries as "Holy, Holy, Holy." (2) *Overpoweringness.* In the first element one has the consciousness of "having been created;" in this, one has the "status of the creature." This is the strain in religion that makes for self-annihilation, and for making God all. (3) *The element of urgency or energy,* an example of which is to be found in the idea of the "wrath" of God or the "consuming flame" of Divine Love of which mystics write. (4) *The wholly other or mysterious,* viz., "that which is quite beyond the sphere of the usual, the intelligible, and the familiar, which therefore falls quite outside the limits of the ' canny ' and is contrasted with it, filling the mind with blank wonder and astonishment." [60] (5) *The element of fascination,* namely that element which impels us not to retreat from the divine but rather to approach and commune with it. Salvation, atonement, reconciliation are all manifestations of this element.

[59] "Das Heilige," English translation by John W. Harvey, 1923, p. 117.   [60] *Ibid.,* p. 26.

In treating each element Professor Otto over and over again insists that there are no concepts or dogmas or rational compartments into which they can be fitted. The transports of the mystic are as unintelligible to the secular mind as the felicity of the lover to the unromantic. The " Holy " lies beyond syllogisms and reasoning processes; it is more deep than logic and far more fundamental. The rational element is only an afterthought or what Professor James called " the outbuilding."

The question which interests our special problem now presents itself. *Does* the religion of *Das Heilige* admit God in the traditional sense of the word? The answer is negative, both from the historical and the philosophical point of view. From the historical point of view, because Professor Otto denies primitive Monotheism, and seems to take a substantial religious evolution for granted, never making a distinction between Buddhistic and Christian mysticism or even attempting a distinction of the true and the spurious.[61] From the philosophical point of view he departs from a belief in a Perfect Being, not only because he has eliminated the rational from religion, but because he seems to make the essence of religion consist in the emotion rather than the object upon which the emotion is directed. At most he will only concede that the "numinous is *felt* as objective and outside the self," [62] which of course gives no guarantee that it is really objective. If religion has an object for Professor Otto it is that element in things which

<hr />

[61] *Ibid.*, p. 133, 135.   [62] *Ibid.*, p. 11.

produces in us an " eerie " sensation of being in the presence of something aweful, mysterious and fascinating.   This element *in things* whatever it may be certainly is not God, the Alpha and Omega of all things; and this one important fact in the religious philosophy of Professor Otto is sufficient to range him with an ever increasing group of present day thinkers who have protested against traditional thought on the subject of God.

Religion according to Mr. Bertrand Russell

In an article entitled "The Essence of Religion"[63] this author develops the idea that in man there is something infinite and something finite. The infinite in him is the principle of union with the world in general by which he knows of it and loves it as something beyond the categories of time and space and *this* and *that*.   It is that in man which transcends the petty selfishness of the ego and goes out in search not for *my* good but for *the good*.

The finite nature in man, on the contrary, is a principle of disunion, for it is that which makes the individual man assert his individuality and consequently his selfishness, and demarcates him from all other men and the rest of the universe.

In proportion as this infinite grows in us we live more completely the life of universal nature.   The finite self is the gaoler of the universal soul and these prison walls of the body must be broken down if life

---

[63] " Das Heilige," English translation by John W. Harvey, 1923, *Hibbert Journal*, Vol. 11, p. 46 ff.

is to be lived at its best. "Sudden beauty in the
midst of strife, uncalculating love, or the nightwind
in the trees, seem to suggest the possibility of a life
free from the conflicts and the pettiness of our every-
day world, a life where there is peace which no mis-
fortune can disturb." [64] But what is this infinite
which at times so overwhelms us? Is it an object
or is it an attitude? "The quality of infinity which
we feel, is not to be accounted for by the perception
of new objects, other than those that at most times
seem finite; it is to be accounted for, rather, by a
different way of regarding the same objects, a contemplation more impersonal, more vast, more filled
with love, than the fragmentary, disquiet consideration we give to things when we view them as means
to help or hinder our own purposes." [65]

All that is required to pass from the life of the
finite self to the life of the infinite is absolute self-
surrender. And from that moment on, when the
finite self appears as a death, "a new life begins,
with a larger vision, a new happiness and wider
hopes."

Now is God necessary for such a surrender? No,
— and this is the important point. The surrender
might possibly be easier for some if they believed in
an all-wise God "but it is not in its essence dependent on this belief or on any other." [66]

God then is not necessary for religion. All that
is required is a communion with our infinite life,
thanks to the crushing of the finite. From this

[64] *Ibid.*, p. 48.   [65] *Ibid.*, p. 49.   [66] *Ibid.*, p. 50.

point, Mr. Russell demonstrates that the three elements of Christian worship, which he enumerates as "worship, acquiescence and love," can get along very well without God. For worship, God is not a necessary object. The object is "the ideal good which creative contemplation imagines."[67] Acquiescence, in its turn, does not demand a God on whose Will we are dependent: "it consists in freedom from anger and indignation and preoccupied grief."[68] Lastly, love, can exist very well in religion without a God Who is Love, as St. John reminds us: "in a religion which is not theistic, love of God is replaced by worship of the ideal good."[69]

Religion then, in conclusion, must be said, according to Mr. Russell, "to derive its power from the sense of union with the universe which it is able to give." Since God's existence is denied, the new religion must be one which "depends only on ourselves. . . . We with our ideals must stand alone, and conquer inwardly the world's indifference."[70] It is man who matters in this subject of religion. "For in all things it is well to exalt the dignity of Man, by freeing him as far as possible from the tyranny of the non-human Power."[71]

Such is the essence of religion as understood by Mr. Bertrand Russell, a conception in which religion dispenses with God and puts man and ideals in His place. If it be the correct explanation of re-

[67] *Ibid.*, p. 52.
[68] *Ibid.*, p. 56.
[69] *Ibid.*, p. 59.
[70] *Ibid.*, p. 62.
[71] "Free Man's Worship" in "Mysticism and Logic," 1925, p. 46 ff.

ligion, then Mr. Russell is right in saying "Man worships at the shrine his own hands have made."

Religion according to Professors Croce and Gentile

Not only is the modern philosophy of France, Germany, England, and America evolving a new religion which leaves no room for the God of reason, but even Italy, which so violently reacted against Naturalism, has also joined the ranks as if to make the demand universal. Italian philosophy like that of France, became tired of Positivism, and reacted against it in an Idealistic fashion as Aliotta has so well shown [72] and then finally developed a philosophy of its own.

The new thought, although Hegelian in inspiration, is not wholly so in its finished product, particularly in so far as religion is concerned. According to Hegel, it is only through a system of concepts that religion can be shown to be true and not by mere subjective intuitions or emotions. The inevitable conclusion is that religion is to be resolved into philosophy.

There is not perfect agreement as to the exact manner in which religion is resolved into philosophy. For Croce [73] spirit must be either theoretical or practical. If theoretical, it is either an intuition which is Æsthetics, or a concept which is Logic; if practical, it is either useful, which is Economics, or Good which is Ethics. The point to be stressed

[72] "The Idealistic Reaction against Science," 1914.
[73] "Filosofia della Pratica," 9th ed., 1923. "Estetica come scienza dell' espressione e linguistica generale," 5 ª ediz., 1922.

here is that there is no room for a specific religious
element; religion is only a hybrid of the above mentioned forms; the Kingdom of God becomes the
Kingdom of Man; and religion becomes the Dialec-
tics of Thought.

Gentile's view of religion agrees with Croce as
far as the fundamental notion is concerned, namely
that Religion is man contemplating his own spirit
idealized. But while Croce tends towards distinc-
tions, Gentile is on fire with Unity, and herein
lies the difference. Gentile [74] is more concerned
with the theory of the Spirit as essentially a self-
realizing act. The Spirit is always becoming aware
of itself as a subject, then of itself as an object, and
finally returning to itself and knowing itself as the
synthesis of both. Religion is that second moment
in which the Spirit discovers itself as an *object*.
The overwhelming sense of the *otherness* of the object blinds the mind to itself as subject. Hence
man forgets himself, annihilates himself before his
object, which now assumes, because of its absoluteness, the very character of God. God then
is the object taken apart from its relation to the
subject.

Further elaboration is unnecessary. The God of
the new Italian religious philosophy is not objective
to the thinker, but like that of Professor Alexander
is a "creature" of Thought or Spirit; or, to para-

[74] *Theory of Mind as Pure Act,* "Discorsi di Religione," 1920.
God for Croce and Gentile is not a Reality separate from the human
spirits. It is the human spirit as conscious of its own identity with the
absolute spirit. Man is God inasmuch as he is the world's self-consciousness.

phrase the words of Mr. Russell, "we worship at the shrine our own spirit has made."

Religion according to Professor Gerald B. Smith

In an article entitled " Is Theism essential to Religion? " [75] Gerald Birney Smith, the Editor of the *Journal of Religion,* declares that Theism as the basis of religion no longer has a cogent appeal, and hence an entirely new concept of religion is necessary to fit in with the temper of the day.

The negative side of the paper is devoted to the proof of the three following propositions: men can be good citizens without appealing to God; they can be good scientists without affirming Theism; and finally, they can be religious without a belief in God.

First, politically, there has been a dissolution of the theological theory of politics. " In the experience of modern nations it was found that the doctrine of the divine right of the ruler could be too easily invoked to sustain a royal tyranny. The democratic movement which has inspired modern political movement has been based upon the primary tenet of the rights of *man.*" [76] The consequence of a struggle for democratic rights is the secularizing of politics. And in terms of practical experience, the secularization of government means that citizenship is complete without any distinctively religious requirements. An atheist has the same rights as a theist. " If, now, in our political

[75] *Journal of Religion,* Vol. 5, No. 4, July 1925.
[76] *Ibid.,* p. 358.

practice, it makes no essential difference whether one is a theist or not, if one can be a good citizen without believing in God, theism comes to be a matter of taste rather than a fundamental doctrine." [77]

Secondly, as theism is not necessary for politics neither is it necessary for science. The old theological supervision of science has passed into the background. It is the detail now rather than "speculations" regarding reality which interests scientists. The conception of God in no way furthers the empirical method, and therefore is unnecessary for it. Furthermore "it is to be noted that scientists generally speak of *religion* rather than of God. Their belief in God, in so far as it persists at all, is a rather vague emotional inheritance." [78] Not only that, the advance of science shows non-theistic explanations of problems. "Epidemics are now averted by controlling sources of infection rather than by prayer. Material prosperity is seen to depend on economic factors rather than on generalized moral attitudes." [79] In short, in the face of practical pluralism, the "appeal to God occupies a decreasing place in modern religion."

Thirdly, men can be religious without Theism. Psychology has shown, Dr. Smith points out, that the fundamental realities in our religious experience are not ideas, but instinctive reactions of the human organism to the stimulus of environment. In

[77] *Journal of Religion*, Vol. 5, No. 4, July 1925. p. 359
[78] *Ibid.*, p. 360.   [79] *Ibid.*, p. 361.

other words "religion exists first, theological ideas are secondary." [80]   Just as the Babylonian religions outgrew a belief in their Shamash, for he was only a symbol of their ideals rather than an actual deity, so too the modern age is outgrowing the old traditional notion of God.

Dr. Smith leans kindly to the ideas of Professor E. S. Ames who would correlate religion with the actual, scientific and social forces dominant in life. God becomes something *in experience,* or as this author puts it: "The character of God will be found in the experienced reciprocity between man and his environment rather than in the realm of metaphysical speculation." [81]   The belief in God means that there may be found, not merely within the circle of human society, but also in the non-human environment on which we are dependent, a quality of the cosmic process akin to the quality of our own spiritual life.   Through communion with this qualitative aspect of the cosmic process human life attains an experience of dignity, and reinforcement of spiritual power." [82]   "Religion for men who think in this fashion will consist in a great mystic experiment rather than in the acceptance of a theological system . . . God will be very real to the religious man, but his reality will be interpreted in terms of social reciprocity with an as yet inadequately defined cosmic support of values, rather than in terms of theistic creatorship and control." [83]

[80] *Ibid.,* p. 362.
[81] *Ibid.,* p. 373.
[82] *Ibid.,* p. 375.
[83] *Ibid.*

Some Modern Definitions of Religion

The foregoing exposition of religion has quite clearly proved to us that today religion is conceived in other terms than those of God and man. Even the word "God," in some cases, is ignored; in others it takes on a new content. A few definitions of religion extracted from current writings bear out this point.

"Indeed the existence of a supreme being as a person external to ourselves and to the world, like a magnified human creature, is not affirmed by the religious consciousness, and if it were known to be a fact, would have no bearing on religion." [84]

"It is probably true that it is best to avoid the term 'God' in purely philosophical writing, just as in the critical discussion of poetry, we need not refer to the Muses." [85]

"I wish you here to agree to my giving the name of God to the sum of the forces acting in the cosmos as perceived and grasped by human mind. We can therefore now say that God is one, but that though one, has several aspects." [86]

"Though the traditional content of the term 'God' is to be denied, the value of that term is not to be denied. Religion needs that word although it needs to overhaul its meaning." [87]

[84] B. Bosanquet, "Value and Destiny of the Individual," 1913, p. 254.

[85] J. Mackenzie, "God as Love and Wisdom and Creative Power," *Hibbert Journal.* Vol. XXIV, no. 2, p. 199.

[86] Julian S. Huxley, "Science and Religion," edited by F. S. Marvin, 1923, Chap. XI.

[87] Julian Huxley, "Essays of a Biologist," p. 235.

"Religion is an emotion resting on a conviction of a harmony between ourselves and the universe at large."[88]

"Religion is the force or faculty prompting to action in accordance with the highest ideals having reference to the future of the individual and the race."[89]

"Religion is due to the interplay of many forces, the family, the community, the priest, the bishop, and other children. . . . The religious experience is best described as the experience of the ideal, the realization of value which comes in an exalted emotional moment that makes us one with our kind, at least with the best of our kind, who might include the whole of them."[90]

Religion is "the pure embodiment of the practical motive — that is, the highly interested desire for a place of action which will secure the maximum of good fortune from the environment as a whole."[91]

"Religion is a projection in the roaring loom of time of a concentration or unified complex of psychical values."[92]

"Whether God exists or not, is not important to the nature of religion."[93]

"Religion is the projection and pursuit of ideal

[88] T. McTaggart, " Some Dogmas of Religion," 1906, p. 3.
[89] G. M. Irvine, " Churches, Religion and Progress," pp. 13, 18.
[90] Ellsworth Faris, *Journal of Religion*, Vol. VI, No. 3, May 1926, p. 241.
[91] Al. Hoernle, *Harvard Theol. Review*, Vol. XI, No. 2, April 1918. R. B. Perry, " Philosophical Tendencies." p. 29.
[92] Jos. A. Leighton, " Man and Cosmos," 1922, p. 545.
[93] R. Eucken, " Truths of Religion," p. 129.

personal relations with the universe and man. . . .
Because it is a process of projection and pursuit, religion is an ever moving process in the direction of
complete personal adjustment and control in man's
total environment." [94]

" In its simplified element religion is thus found
to be the expression of man's mental attitude toward the unknown which is not capable of being
known by any method of investigation available at
the time." [95]

" Any reasoned appreciation of life is — a religion even though there are no conventional religious elements in it." [96]

" *Immanentism*, the conception that God is life-
force, only 'personal' in so far as realizing itself
through successive forms of life, cuts the ground
from under the feet of the Christian appeal; for
where there is not felt to be any distinction, there
can be no desire of union." [97]

" The central dogma of the Christian religion,
finds no support in science. It cannot be said that
either doctrine is essential to religion, since neither
is found in Buddhism. . . . We in the West have
come to think of them as the irreducible minimum
of theology. No doubt people will continue to en-
tertain these beliefs, because they are pleasant, just
as it is pleasant to think ourselves virtuous and our

[94] Edwin E. Aubrey, " The Nature of Religion," *Journal of Religion*, 1925, pp. 189–91.
[95] G. M. Irvine, " Churches, Religion and Progress," pp. 13–18.
[96] G. Santayana, " Reason in Religion," p. 6.
[97] Thomas J. Hardy, " The Present Predicament of Christianity," *Hibbert Journal*, Oct. 1925, Vol. XXIV, No. 1, p. 65.

enemies wicked. But for my part I cannot see any ground for either." [98]

"Religion is the most complete and full-orbed expression of this striving toward action with the widest and fullest environment." [99]

"Religion is, then, *man's sense of the disposition of the universe to himself*." [100]

"God is neither an entity nor an ideal, but always a relation of entity to ideal: *Reality regarded from the standpoint of its favorableness or unfavorableness, to human life, and prescribing for the latter the propriety of a certain attitude*." [101]

"Religion is not mere conformity to moral law, it is an *espousal* of moral ideals, a dedication of the heart, a loyal devotion, the perpetual renewal of a right spirit within us." [102]

"Center of religion is cosmic fortune of values." [103]

"Religion is loyalty and co-operation in the effort to attain the socially approved values involved in the ideal of the satisfactory life." [104]

"Religion is the glorious challenge of human life for the mastery of the planet; the loyal pursuit of the vision of the complete life through the ages." [105]

[98] Bertrand Russell, " What I Believe," 1925, p. 13.
[99] H. W. Wieman, *Journal of Religion*, May 1927, p. 307.
[100] Ralph B. Perry, " The Approach to Philosophy," 1908, p. 66.
[101] *Ibid.*, p. 88.
[102] Durant Drake, " A Definition of Religion," *Journal of Religion*, March 1927, p. 124.
[103] W. G. Everett, " Moral Values," 1918, p. 302.
[104] A. E. Haydon, *Journal of Religion*, March 1927, p. 127.
[105] *Ibid.*, p. 133.

"Faith in God is synonymous with the brave hope that the universe is friendly to the ideals of man." [106]

Psychological Negations of the Traditional Object of Religion

Psychological arguments are not wanting to bolster up the contemporary negation of God as the object of religion. In making such an assertion there is grave danger of being misunderstood. Psychology, as such, does not hold nor even make for such a position any more than does modern physics or modern biology; it merely attempts to describe the by-products of religion, its emotions, its states and its reactions. In doing this it has rendered much service to the proper understanding of religion. In the words of Professor Flournoy: "Psychology neither rejects nor affirms the transcendental existence of the religious objects; it simply ignores that problem as being outside its field." [107] Dr. James Bislett Pratt, of Williams College, is an American psychologist who has well understood the boundaries and frontiers of his science when he writes "My purpose is to *describe the religious consciousness,* and to do so without having any point of view. . . . My aim in short has been purely descriptive, and my method purely empirical. Like other men I have my own theories about the philosophy of religion, but I have made unremitting ef-

---

[106] A. E. Haydon, *Journal of Religion*, March 1927, p. 128.

[107] "Principes de la Psychologie Religieuse," in *Archives de Psychologie,* Vol. II, pp. 37–41.

forts to describe the religious consciousness without undue influence from my philosophical theories, but merely by going to experience and writing down what I find." [108] Even better still has Dr. Gerald B. Phelan outlined the frontiers of psychology and philosophy of religion. In an excellent paper read at the American Catholic Philosophical Association, he said: "When the psychologist follows the methods of his science in dealing with the phenomena of religious life as they affect the individual mind and the social group, he is quite within the confines of his territory and philosophy should look across at him smiling her approval on his energetic efforts. Only when the empirical investigator surreptitiously appropriates the findings of philosophy and distorts them to accommodate the findings of his science should the voice of Dame Philosophy be heard in protest. . . . Whatever explanations he may offer, the authority of the psychologist extends no further than the data of his science, which being definitely phenomenological, furnish no grounds for conclusions about the transcendental." [109]

If psychologists remained psychologists there would be no reason for introducing them here, but unfortunately there is often an itch among them, as there is among physicists and mathematicians, to become philosophers and to discourse

[108] "The Religious Consciousness," 2d ed., 1927, p. vii.
[109] "Proceedings of the Second Annual Meeting," 1926, pp. 85, 86. Cf. p. 17 of "Feeling Experience and Its Modalities" by the same author, London, 1925.

about the nature of God and His existence. When this inclination so masters them that their descriptions become explanations, then they become philosophers of religion and as such must be treated.

There is probably no psychologist of religion who has so far over-stepped the limits of his science as Professor James Leuba. His particular theories of conversion and mysticism and the like do not interest us, but his denial of anything beyond psychological causes of religion is of vital interest. There is no misunderstanding his position. He comes out very clearly against Flournoy's statement that "Psychology neither rejects nor affirms the transcendental existence of the religious objects"; and asserts that such a position nullifies the science of which he is an exponent. "The principle," he writes, " of irrelevance of science to the transcendent, shields the cardinal belief of the established religions only if their gods are transcendental objects. In taking for granted that there are such objects, an error has been committed and grave confusion has been introduced in the discussion of the relation of science to religion." Very justly, he adds, that if the object of religion is a god whose source is in the naïve interpretation of phenomena then religion is not outside science. But he believes every notion of God to be such an interpretation. "Should there be no ground of belief other than physical phenomena and inner experiences, then, for those who are acquainted with the modern scientific conception, there would be no belief in God." [110]

It is quite evident that for Professor Leuba there is very little reason for introducing the traditional notion of God into religion, for that notion has since been dissolved by scientific study. If there were super-human beings, their existence, he tells us, should have become increasingly evident. "Yet the converse is apparently true; the supernatural world of the savage has become a natural world to the civilized man; the miraculous of yesterday is the explicable of today. In religious lives accessible to psychological investigation, nothing requiring the admission of super-human influences has been found. There is nothing, for example, in the life of the great Spanish mystic whose celebrity is being renewed by contemporary psychologists — not a desire, not a feeling, not a thought, not a vision, not an illumination, that can seriously make us look to transcendental causes." [111]

That Professor Leuba means these shafts of naturalism to be the undoing of traditional religion is quite clear from the following passage: "The evils bred by the traditional conception of God may be called by the general name of ' otherworldliness.' It would be difficult to evaluate the harm done to humanity in the past by the conviction that the real destination of man is the World to Come, and equally difficult to estimate the harm done by the

[110] " The Psychology of Religious Mysticism," 1925, pp. 300, 302, 304.

[111] " Psychological Study of Religion," p. 272.

conviction that for its ethical improvement society is dependent upon a personal God. If these evils are of lesser magnitude now than in the past, it is because the traditional belief has lost some of its ancient potency, and because the sense of responsibility of the individual for the natural and the spiritual welfare of society has grown correspondingly greater. In order that we may come to a full realization that he and he alone is his brother's keeper, it is necessary that man should entirely give up the belief in personal super-human causation. Divided responsibility works no better in religion than in business." [112]   "It need hardly be said here that the abandonment of the belief in a personal God and in personal immortality, though it involves the disappearance of existing religions, need not bring to an end religious life." [113]

The God-less religion of this psychologist is defined as follows: "Religion is that part of human experience in which man feels himself in relation with the power of psychic nature, usually personal powers, and makes use of them. . . . In its objective aspect, active religion consists then, of attitudes, practices, rites, ceremonies, institutions; in its subjective aspect, it consists of desires, emotions and ideas, instigating and accompanying these objective manifestations. The reason for the existence of religion is not the objective truth of its conception, but its biological value." [114]

[112] "Psychology of Religious Mysticism," pp. 329-330.
[113] J. H. Leuba, "The Belief in God and Immortality," 1916, p. X.
[114] "Psychological Study of Religion," pp. 52, 53.

While Professor Leuba rules God out of court and relegates such belief to non-psychological ages of human existence, there are others who are more inclined to exclude God from religion altogether by reducing Him to a psychic state. "The theory of projection" is the popular fashion of doing this among the latter group of psychological-philosophers. Professor A. G. Tansley, for example, makes religion God-less by making God a mental projection:

"In a primitive state of culture man projects parts of his own personality upon the forces of nature and thus personifies and defies them. . . . At a later state of development the process of projection is gradually simplified, in accordance with the persistent need of unification, and finally crystalized into a dualism, a personification of good and evil, of what is beneficial or harmful to the human race, and instead of polytheism we have the antithesis of God and the Devil. . . . At a later stage still we have a further unification; the Devil is banished from the cosmology, and God is represented as responsible for everything — even for the evil in the human heart. . . . So far God is essentially a social God, a concentrated projection of all the qualities useful to the herd in a supreme supernatural personality — the supreme herd leader of humanity, just as the tribal gods were the tribal leaders." [115]

[115] "The New Psychology and its Relation to Life," 7th ed., 1922. W. R. Matthews while denying that the idea of God is a pure projection believes that it should be retained because it has a " survival

Sociological Negations of the Traditional Object of Religion

In addition to the purely metaphysical or psychological explanations of religion there is yet another which may be called the sociological or the humanitarian. Among European thinkers this explanation takes a double form: either that of Durkheim for whom God is " a divinized society " or that of Wundt for whom God is the term which represents the values of life as estimated either by the folk or the community. Professor Alfred Hoernle, who knows so well the currents of contemporary philosophy, describes the humanitarian view as follows: " For the ineffective love of a supernatural or even non-existent God it seeks to substitute the effective love of actual men and women. From preoccupation with the salvation of his soul in a life after death, it seeks to turn man to the service of his kind in this life. It aims at making the energy of

---

value ": " This idea, no less than the idea of nature, has value for life, and has helped man to gain command of the circumstances in which his existence is cast." " The Psychological Approach to Religion," 1925, p. 21; cf. Jung, " The Psychology of the Unconscious "; T. W. Pym, "Psychology and the Christian Life," 1921, Chaps. 2, 3. " The psycho-analyst is satisfied with the theory that religious beliefs are produced by disused, displaced and projected libido." " The ' one God ' satisfied the narcissistic craving of the beloved Ego for an omnipotent projection for its own adoration." Cavendish Moxon, M.A. (Oxon). " Freudian Essays on Religion and Science," 1925, pp. 18, 20. " Religion is primarily emotional and therefore is in the broadest sense of sex-origin." S. Swisher, " Religion and the New Psychology," 1923, p. 19. J. Cyril Flower, "Psychological Studies of Religious Questions," 1924, p. 224 ff. " The constitutive character of religion lies in the psychical's successful attempt to assert itself physically." Jacques Cohen, " Religion," 1923, p. 35.

religion available in the cause of human progress, for the fight against disease, poverty, ignorance, crime. It preaches a crusade against remediable ills in the cause of a better future for the human race on this earth." [116]

There are few contemporary thinkers who have done more to further this natural kind of religion than Professor E. S. Ames of the University of Chicago. He believes that the Christian conception of a future life is gradually losing its hold on mankind. "At last religion has come," he says, "to reckon with the fact that its highest quest is not for a supernatural order but just for natural goodness in the largest and fullest measure. . . . What then is the goal of religion? . . . The goal of religion is the fulfillment of the normal duties and opportunities of life as we experience it, with sympathy and idealism and passionately unselfish devotion." [117]

The notion of worshipping a Supreme Being in another world is therefore quite out of the question. It smacks of the "adoration and flattery such as were formerly given to tyrants and despots." [118] "In our democracies men do not bow themselves to the ground nor prostrate themselves even before the mightiest individuals." [119]

More or less the same sentiments are expressed by Professor Charles A. Ellwood of the University of Missouri. "The crisis in the religious world," he

[116] "Matter, Life, Mind, God," 1923, p. 176.
[117] "The New Orthodoxy," 1925, pp. 93, 101.
[118] Ibid., p. 117.   [119] Ibid., p. 121.

writes, "has been brought about by the failure of existing religion to adapt itself to two outstanding facts in our civilization — science and democracy." [120] He believes that a religious revolution is in the air, and that it is concerned with a transition from ethical monotheism to a scientific and social conception of religion. And "the real religious problem of our society is to secure the general acceptance of a religion adapted to the requirements of continuous progress toward an ideal, consisting of all humanity." [121] "Service of God must consist in service of man." [122] The traditional notion of God will then be done away with. Professor Ellwood calls it a Santa Claus notion. "The autocratic conception of God, as a force outside the universe, who rules by arbitrary will both physical nature and human history, will be replaced by the conception of a spirit immanent in nature and in humanity, which is gradually working out the supreme good in the form of an ideal society consisting of all humanity. And since service of God is in reality service of man, there will be sin in this new religion of democracy; it will be a failure to serve mankind. In other words it will be "disloyalty to society." [123] "Religion means the consecration of individual life, at first for love and spiritual ends, but finally for humanitarian ends." [124]

[120] "The Reconstruction of Religion," 1922, p. 2.
[121] Ibid., p. 64.
[122] Ibid., p. 100.
[123] Ibid., pp. 139, 143.
[124] Ibid., p. 45. "This new spirit, forming itself, as it were, upon the restless sea of humanity, will, without doubt, determine the

Professor R. W. Sellars expresses similar ideas on the nature of religion, believing that "religion must be separated from the other worldly pull of the traditional theologies and be sanely grounded in the outlook of modern knowledge. . . . The Humanist's religion, is the religion of one who says yea to the life here and now, of one who is self-reliant and fearless, intelligent and creative. . . . Its Goal is the mastery of things that they may become servants and instrumentalities to man's spiritual comradeship." [125]

Mr. Thomas J. Hardy, noting this growing religion in which mankind is both worshipper and worshipped, has said " If immanentism means the apotheosis of Man there are few who need much converting. . . . Man is emerging from the cumbrous trappings of Divinity and 'the Service of

---

future sense of God and destiny. The deistic conception of an age now completely past, that God is some distant monarch, will fade into the darkness with the social system which gave it rise; and society as a federal union, in which each individual and every form of human association shall find free and full scope for a more abundant life, will be the large figure from which is projected the conception of God in whom we live and move and have our being." (Robert A. Woods, *Democracy: A New Unfolding of Human Power*, a chapter in "Studies in Philosophy and Psychology," 1906. "Society, democratic from end to end, can brook no such radical class distinction as that between a supreme being favored with eternal and absolute perfection and the man of beings doomed to the lower ways of imperfect struggle. It is the large figure out of which is projected the conception of the God *that is ourselves*, in whom and of whom we literally are; the God that, in every act and intention, *we, with all our countless fellows are realising*. . . . It is a God that in one respect is in the making, growing with the growth of the world; suffering and sinning and conquering with it; a God, in short, that *is* the world in the spiritual unity of its mass-life." H. A. Overstreet, "The Democratic Conception of God," *Hibbert Journal*, Vol. XI, p. 410.

[125] "The Next Step in Religion," 1918, pp. 211, 212, 217.

Man,' rejected in its doctrinaire presentment, has become the Established Religion." [126]

The foregoing survey of the field of philosophy of religion, though it does betray a great want of uniformity of teaching, does nevertheless very clearly reveal a tendency to dispense with God as the goal of religion and the end of life. The term "God" may still be retained, and in some cases is, but it is emptied of all the content ascribed to it by the greatest minds of the past. In other words, the conclusion to be drawn from the philosophical theories just presented is not that there is no God in modern religion, but only that God as traditionally understood is no longer considered the object of religion. The reasons for such a conclusion, as we have seen, are generally either philosophical, psychological or sociological, but underlying them all is the inability to reconcile the old concept of God and religion with

[126] "The Present Predicament," *Hibbert Journal*, Oct. 1925, Vol. 24, No. 1, pp. 66, 69. "The new faith will be neither Buddhist nor Christian, nor Mohammedan; it will be an outcome of the wants, the hopes and the aspirations of these our times and the near future; it will involve the fraternal love of man to all beings." C. A. F. Rhys Davids, D.Litt., "Old Creeds and New Needs," 1923, p. 178. "The object of humanistic religion is the enhancement of the human estate. . . . The old religion judges man by his contribution to the gods; humanism judges the gods by their contribution to man . . . we are loyal to our ideas of right and wrong, to our ideas of value, not in order to measure up to an ultimate standard but in order to promote human welfare. . . ." Curtis W. Reese, 1926, pp. 17, 23, 35. Among other interpretations of religion which reduce religion to a purely human thing is the historical, e.g., Alfred W. Martin, "The World's Great Religions and the Religion of the Future," 1921. E. Washburn Hopkins, Ph.D., "Origin and Evolution of Religion," 1923, writes, "Every religion is a product of human evolution and has been conditioned by social environment." p. 1. A. N. Whitehead, "Religion in the Making," 1926, Chap. II.

the latest discoveries of science.   This conclusion is, of course, negative, and tells us nothing positive of the content of modern religion.   A more interesting inquiry is the nature of the substitute offered and this is the burden of the following chapter.

CHAPTER II

MODERN RELIGION IN ITS POSITIVE ASPECT

WHILE it is a difficult task to group the multiple and varied theories of religion which are now seeing the light of day, under some specific heading, it does nevertheless seem true that they are all quite agreed in regarding *values* as the object of religion. The varied and colorful interpretations of God which were substituted for the traditional notion now merge on a common ground: God is subordinated, at least in some way, to the supreme task of conserving values. It is true that for some, God still remains the object of religion, but only in relation to values. Thus Professor Whitehead, for example, although admitting the necessity of some "harmonizer" or "principle of concretion" in this world of relations, makes God subserve value. "The purpose of God," he writes, "is the attainment of value in the temporal world." [1]

There is no danger of exaggerating the place which the philosophy of values holds in the world today. Only a few decades ago the term "Value" would have suggested nothing more than a term of economics, signifying the price of things. "The

[1] "Religion in the Making," p. 100.

value of a thing is just as much as it will bring."
Now the term is applied in the field of education,
art, religion and all the aspects of human life.[2] Professor Pringle Pattison says that "At the present
time philosophy is carried on more explicitly in
terms of value than at any other time."[3] To take
another of the vast host of testimonies to this fact,
Professor D. S. Robinson affirms that: "Since the
time of Kant all progressive theologians have shifted
the emphasis away from the abstract philosophical
arguments for the existence of God to the searching
question: What value does God have in human
experience?"[4] The philosophy of value up to the
present day has been a by-product of thought; now
it is the essential. Writing in 1885, Herman Lotze
saw the possibility of its development when he
wrote in reference to æsthetics and ethics: "and
for these two investigations a third common to
both may be conceived, which has hitherto never
been carried out, namely, an investigation concerning the nature of all the determinations of
value."[5]

But what is the reason for the popularity of a
philosophy of value? Only a few have attempted
to answer this question. Professor R. B. Perry and
Professor J. S. Mackenzie are notable exceptions.
The former believes that the philosophy of value is

[2] J. S. Mackenzie, "Ultimate Values," 1926, p. 13.
[3] "The Idea of God," p. 39.
[4] "The God of the Liberal Christian," 1926, p. 118.
[5] "Gründzuge der Logik und Encyclopädie der Philosophie,"
quoted by Perry, "General Theory of Value," p. 5.

the culminating phase of the modern scientific movement in which science not only studies nature but man, and the study of man means the study of his values. The old Baconian program of science which promised man conquest over the powers of nature has given place to the new program which promises power through the conquest of himself. Sciences which before studied only the physical world now include man within their scope; biology, for example, now studies the "descent of man." "The theory of value belongs to this general intellectual movement—shares its aspirations, and participates in its efforts." It is really an attempt to apply science to life, and to discover that age-old problem of living together with a minimum of friction and a maximum of mutual aid.[6]

Professor Perry gives a still more interesting explanation of the importance of the philosophy of values. It is founded on the contrast between the outlook of the ancient and medieval world and that of the modern world. The fact is that in the modern world there has been such a multiplication of diverse objects, thanks to the development of industry and commerce, that the needs and the wants of man are constantly increasing. What our grandparents looked upon as luxuries, are necessities for us. The standard of living has mounted; what once was a luxury is now a need, and what is presently a luxury will some day be a necessity. Coupled with this vast increase of values there has grown a great

[6] "General Theory of Values," pp. 12, 13.

confidence in the attainability of these things. Men are becoming more certain that the world is at their service and that as time passes on newer and better conveniences will reveal themselves which will make life better and more worth living. The world is a good place to live in. "There is something in the modern spirit that prevents a man's washing his hands of the whole matter and retiring from the world."

Set now in contrast with this modern spirit is that of the ancient or the medieval world. The idea of the ancient world was that man should be content with what he has. Stoics proclaimed the doctrine of disillusionment. The medieval world continued to do the same but introduced a new element which was not found in paganism; namely, the doctrine of the future life where the losses of time would be compensated by the gains of eternity. There was still a common element between the two, namely the disproportion between man's desires and his powers and the consequent need of renunciation. Its wisdom, continues Professor Perry, "was pervaded with a sense of doom, of ironic fate, of incurable failure, or of divine intervention. It taught men to believe that worldly attainments could never be more than provisional. . . ." But the triumphs of modern science have, for better or for worse, resulted in a sort of re-illusionment of the modern European. He proposes to increase production rather than reduce consumption. He has undertaken an aggressive campaign in the open. . . . If

he remembers the fate which overtook the Tower of
Babel he attributes it to ignorance of modern engineering. If he summons faith to his aid it is not to
compensate resignation, but to invigorate his effort
or confirm his illusions. . . .[7]

Hence the broad difference between the theory of
value in the contemporary and European sense, and
the theory of value in the earlier and non-European
sense.   Value today springs from a kind of embar-
rassment of riches. How shall a man choose from
what is offered him? How shall their conflict be reduced or eliminated? The problem, in other words,
is that " of establishing a principle of selection and
a method of reconciliation by which order and harmony shall be brought out of a bewildering chaos
and a confusion of values."[8] Since the world has
changed its outlook on life, and is more bent on
enlarging man's powers than reducing his desires,
a new theory of values is necessary to adjust properly the details of the new vision.

Value, in some way or other, has become the
primary object of religion, regardless of the kind of
God any contemporary philosopher may 'create.
Those who are well versed in contemporary religious philosophy will recall the frequency with which
Höffding's definition of religion is quoted.[9] It
would be interesting to know who has not quoted
it. Höffding has defined religion as " faith in the
conservation of values," or " the conviction that no'

[7] *Op. cit.* p. 13.
[8] *Op. cit.* pp. 14-16.
[9] J. S. Mackenzie, " Ultimate Values," 1924, p. 172.

value perishes out of the world." [10]   Windelbrand, who is no less an authority, sums up the present philosophical situation in these words: "We do not so much expect from philosophy what it was formerly supposed to give, a theoretic scheme of the world, a synthesis of the results of the separate sciences, or of transcending them on lines of its own, a scheme harmoniously complete in itself; what we expect from philosophy today is reflection on those permanent values which have their foundation in a higher spiritual reality above the changing interests of the times." [11]

One might go on through the field of contemporary philosophy seeking positive definitions of religion and in the end would find they would be variations of Höffding.   Thus Professor E. G. Spaulding finds in religion "the factor of value, of something that is of worth to the individual, of something that means to him betterment and goodness." [12]   "The essence of religion," according to Viscount Haldane, "is the claim that the world has value." [13]

But what is value?   While contemporary philosophy agrees that religion is destined for the conservation of values, there is not a perfect agreement as to what constitutes value. Professor Whitehead,

[10] "Philosophy of Religion," English translation, p. 6.

[11] "Die Philosophie im Deutschen Geistesleben des 19ten Jahrhunderts," 1909, p. 119.

[12] "Christianity and Modern Thought," foreword by Ralph G. Gabriel.   Chap. 4; *Psychology of Religion* by Professor Spaulding, p. 72.

[13] "The Reign of Relativity," 1921, p. 305; cf. W. K. Wright, "A Student's Philosophy of Religion," 1922, p. 41.

for example, defines it as "the intrinsic reality of an event."[14] Meinong, on the contrary, says the value of an object lies in the total reaction of the subject in terms of the feeling aroused by the judgment or supposition of its existence or non-existence.[15] Professor John Dewey tells us that "value is constituted by interest, liking, vital bias,"[16] which is something similar to Professor R. B. Perry's notion that value is intelligible in function of interest.[17] Professor E. S Brightman likes the psychological explanation and defines it as "what is liked or desired or approved in the light of our highest ideals."[18] "Value is at any stage the distinction between what on that level is fitting and what is defeated in the contrast or the struggle with it."[19]

And so one might go on elaborating definitions. Ultimately some classification would have to be made. This classification might be based on the distinction between objective and subjective values, or between instrumental and intrinsic values, or else a classification founded on the several sciences which would give such values as ethical, moral, artistic and the like. While admitting the validity of all these classifications and divisions, there is yet another one which far better serves the purpose this work has in view. It is a classification in

---

[14] "Science and the Modern World," p. 136.

[15] "Ueber Annahmen," 1910, p. 182.

[16] "Valuation and Experimental Knowledge," *Phil. Review*, Vol. XXXI, 1922, p. 334.

[17] "General Theory of Value," 1926, Chap. 5.

[18] Professor S. Alexander, "Religious Values," 1925, p. 15.

[19] "Space, Time and Deity," Vol. 2, p. 410.

answer to a problem which has been well expressed
by Professor E. S. Brightman: "Can we give a
complete account of what religious values mean
merely in terms of our psychological life, our actual
or possible immediate experience, or does the meaning of our religious experience depend on our relation to a real order which is more and other than our
human life?"[20]   In other words, is God necessary
for the conservation of values?

There is no violence done to the philosophy of
value in classifying its various schools according
to their answer to this question, for here we are not
taking sides, but merely treating values in relation
to religion.   In this connection it may be said that
there are two groups of Value-Philosophers, one
holding that God is necessary as the ground of
values; the other either ignoring God or denying
His necessity as their foundation.

1. First Group of Value-Philosophers

In his work, "Moral Values and the Idea of
God," which may be said to be the finest contribution contemporary philosophy has made to the
problem of value, Professor R. S. Sorley gives a very
orderly and coherent background for values.   He
holds that the mind has a double interest, first that
of interest in the individual, the other that of interest in universals.   Natural sciences study the
universals; the historical and moral sciences study
the individuals.   In other words, natural sciences

[20] "Religious Values," p. 103.

study causes and moral sciences study values, because values are essentially personal. There is objectivity in both spheres. Ethical principles are as valid for persons as physical principles are valid for material things.

There is no absolutely independent unit among the objects of experience; reality is known to us as a whole. The problem is to understand this whole, for each thing is a part of a great whole. Reality includes diversity. The problem then is how are these diversities reconciled into a whole, i.e., the diversities in the realm of causes and the diversities in the realm of ends. The two meet in man and there seem to be in conflict.

From this conflict there arises a difficulty which may be put in the form of two questions. Why do persons realize their ideals so imperfectly? and why is the causal system so indifferent to them?

The answer to the first is Freedom; the answer to the second is Purpose.

"How is it that persons do not realize the moral order of the universe? and the answer is that moral values can be realized by free beings only; that freedom is necessary for goodness . . . and that the world would be a less noble and worthy event than it is if it did not contain the values which can be realized only by free beings, and therefore cannot be purchased except by the gift which makes evil possible as well as good." [21]

Why is the world apparently so indifferent to

[21] "Moral Values and the Idea of God," p. 503.

our ideals? This difficulty "can be explained only by the interpretation of the world as a purposive system. . . . We must postulate purpose in the world as well as freedom in man. The world with its order of natural law cannot be explained from its present appearance only; not only its justification but also its explanation depends upon the final issue; and we must have regard to the ends which it is adapted to serve. . . . The order of nature intends a result which is not found at any particular stage in the process of existence. It requires an idea of the process as a whole and of the moral order to which nature is being made subservient. It means therefore intelligence and the will to good as well as the ultimate source of power. In this way the recognition of the moral order and of its relation to nature and man, involves the acknowledgment of the Supreme Mind or God as the ground of all reality." [22]

Although arguing that the "idea of value is fundamental," [23] Professor Sorley does not say that God is good because there is goodness in things. "We have not argued," he writes, "that God is good because we find goodness in man, but that he is good because we find the idea of goodness to be valid for that universal order which we are trying to understand." [24] In this same favorable connection must be mentioned Professor E. S. Brightman, who is thoroughly unsympathetic to any theory of values which outlaws God. "Man-made values are

---

[22] *Ibid.*, p. 503-504.   [23] *Ibid.*, p. 487.   [24] *Ibid.*, p. 488.

not only unsatisfying, but they are groundless. God alone can give fixity and permanency to values and hence is to be defined as "The Supreme Value of the Universe." [25]

The problem of the foundation of values has been taken up by another justly celebrated moral philosopher, Professor Hastings Rashdall in his two volume work: "The Theory of Good and Evil." [26] Well done in its criticism of psychological and rational utilitarianism and the Kantian categorical imperative, it is less satisfying in its constructive part. His own theory is that goods of different kinds (pleasure, virtue and the like) are capable of quantitative reckoning and admit of being measured in respect to their ultimate value. But there must be some ultimate postulate for morality, otherwise there is no reason for being moral. Now God is such a postulate. Moral values are in close connection with the doctrine of the love of God. "For God to be loved He must be thought of as worthy of love, and it is difficult to believe that He is worthy of love if He wills such a world as ours except as a means to some better one, for those at least of his creatures who are worthy of it. . . . In the love of God the two strongest emotional forces which make for Morality in this world find their fullest and most harmonious satisfaction — reverence for the moral ideal and love of humanity." [27]

[25] "Religious Values," 1925, p. 16.
[26] 2d ed., 1924.
[27] *Ibid.*, Vol. 2, pp. 212, 243, 267, 299.

But when one asks what is the nature of God Who is so necessary for the conservation of values, we are surprised to learn that it is a God Who is not omnipotent.[28]   God is not the Absolute, but "the absolute must include God and all other consciousness, not as isolated and unrelated beings, but as intimately related (in whatever way) to Him and to one another and as forming with Him a system or Unity."[29]   Thus the God Who conserves values is not the God of traditional thought, but the God Who with us goes to make up the Absolute.

Professor Pringle Pattison joins the rank of those who believe in the necessity of God for the conservation of values. He wars against finite personalities constituting the final purpose or the central fact of the universe. "All claims made on man's behalf, must be based on the objectivity of values revealed in his experience and brokenly realized there. Man does not make values any more than he makes reality."[30] But what is the nature of this God who sustains values? It is certainly not the traditional notion, for that must be "profoundly transformed," it being "a fusion of the primitive monarchical ideal with Aristotle's conception of the Eternal Thinker."[31] His own idea of God is not that of "two independent acts, but the experienced fact which is the *existence of*

---

[28] *Ibid.*, p. 237.
[29] *Ibid.*, p. 239.
[30] "The Idea of God," 2d ed., 1920, pp. 43, 239.
[31] *Ibid.*, p. 407.

the one in the other and through the other." [32]   God
is transcendent, if you will, but this transcendence
refers "to a distinction of value or of quality, not
to the ontological separateness of one being from
another." [33]   Professor Hocking says "The use of
the God idea . . . will be the chief *determinant of
the value level in any consciousness.* . . . Whatever value religion has for man will be founded, we
now judge, in the religious ideas . . . the idea of
God."   And yet, God is not so important after all,
for later on he writes: "The world would be consistent without God; it would also be consistent with
God; whichever hypothesis a man adopts will fit
experience equally well; neither one, so far as accounting for visible facts is concerned works better
than the other." [34]

Hugo Münsterberg believes that Religion demands "a progression over the limits of the experi-
enceable." [35]   Values are found in the region of the
human will and value implies an over-personal,
metaphysically absolute will.   But this absolute
will is not to be interpreted as a Perfect God for he
adds: "Whether God stands above the things or
lives in the things themselves, whether there is one
God or many, remains a consideration of secondary
importance." [36]

There is also a group of philosophers inspired by
the Kantian "Critique of Practical Reason," who

[32] "The Idea of God," 2d ed., 1920, p. 254.   [33] *Ibid.,* p. 255.
[34] "The Meaning of God in Human Experience," 1921, pp. 136,
139, 143.
[35] "Eternal Values," 1909, p. 355.   [36] *Ibid.,* p. 362.

believe that God is a postulate for moral values. Such is the idea of Professor Joseph A. Leighton, whose position may be summed up as follows: "The true meaning of postulating a God, 'the animating principle of faith in God and the higher order of which He is the guardian and sustainer, is this affirmative response to the very cry of mankind for the assurance or promise of the *permanence of the life of most worth.*'" [37] This is similar to the views of Lord Balfour: "Divine Guidance must be postulated if we are to maintain the three great values — knowledge, love and beauty." [38]

2. *Second Group of Value-Philosophers*

There is yet another group of philosophers for whom an existent God is not necessary for the conservation of values, and this for varying reasons, either psychological or metaphysical. An example of the psychological point of view is furnished by Professor Ralph Barton Perry in his "General Theory of Value." [39] Instead of starting with a category and then seeking for instances of it, he prefers to proceed in the reverse direction, by collecting instances and then distilling out their common characteristics.

The discussion of value opens with the search for a term which will be broad enough to embrace the varieties of the motor-affective life, and this

[37] "The Field of Philosophy," 1923, p. 475.
[38] "Theism and Thought," 1923, p. 248.
[39] 1926.

term is *interest*. Professor Perry here separates himself from Santayana for whom value is absolutely indefinable, and from Brogan and Dewey for whom it is relatively definable. His own theory is that the value of an object lies in its relation to interest, but not in terms of a peculiarly qualified will or interest. But how are we to conceive this relation between value and interest? Does interest direct itself towards the object, as the marksman directs his arrow to the target, or does the object draw the interest towards itself like a magnet? In the first case value springs from interest and would be conferred on the subject; in the second case value would reside in the object according to its capacity to command interest. Professor Perry inclines to the first view: "That which is an object of interest is *eo ipso* invested with value. Any object whatever it be, acquires value when any interest, whatever it be, is taken in it; just as anything whatever becomes a target when anyone aims at it." [40] He believes that Aristotle was "fundamentally mistaken when he said that the apparent good of a thing makes it an object of appetite, as its real good makes it the object of rational desire, and that Spinoza was right in asserting that a thing is good because we desire it and not vice versa.

Since interest is constitutive of value in the basic sense, the theory of value will take interest as its point of departure and centre of reference. Interest is then analyzed biologically, psychologically, and

[40] "Theism and Thought," 1923, p. 116.

cognitionally. The foundation of interest is biology. This science has definitely established the fact that the living organism provides the context of interest for there is found in it a capacity of *prospiciently* determined action. The dog who anticipates a beating behaves in such a way not only to avert the beating, but also in a way appropriate to a possible future beating which the whip represents to him. (Animals not only *possess* adaptation to environment; they also *acquire* it.) This anticipatory response, along with adaptation to environment and the like are kinds of interest. What is lacking is *prescience* and this leads one into the psychological consideration of interest.

Psychology defines an interested or purposive action as an " action adopted because the anticipatory response which it arouses coincides with the unfulfilled or implicit phase of a governing propensity." [41] A chess player for example has a series of moves all ready in advance; there is in him a coincidence of the expected sequel and the governing tendency.

Interest may be studied not only in its basic relations, biology and psychology, but also in relation to cognition. Interest is related to cognition inasmuch as the satisfaction varies with the truth of a judgment. This is very different from saying that the act of interest is the same as the act of judgment. "The nerve of the judgment is the connection between the index and the predicate,

[41] *Ibid.*, p. 209.

whereas the nerve of interest is the connection between the predicate and the governing propensity.[42]

The conclusion which Professor Perry draws from this long study of interest is that "All values are subjective in the sense of being functions of interest and objective in the sense of being independent of judgments about them."[43]

Passing on to the Critique of Value, the author then asks the question: What is that condition of an object in virtue of which it may be said to be better or worse than another object, or the best or worst among several objects? In other words, what is the standard of comparative value? In answer he gives three irreducible standards — *intensity, preference* and *inclusiveness.* "An object, wine, is better than an object, water: first, if the interest in the wine is more intense than the interest in the water; and secondly, if the wine is preferred to the water; and thirdly, if the interest in the wine is more inclusive than the interest in the water."[44] The intensive principle is emphasized by the hedonistic school; the preferential principle by the humanistic school, or in the cult of rationality and taste; and the principle of inclusiveness by the school of moral rigorism.

So much for the comparative values; but what will be the greatest good? "The greatest good will be the object of an all-inclusive and harmonious system of interests."[45] In the individual, for ex-

[42] "Theism and Thoughts," 1923, p. 357
[43] *Ibid.*, p. 605.
[44] *Ibid.*, p. 616.
[45] *Ibid.*, p. 659.

ample, harmonious interests constitute a better
person than antagonistic interests. In the "harmonious person" there is subordination of a lesser
to a greater interest and there is also mutuality of
which love is a special case. But there is also such
a thing as a "harmonious society," the harmonization of which is effected through universal love.
"An all-benevolent will, or a benevolence of which
all persons are the object, and which is each person's controlling purpose, is a unique mode of life
— an integration *sui generis.* . . . It is the characteristic product of a personal life in which all interests are subordinated to the love of the aggre-
gate of persons, a will resulting from the catalytic
action of universal benevolence within the chemism
of that complexus of appetites and desires that is
rooted in one organism."[46] This integration does
not make a person; it is rather a benevolent will,
"everybody's good toward everybody." "It is the
will in which it is reasonable for all to concur, not
because of some occult property or authoritative
sanction, but because such general concurrence is
reasonable."[47] And this all-benevolent will, according to Professor Perry, is God. And this God
is not a person. "The demand that God shall be a
person is only the last of the anthropomorphisms by
which man has compromised God by the desire to
worship him. When persons live in accord the total
situation is something greater than a person, as truly
as an organism is something greater than a cell."[48]

[46] *Ibid.*, p. 685.   [47] *Ibid.*, p. 685.   [48] *Ibid.*, p. 686.

Professor Perry believes that such a concept leaves no room for such troublesome questions as: does the supreme good consist in utility and pleasure, or in some deeper well-being, such as virtue, self-perfection, or saintliness? " In the conception of a happiness of all which is the condition of the happiness of each one, there is standing room alike for Stoics and Epicureans, for Kantians and Utilitarians, for Christians and pagans." [49]

Naturally a further question arises. Does such a harmonious, all-benevolent and enlightened unanimity exist? Does God exist, if you will? Professor Perry does not fly from the difficulty. In a note to page 686 of this same work he states that he believes in Alexander's emergent deity, which, of course, does not exist but is the nisus towards existence. We can therefore expect a like solution, and our expectations are not unfulfilled. Unanimity *should* exist, is Professor Perry's contention. "The best so defined is a hypothetical and not a historical fact. . . . If I say that another world war *would be* a supreme catastrophe, or that a man having a stature of ten feet *would be taller* than any man now alive, I affirm what is true despite the non-occurrence of war or the non-existence of giants. . . . So if one asks generally what would be best, and is answered in terms of that which neither did, nor does, nor even will exist, such an answer is not on that account inapt or untrue." [50]

In that sense God (the all-benevolent will of

[49] " Theism and Thoughts, 1923 p. 687.   [50] *Ibid.*, p. 688.

mankind) is helpful for values. "God defined as a will which *would* make all demands harmonious and commensurable *if* it existed, is so defined by combining the *facts* of discord and incommensurability with the *principles* of comparative value. . . . God is that being whose nature may be judged to be highest, in the sense proper to goal as yet unattained but rationally binding on the will. God is a being far exceeding and surpassing man, and yet dependent on man's moral effort. The world becomes divine through being willed to be divine, and hence its being divine is conditioned by the dynamic faith through which high resolves are carried into effect. God's existence may in this sense result from belief *in* God, though not from a belief that God already exists." [51] "The persistent danger of religion is that through excess of faith in his existence God should cease in any moral or intelligible sense to be divine." [52]

Professor J. D. Mackenzie, in his "Ultimate Values," after rejecting the notion of Dr. G. E. Moore that values are objective, as well as the view of Sedgwick that they are purely subjective, inclines to a compromise position that they are both objective and subjective. The difficulty with the first view — and here he resembles Professor Perry — is "that in every case of intrinsic value it seems to be true that a change in the subjective attitude produces a change in the object." [53] The objection

[51] *Ibid.*, p. 689.   [52] *Ibid.*, p. 690 and cf. p. 691.
[53] "Ultimate Values," p. 123.

he raises against the subjective view is that "to be pleased we must be pleased with something."

Among other theories of value, which ignore God as their foundation, though not necessarily excluding Him, are those of Meinong, Ehrenfels, and Urban.

For Meinong value is the content of feeling when this is mediated by a judgment. The measure of the value of an object is the pleasure and pain felt on the assumption of its existence or non-existence. The particular kind of *objective,* or what one feels *should* exist, he calls a "dignitative," just as he terms what one *desires* to exist a "desiderative." Values have in other words that non-existent objectivity which is so basic in Meinong's system.[54]

Ehrenfels adopts the psychological method like Meinong. His theory is something like Perry's. "Value is a relation between an object and a subject, which expresses the fact that the subject either actually desired the object or would desire it, in case he were convinced of its existence."[55]

For Urban value in the sense of *ought to be* is an ultimate category, under which in the last analysis, must be subordinated even the categories of existence and truth.[56]

Value does not attach itself uniquely to will. It is not relative to any actual will either divine or human, for then value would become a question of existence and nature. He argues that the whole,

---

54 " Ueber Annahmen," 1910, pp. 182, 183.
55 " System der Werttheorie," 1897, Vol. I, p. 65.
56 " Value and Existence," *Journal of Philosophy,* Vol. 13, 1906, p. 449.

perfect happiness *ought-to-be*, which following Meinong, he calls an "objective." Urban says that when we know a value we need know nothing of being or possibility. Thus I may say that "perfect happiness" ought to be whether or not there is such a thing, or even though it would be impossible. Ideals ought to be, and they possess regulative value, even when like "complete self-realization," they are essentially unattainable; just as impossible fictions such as the "infinitely little" or the "ether conceived as a perfect fluid" may have value in science.[57]

To be added to this group, whose ultimate is the ought-to-be, there are others for whom value is purely human. Bertrand Russell, for example, asserts, "It is we who create value and our desires which confer value. In this realm we are kings, and we debase our kingship if we bow down to Nature."[58] Professor Sellars writes, "Values concern man's response to, and estimation of things. . . . Though they are conditioned objectively by the nature of their objects, they are yet primarily personal and social, that is human."[59] Finally, there is Dr. Walter G. Everett, who is so much wedded to an earthly ground for values. "For the realization of all values," he writes, "we are directly dependent upon the cosmic Power."[60] The world has outgrown the Palestinian and Mediæval

---

[57] "Value and Existence," *Journal of Philosophy*, Vol. 13, 1906, p. 463. "Valuation," 1909, p. 16 ff.
[58] "What I Believe," 1925, p. 25.
[59] "Evolutionary Naturalism," p. 342.
[60] "Moral Values," p. 422.

idea of a double world — heaven and earth. "The two worlds of value are here and now — they are with us in each hour, nay in each moment of choice, as we consciously will to dwell in the world of knowledge or ignorance, of love or hate, of beauty or ugliness, of generous aims or ignoble passions. . . . The feeling that what is won in this process is unspeakably precious is the true basis of religious reverence and confidence in the extension and growth of these values as the true ground of religious faith and hope. . . . He who does not find God here is in danger of finding Him nowhere." [61]

In light of the foregoing presentation two conclusions emerge: (1) There is a growing tendency in contemporary philosophy to present a religion without God. This is done either by denying God altogether, which is rare, or else by emptying the God-idea of all traditional content and identifying it with anything as vague as a "nisus" and as vaporous as "society divinized." (2) As a substitute for religion in terms of God and man, the majority of philosophers of religion offer a religion in terms of value or friendliness of the universe. These views are new; they are forcing themselves upon intellects and are meeting with favorable reception. It is not enough to dismiss them as "modern," or "foolish" for they are offered in all sincerity. It is the purpose of this book to pass a reasoned judgment on them in the light of history and the philosophy of the "most learned of the saintly and the most saintly of the learned," St. Thomas.

[61] "Moral Values," pp. 427, 428, 431.

PART II

The Historical Origins of the
Contemporary Idea of Religion

PART II

The Historical Origins of the Contemporary Idea of Religion

CHAPTER III

THE SPIRITUAL PRINCIPLES BEHIND THE EVOLUTION OF THE CONTEMPORARY IDEA OF RELIGION

THE problem before us is to account historically for the contemporary idea of religion, which has been reviewed in the preceding chapters. The mass of historical data of the last four centuries, representing the raw material of this study, is capable of manifold and diverse interpretations. A survey of the democratizing movement in religion, for example, would not embrace the same historical data as would the study of the development of dogmas. In like manner, a study of the origins of the contemporary conception of religion will not include those elements which are foreign to the subject even though contemporaneous with it. Our interest lies only in those particular and definite threads of the past which have been woven into the fabric of what is now called "modern religion."

Since there are no hard and fast lines in the evolution or progress of religious thinking, it is only natural that, here and there, we should find certain cross-currents of thought, cutting diagonally through what appears to be a natural line of development. When Newton gave his physics to the world, and Galileo his astronomy, there were waves of opposition, which probably confused their contemporaries. But for us, these events are sufficiently in retrospect to permit us to separate the wheat from the chaff, and to outline the story of the development of the new physics and the new astronomy. So too, there are cross currents in philosophical thinking; there are tangents of idealism cutting through materialism, as there are reactions to Lutheran Protestantism among reformers themselves. But from all these reactions, and cross currents, there still remains a very definite line of thought which has brought its heritage to the doors of the twentieth century and enriched, if not created, our new ideas concerning man's relation to God.

Our task is not to trace the development of religious thinking in a strictly chronological way, nor is it to localize the thought according to the countries in which it took its rise. Rather, we shall seek out those *spiritual principles* buried in the past which have been germinal in the development of modern religion. We are *solidaire* with the past intellectually as well as physically. We are not only children of our age but we are children of every age. The principles born *in acie mentis* of our intellectual forebears is the germ of the " spirit of modern progress."

Spiritual principles — it is these we seek, for religion, whatever else it may be, involves spiritual elements, which transcend the gross materialities of life. Spiritual principles are sought for still another reason, and that is because they are fundamental. It is the thought which inspires action; "the thinker lives forever; the toiler dies in a day." The Marathon racers of Greece are dead and forgotten, but Plato and Aristotle live and are venerated. The mere search after the origin of the supposed conflict between science and religion, monism and pluralism, vitalism and mechanism, would always leave something to be desired. Such history might explain the growth of the fact, but it would not explain the fundamental principles behind it.

Now there are three fundamental spiritual concepts with which religion and philosophy are concerned. One of these belongs to the supernatural order, the other two to the natural. They are: *grace, intellect* and *will*. Grace is a participation in the intimate life of God; intellect and will are likenesses of the Divine Life. We are like God inasmuch as we have an intellect and a will; we are like to the animals inasmuch as we have a body. It is around these three concepts that the whole religious and philosophical life of man revolves. Other problems are subsidiary; materialism, for example, is only secondarily a glorification of matter; primarily, it is the denial of the spiritual.

The treatment these spiritual realities have received from the hands of thinkers since the beginning of the Christian era has been as varied as it has been bewildering. The Pelagians and Augustine in the past, Fundamentalists and Modernists in our own day, are not agreed on the nature of grace. Bergsonians and Thomists have different notions of the intellect while Fouillé and Nietzsche have given us quite diverse conceptions of the will. It is necessary then (under penalty of never tracing out a coherent history of modern religious ideas) to have some fixed meaning for these great spiritual realities. A standard is necessary. If the carpenter's rule changed with each beam even the pragmatist would not want to live in a modern house. If everything changes we should never know there was a change.

Without prejudicing the case, but merely to have a certain norm by which to judge these spiritual realities, we take the definitions given them by the *philosophia perennis*. Whether or not a contemporary philosopher agrees or differs with this standard does not matter. He may disagree, but he knows very definitely with what he disagrees. The Scholastic meaning of these terms is taken as a norm, and if there were any other norm equally inelastic and permanent, it would serve our present purpose just as well, but there is none. The justification of this norm on the grounds of its logical consistency is quite another problem than that of its fixity, though fixity does make us suspect its consistency. The problem of its justification we shall touch on in the following section.

A brief explanation of what the *philosophia per-*

ennis and the *theologia perennis* mean by grace, intellect and will, will not only clear the mist of misunderstanding which hangs about these terms in the minds of many contemporaries, but will also serve to make clear the modern ideas themselves, inasmuch as they are reactions from the traditional notions; and we can never know what a man has fallen to until we know what he has fallen from.

Grace

Grace. Creation had for its purpose the communication of the infinite riches of Divine perfection. And since the perfections of God have no limits it was impossible that they be fully represented by one creature. That is why, St. Thomas tells us, God has multiplied and diversified creatures, in order that what one lacked in the manifestation of Divine Goodness the other might supply. The Goodness which is in God is simple, but it broke up, so to speak, much like the rays of the sun break up into the seven colors of the spectrum when shining through a prism. That is the reason why the infinite perfections of God are better represented by the totality of the cosmos, than by any one nature, however perfect it might be.[1] Just as the infirmity of our human language obliges us to multiply words in order to express something of the nature of God, which He Himself speaks in a single and unique Word; just as a teacher breaks

---

[1] 1. q. 47 art. 1. References to St. Thomas will be given throughout this work in this manner, i.e., without nominal reference.

up abstract principles into the crumbs of concrete examples for his pupils, so too does God break into fragments His infinite yet simple perfection, in order that our finite minds might grasp and understand it.

Thus it is that the whole world is an ensemble of the participations of this Divine Beauty. If all things in this universe exist, it is because they participate in the Being of God; if there are some things with life, it is because they are reflections of the life of God; if there are beings endowed with an intellect and a will — like men and angels — it is because they are a participation of the Sovereign Intellect which is God.

And yet none of these participations, however excellent they may be, suffices to constitute creatures children of God; none of them permits man to become partaker of the Divine Nature itself. The stone, for example, is like man, inasmuch as it has existence; the plant is like man, inasmuch as it lives; the animal is like man, inasmuch as it is conscious, but there is nothing in the universe which is like man inasmuch as he is possessed of an intellect and a will. So too, there is nothing in the world like to God in His most intimate nature, in that by which He is God. By nature we are *creatures*, not *children*.

If God, out of the fullness of His love for men, wills to communicate to us a participation of His nature which will make us not merely creatures but children, such a gift will be above the due nature of

man without being contrary to it.[2] It will be supernatural in the strict sense of the word. It would be
a "supernatural" act for marble, if it bore fruit;
it would be a "supernatural" act for a flower if it
were conscious with the consciousness of the five
senses; it would be a "supernatural" act for an
animal if it were endowed with the power of reasoning like an Aristotle or an Aquinas . . . "supernatural," because these gifts transcend, in a vague
way, the exigencies and powers and nature of these
creatures. But, in a *far more rigorous way* would
it be a supernatural gift for man, if God communicated to him the power of becoming a member of
the family of the Trinity, an adopted son of God,
consortes divinæ naturæ.[3] This participation in
the very intimate life of God, is called *grace* and has
been defined as "a supernatural gift of God be-
stowed on us through the merits of Jesus Christ
for our salvation." And the least gift of this Life,
according to St. Thomas, is worth more than all
created things. It is *grace* which makes the difference between creature of God and son of God.
The same learned Doctor tells us that there is more

[2] Sic enim fides præsupponit cognitionem naturalem, sicut gratia
naturam, et ut perfectio perfectibile. 1. q. 2 art. 2 ad. 1.

[3] Those who wish something more than a mere analogical expression of the natural and the supernatural will find an excellent exposition in the work of P. Garrigou Lagrange, "De Revelatione,"
Vol. 2, p. 198.

1. *Natura* in qualibet re est eius essentia, ut principium radicale
operationum et passionum quæ ei per se conveniunt.

2. *Supernaturale* dicitur pro qualibet ente finito *id quod* excidit
proportionem eius naturæ, et id quod superat eius essentialia, eius naturales passivitates, vires, exigentias, immo eius meritum naturale, eam-
que gratuito perficere potest.

difference between a soul in the state of grace and a soul not in the state of grace on this earth, than there is between a soul in the state of grace on earth and a soul in heaven. Grace is the germ of glory; it has the potencies of the beatific vision within it, in a far more remarkable way than the acorn has the potencies of the oak within itself.

Intellect[4]

The intellect has two important characteristics: its *realism*, and its *transcendentalism*.[5] *Realism*, because it knows things before knowing the ideas of things, it being only by a reflex act that it grasps the ideas. That with which it is in direct contact is the real. *Transcendentalism*, because of its power to know things above the sensible order. The intellect is spiritual; being spiritual it can be actuated spiritually, and the more spiritual the object

---

[4] It is worth noting at the outset that intellect and reason are not syonymous terms — a confusion into which Professor Bergson hopelessly fell. The intellect simply apprehends truth; reason moves from a known truth to a truth hitherto unknown. Intelligere enim est simpliciter veritatem intelligibilem apprehendere; ratiocinari autem est procedere de uno intellecto ad aliud ad veritatem cognoscendam. 1. q. 79 art. 8; 1-2. q. 93 art. 4; 3d4 q. art. 1 ad 5; C.G. lib. 4 c. 11; De Veritate, q. 15 art. 1; Post Analy. lib. 1 art. 1. Intellect and reason are related as being and becoming, or as the centre of a circle to its circumference. Et sic motus comparatur ad quietem, et ut ad principium et ut ad terminum; ita et ratio comparatur ad intellectum ut motus ad quietem et ut generatio ad esse. De Veritate, q. 15 art. 1. The intellect does not explain, does not argue, it grasps. It knows an intelligible object as the eye knows a sensible object. Reason is related to the intellect as movement is related to rest; or as acquiring a thing is related to having a thing; as going is related to arriving. Furthermore, just as going and arriving do not mean two journeys, so reason and intellect are not two distinct faculties.

[5] See Part III, Chap. I for a fuller explanation of these points.

the more adequate it is for the intellect. The factors disclosed by experience do not limit its power of knowledge any more than all the colors of the rainbow exhaust the possibilities of vision. The intellect never finds an object adequate to itself until it rests in God.

Will

The will is the faculty of the good as the intellect is the faculty of being. Everything in this universe has a curve which it must trace. The target for every one of nature's projectiles varies with its nature; in like manner the propulsion which traces its curve and directs it to its targets, varies from thing to thing. Material things, for example, are directed to their end by *laws of nature;* animals are directed to their end by *instincts,* and man is directed to his end by *reason.* Pleasure is the attainment of the end for which a thing is created; pain is caused by being out of joint with that end. The will is that tendency towards a thing suitable to its nature.[6] Desire is the mainspring or the impulsion of the projectile and is founded on — first, an actual indigence, and secondly, a potential richness.

Relation of the Intellect and the Will

Whence does the will receive its end or its object, or what constitutes its target? It is quite easy to see that material things receive their end

[6] Quasi tendere in aliquid ad ipsum ordinatum. De Veritate, q. 22 art. 1.

from nature, and animals their end from instincts. But whence does man receive his? In addition to his own nature with its native inclinations common to the whole human family, man, in virtue of his spiritual soul, is capable of receiving the natures of other things within himself by an act of knowledge, knowledge being an assimilation and a possession of the outside world. Of course he does not possess the natures of these things in a material way, but in a spiritual or "intentional" way, for everything assimilates according to its own nature.

Now, since these natures or "forms" as they are more technically called, exist in man in a nobler way than in things, it follows that the inclination derived from these natures or "forms" will be more elevated than in the material world. In lower creatures where these "forms" are natural, the inclination is called *appetite;* in man, where the forms are acquired, the inclination is called the *will.* It is clear then that unless there was knowledge there would never be a desire — *ignoti nulla cupido.*

Knowledge is the condition of desire,[7] and the more lofty and noble the knowledge the more elevated the desire. If our thoughts are low and base we tend to that which is low and base; if they are sublime and virtuous we tend to that which is sublime and virtuous. Hence the necessity in the Scholastic synthesis for clear and clean thinking. Sound pedagogy cannot overlook this point. It

[7] Bonum autem appetibile cujus ratio est in intellectu est objectum voluntatis. 1. q. 82 art. 3. c.

is not enough to legislate on a desire when it has passed into act; it is far better to crush the thought before it is desired. The proper therapeutic for bad living is clear thinking. We must supply the will with the right kind of projectiles, and trace for it the proper trajectory, for the will, by its nature, is inspired by the intellect.

This brings us to the question: which is the higher, the intellect or the will? It is in answer to this question that we find the source of many of our erroneous ideas on religion.[8]

A very manifest distinction must be made at the beginning: the intellect and will may be considered in relation to things above the soul in nobility, or below it.

1. *In relation to things below the soul, in nature and nobility,* the intellect is nobler than the will.[9] The reason is that the intellect and the will act differently toward material things. The intellect elevates things by knowing them, for it confers on them a new existence, but the will steps down to meet the requirements of the thing. The intellect in knowing assimilates, and since it is spiritual,

---

[8] Absolutely speaking, the intellect is higher than the will, for the reason that its object is more simple. Though the intellect must use the senses, yet in its movement toward the intelligible it leaves behind it as many images as possible, whereas the will carries them with it in its movement toward the object which it loves, that is, carries with it the affections of the sensible appetite. Even in a practical way, knowledge is imperfect as long as it carries subjective dispositions and prejudices with it. Furthermore, the object of the intellect is within itself, whereas the object of the will is that which is presented by the intellect. I. q. 83 art. 2 c.; De Veritate, q. 22 art. 11.

[9] Quando vero res, in qua est bonum, est infra animam, tunc etiam in comparatione ad talem rem intellectus est altior voluntate. I. q. 82 art. 3. c.

it assimilates spiritually. Thus the tree endowed
with a mere material existence is ennobled and perfected when it enters into a knowing mind for there
it becomes endowed with intellectual being. The
will, on the contrary, instead of drawing the thing
in to itself, goes out to meet the object of its love.
Lovers always accommodate themselves to and
meet the demands of the one loved, and for this
reason love is often synonymous with sacrifice.
And since *here* the object loved is beneath the soul
in dignity, the will by taking leave of its spiritual
demands and descending to mere material satisfac-
tions would be degrading itself.

For this reason, the intellect as far as material
things are concerned, is nobler than the will and a
practical conclusion to be deduced is that, in accordance with the Thomistic position, it is much
better to be a scientist than a worldling; for the scientist ennobles the universe by knowing it, while
the worldling degrades himself by loving it.

2. *In relation to things above the soul in dignity*,
however, the will is superior to the intellect.[10]
Again, the reason is that the intellect and will act
differently towards things above the soul, as they
do towards things beneath it. The intellect in attempting to grasp truths which are difficult and
above its capacities, splits them up, makes use of
examples, concretizes them and brings them down
to its own level. This every teacher must do who

---

[10] Quando igitur res, in qua est bonum, est nobilior ipsa anima,
in qua est ratio intellecta, per comparationem ad talem rem voluntas
est altior intellectu. 1. q. 83 ad 2 c.

has the task of presenting abstruse truths to others. The intellect thus runs true to its form, assimilating knowledge according to its nature, splitting up the simple and the abstract.

But the will, on the contrary, since it always goes out to the object loved and tends to become one with it, is ennobled inasmuch as the object loved is nobler than itself. It becomes heavenly in loving heavenly things as it becomes earthly in loving earthly things, forever manifesting the law that love tends to become like or one with the object loved. Thus philosophy disposes the mind for the acceptance of the Incarnation, wherein God became man and like to man because He loved man.

A practical conclusion from this doctrine of St. Thomas is one which he himself draws; namely, it is better to love God than to know Him, just as it is better to know the material things than to love them. *Melior est amor Dei quam cognitio; e contrario melior est cognitio rerum corporalium, quam amor.* We ennoble things in knowing them; we ennoble ourselves in loving God. Hence the necessity for loving something nobler than ourselves in order that we might be perfected by that love. Not only that; our knowledge and our love should be harmonious. We should love what we know only according to the degree of nobility which that thing possesses. Thus we reflect the Trinity in which Knowledge and Love are in harmonious eternal balance — the Son and the Spirit being *equal.*

The origin of the contemporary idea of religion is to be found in the historical reactions to these three fundamental ideas of the spiritual life — grace, intellect and will. It is admitted on all sides that during the last four centuries there has been a gradual misunderstanding, dissatisfaction with, and finally the elimination of each of these realities, the denial being accompanied in each case by the assertion of some substitute to fill the void.

The general principle which has been implicit in religious thinking for the past four centuries has been the *denial of the transcendent and the assertion of the immanent*. In the normal order of things there is a balance between the transcendent and the immanent, for all life is an equilibrium between the forces of within and the forces of without. The negation of the transcendent under the plea that it is an oppression and a violence to our nature, always has for its counterpart an insistence on immanence, on the plea that it makes for independence.

The Denial of the Transcendent: By this is meant the tendency to ignore or disregard those spiritual realities which lie beyond the phenomenal world about us. What traditional thought has called *transcendent* (not in the Kantian sense) our contemporaries regard as *extrinsic;* and what is extrinsic is considered as an attack against liberty of mind and freedom of thought, as something which stands between us and our power to work out our own salvation, as something which is unnatural for the very reason that it is transcendent, and as a force whose sole end and purpose is opposition to the ego. Every *mean* which common sense regards as uniting the " within " to the " without " is looked upon as an " intermediary " which separates us from the real — such are ideas in the realm of knowledge and the Church in the kingdom of grace.[11]

The Assertion of the Immanent: The denial of the perfectible as something extrinsic has as its counterpart the glorification of the " within " as contrasted with the " without." The Immanent principle asserts that there is nothing which dominates man, nothing which measures man, no Supreme End toward which he tends. Man is independent as regards powers above him; he possesses license as regards laws which reason may press upon him; he is supreme and free as regards the choice of values. Nothing above man, nothing above mind, nothing above matter — these are the dictates and maxims of the immanent principle carried to its logical conclusion.

This principle of the denial of the transcendent and the assertion of the immanent has been progressively applied to the three great spiritual realities of all religion: Grace, Intellect, and Will. Each in its turn has been denied as " extrinsic," and a something foreign and exotic has been erected in its place.

[11] Jacques Maritain, " Anti-Moderne," Introduction.

DENIAL OF THE TRANSCENDENT ASSERTION OF THE IMMANENT

Grace	The Philosophy of Individualism
Intellect	The Philosophy of Fact
Will	The Philosophy of Value

The three great periods roughly corresponding to these three stages are the Reformation, Rationalism and Romanticism. The problem of each of these periods was formulated in terms of the ego. The Protestant Reformation asked the question: "How am I justified? "; Rationalism asked the question: "How do I know? " and Romanticism, "What am I worth? " The problem of grace, the problem of the intellect, the problem of the will were no longer formulated in the third person as with the Scholastics, but in the first. In a word, the history of Theology ceased to be Christo-centric and became anthropo-centric; the history of philosophy ceased to be theo-centric and became ego-centric.

The three great prophets of the religious reform who have prepared the way for twentieth century ideas are Luther, Descartes and Kant.

Luther distorted grace by making it extrinsic to an intrinsically corrupt human nature, and through his doctrine of private interpretation prepared the way for the Philosophy of *Individualism*.

Descartes distorted intellect by making it intuitive and independent of the sensible, and through his rational principle of the clear and distinct prepared the way for the Philosophy of *Fact*.

Kant distorted the will by making it blind, and separating it from the intellect and through his doctrine of the moral sense ushered in the Philosophy of *Value*.

The combination of these three philosophies, — subjectivism, rationalism and pragmatism lie at the roots, we believe, of our contemporary idea of religion.

CHAPTER IV

THE PHILOSOPHY OF INDIVIDUALISM

LONG before the sixteenth century the supernatural was the object of attack and misunderstanding. St. Augustine found it necessary to defend it against the Pelagians. In the year 1311 the Council of Vienne defended the supernatural against the Beguards and Beguins who asserted that every intellectual nature has naturally its beatitude within itself and therefore has no need of glory to lift it to the beatific vision. Later, under the Pontificate of John XXII, certain propositions of John Eckhart were condemned because they tended to a pantheistic suppression of the natural in favor of the supernatural.

But none of these errors ever succeeded in becoming a tradition like those which arose at the time of the Reformation. The theology of Luther marks formally the first seed of a tradition touching on the supernatural which ultimately bore the fruit of an entire elimination of the whole order of grace and justification.

Luther, of course, did not draw his theology of the supernatural out of the void, for the very reason that no man is completely isolated from the time in which he lives. There were certain antecedents both in his life and doctrine as well as in history which prepared the way for it.

The two principal ideas which formed the background of Luther's doctrine concerning the relation of grace to nature are:

1. The doctrine of the essential corruption of human nature.
2. The nominalism of the decadent Scholastics.

1. *Essential Corruption of Human Nature*

Whether it was Luther's own experience of the invincibility of concupiscence, or the rational conviction of the inability to perform good works which led him to the doctrine of essential corruption of human nature in no way affects the certainty that he held such a doctrine.[1]

[1] A problem of secondary importance is the psychological elements which gave birth to his doctrine on concupiscence. Two principal theories are those of Grisar and Denifle who are divided on the priority of the idea and the fact. Denifle believes that Luther's inner experience paved the way for the doctrine. Grisar denied that it did. cf. Grisar, " Luther," English edition, Vol. 1, p. 110 ff: Denifle, " Luther," French ed., Vol. 2, p. 391 ff. There seems much in the life of Luther which would indicate that he arrived at this doctrine through experience. (1) He often equated being in the state of *grace* with feeling himself in the state of grace. (2) He relied over-much on his own forces, much more than on grace, in his attempt to overcome the revolts of lower nature. " Presumptuossimus justitiarius," quoted by Janssen, " L'Allemagne et la Reforme," Vol. 2, p. 71. (See notes 4 and 5 in Maritain, Les 3 Reformateurs," p. 241.) (3 Added to both of these was a dedication to work which took him away from all prayer. Maritain *op. cit.* pp. 10, 11. See Denifle, Vol. 2, pp. 433, 434; also pp. 391, 392 for comparison of his ideas with Grisar's on the question of the priority of experience over doctrine, also note by French translator J. Paquier: For Grisar; Vol. 1, English edition, pp. 110-117: Luther's belief in its irresistibility is not to be alleged as a proof of his moral perversity. In favor of his thesis Grisar gives two reasons: —

1. Luther strove to overcome bad tendencies.
2. He wished that justification be crowned by the fulfillment of the commandments.

It is quite clear that in the year 1514 Luther held
to the traditional notion of original sin, and upheld
the freedom of man in face of his passions.[2]   In his
" Commentary on the Romans " he sacrifices this
freedom a little, but insists that prayer will overcome everything.   His sermons at this particular
time are full of exhortations to prayer as the great
help in overcoming the burning fires of concupiscence.   In 1515 he comes out very clearly and
asserts that evil, concupiscence and sin are "invincible."[3]   Experience, he asserts, teaches us
that.[4]

This invincibility of concupiscence which " cannot be removed from us by any counsel or work," is
another way of saying that human nature is intrinsically corrupt.   Grace, Baptism and Penance
in no way affect this essential corruption.   The
Scholastics he upbraided because " in their arbitrary fashion, they make out that on the infusion
of grace, the whole of original sin is remitted in
everyone."[5]

Grisar weaves the whole story of Luther around abnormal psychology.   That he opened a fertile field for investigation is shown by works
written since, e.g., H. Strohl, " L'evolution Religieuse de Luther jus-
qu'en 1515," 1922, in which he shows that Luther's boyhood was clouded
by religious fear.   P. Smith also in the preface to the second edition
of " Life and Letters of Martin Luther " admits a " neurotic vein "
in Luther.   Finally, R. Will in " La Liberté Chrétienne, étude sur le
principe de la pieté chez Luther," 1922, believes that Luther is a problem
for religious psychology.

[2] " Werke," Weimar ed. III, p. 215.

[3] " Invincibilem esse concupiscentiam penitus," Weimar, I, p. 35.

[4] Sic enim passio, ire, superbie, luxurie, cum absens est, facilis
præsumitur victu ab inexpertis; sed cum præsens est, sentitur difficillima,
immo insuperabilis, ut experientia docet.   Weimar, IV, pp. 207, 7, 32.

[5] " Schol. Rom.," p. 108.

At one time, he says, he had believed that the Sacrament of Penance removed everything, and therefore in his madness thought himself better after confession than those who had not confessed.[6] But now he knows that sin remains even after absolution. "Sin therefore," he writes, "still *remains in the spiritual man* for his exercise in the life of grace, for the humbling of his pride. . . . We must carry on a war with our desires for they are culpable; they are really sins and render us worthy of damnation."[7]

If grace, absolution, and baptism do not affect the soul intrinsically, neither do good works. 'Works, do not render us good, but our goodness, or rather the goodness of God, makes us good and makes our works good, for in themselves they would not be good, and they are or are not good in so far as God accounts them or does not account them good."[8]

Concupiscence then, with Luther, is not something which solicits the will without determining it, but on the contrary, is an essential evil of human nature which corrupts the interior man, his reason, will, and his appetites. In other words, concupiscence is original sin itself. Nothing can remove it or alter it intrinsically. It remains even after the administration of the sacraments. Human nature is essentially bad. "We are all a lost lump."[9]

Sin and grace then co-exist in the same being, for

---

[6] Omnia ablata putabam et evacuata, etiam intrinsece, *Ibid.*, p. 109.
[7] *Ibid.*, p. 178.   [8] *Ibid.*, p. 221.   [9] Weimar, p. 343.

the human nature is essentially sinful, and grace is merely a covering for that sinfulness and in no way affects human nature intrinsically. A conclusion which follows is that virtue and vice may co-exist, and Luther admitted this.[10]

The teaching of Luther on human nature may be summed up in the following propositions:

1. Original justice in the Garden of Paradise was the *natural state* of man. What traditional thought called gifts were "just as natural for man as to receive light through the eyes."

2. Now when man lost these gifts through the fall, he lost that which was natural for him, and forever after became "de-naturalized," so to speak, in this sense that his nature became intrinsically and essentially vitiated and corrupted.

3. Concupiscence which is the inclination to sin and which is "invincible" is identical with original sin.

4. Concupiscence remains all through life, so does original sin. Grace, Baptism, Penance in no way affect our intrinsic corruption. Hence every act which proceeds from our nature is sinful for reason that our nature is sinful. "We are all a lost lump."

2. *Nominalism*

The first source of Luther's peculiar notion of the super-natural is to be found in his theory of human nature. The second source is to be found in

---

[10] "Vera castitas est in luxuria." Weimar, I, p. 486.

the Nominalism of the decadent Scholastics. William of Occam is known as *Venerabilis Inceptor Nominalium.* " On theological questions concerning poverty he came in conflict with the Pope; his sentences were condemned by the University of Paris, he appealed from the Holy See to a General Council; was excommunicated in 1328, protested against the decisions of the General Chapter of the Order, and then took refuge with Lewis of Bavaria, the schismatic, whose literary defender he became." [11]

Now what were some of the doctrines of the Occamists? To their justice let it be said that they recognized that the natural and the supernatural order were distinct from each other. But the two principal doctrines which bear on the present consideration are the following:

1. Grace is not absolutely necessary; it is necessary only in the present condition of things. Any act of charity which we perform in the ordinary course of our mortal life does not differ essentially from any act of nature. It is not therefore anything above our natural forces. [12]

2. God *accepts* our supernatural acts as such, simply because He has willed to do so. They are not necessarily and in themselves meritorious. It is in the nature of no act to be meritorious, even though it be infused with charity. The merit comes from the free acceptance by God. [13]

---

[11] Grisar, *op. cit.,* Vol. 1, p. 131.
[12] Occam. 1, Sentences d. 17, q. 2, ad 1.
[13] *Ibid.,* Sentences d. 17, q. 1.

Luther was influenced by theology of Occam. He states that he belonged to the School of Occam, [14] and considered Occam as the most gifted of all Schoolmen. [15] He was very familiar with the Commentary of d'Ailli on the Sentences, and in his marginal notes on the Sentences of Peter Lombard often cites d'Ailli under the name Cameracensis, Bishop of Cambrai. It is a little early yet to say definitely whether the whole of the Nominalist doctrine of Luther was derived from the Occamists. There is a growing suspicion on the part of some, in the light of researches by Professor Etienne Gilson, that Luther may have derived his Nominalism from a distinct Augustinian Tradition of thought which was current in his community. But whatever be the source, there is no disputing the fact that Nominalism colored and influenced all his teachings.

In taking over doctrines from the Nominalists Luther magnified them considerably. Occam, for example, taught that it was possible for nature to produce the same effects as grace; it was only in the present ordering of things that it was necessary. What Occam taught as possible, Luther taught as a fact.

Furthermore, the *theory of acceptation* in the Occamist theology, became the *theory of imputation* in the Lutheran, and was applied, not only to grace,

[14] Sum occamicæ factionis. Denifle, "Werke," Weimar ed., VI, 600.

[15] Summus dialecticus, scholasticorum doctorum sine dubio princeps et ingeniossimus — *Ibid.*, p. 183.

but to good works. Our works are good only because God accepts them as such and imputes His
goodness to us. [16]

This doctrine of imputation is found scattered
throughout the whole of Lutheran theology. Even
in his Commentary on the Romans, Luther en-
deavors to show that imputed righteousness is the
principal doctrine advocated by St. Paul. "God
has willed to save us, not by our own, but *by extrane-
ous righteousness and wisdom,* not by such as is
in us or produced by our inner self, but by that
which comes to us from elsewhere. . . . "Again,
he writes, "we must rest altogether on an *extrane-
ous and foreign righteousness."* [17]

Since righteousness does not come from works, for
works come from a corrupted human nature which
can produce nothing good, we should therefore, and
so much the more, cling to imputation. "Our works
are nothing, we find in ourselves nothing but
thoughts which accuse us — where shall we find
defenders? Nowhere but in Christ. . . . He has
done enough." [18]

Man ever remains sinful, but the sin is not imputed to him; he is accounted righteous by the
imputation of something which is quite foreign to
him, namely the righteousness of Christ. "The
Christian faith differs from the faith and religion
of the Popes and the Turks, etc., for by it, in spite of

[16] Quia non essent in se bona, nisi quia Deus reputat ea bona. Et tantum sunt vel non sunt quantum ille reputat vel non reputat. (Denifle),
Fecker 11, 196.   [17] (Grisar), "Cod. Vat. Palat." 1826 fol. 77.
[18] (Grisar), "Schol. Rom." p. 44.

his consciousness of sin, a man, amidst afflictions and the fear of death continues to hope that God for Christ's sake will not impute to him his sin." [19]

"We hide our injustice behind God as a screen"; Christ's merits cover us like the wings of a hen. Christ is our "mother-hen." [20] The justice of Christ covers us, and when we go before God to be judged it is not the sinner He perceives but the screen — Christ. Our justification then is something *extrinsic* to our sinfulness, [21] it is a covering over that which on the inside is full of filth and corruption. In other words, we are really like "whitened sepulchres," outside clean, but inside full of dead men's bones. The imputation saves, and not righteousness. We need have faith in Christ, and despite our sinfulness we shall be saved in the next world and imputed righteous in this. It is just this kind of theology which exaggerated itself into that remarkable letter he wrote to Melanchton on August 1, 1521. "God does not save those who merely fancy themselves sinners. Be a sinner and sin boldly, but believe more boldly still. ("*Esto peccator et pecca fortiter, sed fortius in fide*.") [22]

These are the two forces which prepared the way

---

[19] (Grisar), Weimar ed., p. 360.
[20] "Einer muss des andern Schanddeckel sein." Fecker 11, p. 334. Et ego semper prædico de Christo, gallina nostra. (Grisar), Weimar ed., p. 31. Ecce impossibilis est lex propter carnem; verumtamen Christus impletionem suam nobis impertit, dum se ipsum gallinam nobis exhibet, ut sub alas eius confugiamus et per eius impletionem nos quoque legem impleamus. *Ibid.*, p. 35.
[21] "Ideo recte dixi, quod extrinsecum nobis est omne bonum nostrum, quod est Christus." (Denifle), Fecker 11, pp. 114–115.
[22] (Grisar), "Briefwechsel," 3, p. 208.

for the Lutheran distortion of the notion of grace,
viz., his doctrine concerning the invincibility of
concupisence and the intrinsic corruption of human
nature, and which may possibly have been derived
from his experience, and secondly, the Nominalist
influence which asserted that the supernatural was
acceptable, not because it was really worth more
than the natural, but merely because God willed to
accept it as such.   From this Luther derived his
notion of the *imputability* of the merits of Christ.

Two consequences flow from these influences,
both of which endure to the present day, but under
different forms:

1. Religion ceases to be the sum of man's service to God,
but becomes the sum of God's service to man.   In other
words, religion becomes anthropo-centric, instead of theo-
centric.
2. The traditional notion of the supra-position of nature
and grace gives way to the notion of their juxtaposition.

1. *Religion becomes God's service to man.*   Nominalism in philosophy denies that the mind can
attain the real, and asserts that that with which we
are in contact is only an effigy of the real.   Mediæval
Nominalism is modern subjectivism.   Nominalism
in theology asserts that the divine never really attains the natural; it is *imputed to it;* it is something
extrinsic to it, but never one with it.

Now, if the mind knows not the real, but only its
effigy, then, as St. Thomas says, in his Summa,[23]
all knowledge is mental instead of real.   The mind

[23] i. q. 76 art. 2 ad 4.

then becomes the centre around which the world revolves. This is a Copernican Revolution long before the time of Kant, it being in germ in the decadent Scholastics. So too, in the spiritual order, if the divine, the supernatural, and grace, do not attain the natural in its inmost being, then there can be nothing in the natural as such which can make it pleasing to God, but there is much in the supernatural which may make it pleasing for the natural. It was this very implication hidden in the theology of the Reformer, which his friend Staupitz pointed out to him in a letter: "You see that the grace by which we are in *the friendship of God is not that by which we please God, but that by which God pleases us and makes Himself agreeable to us.*" [24] It is Christ who pleases us; we can do nothing, for "we are a lost lump." Righteousness is nothing intrinsic, and organic, entering into the very life of our soul; it is something extrinsic, mechanical, crystalline, remaining ever outside ourselves like a cloak. We cannot please God, but God can please us, and this in so many words means that man and not God is the centre and object of religion.

This of course is not openly manifest in Lutheran principles of reform, but the germ of it is there as Staupitz well saw. The explication comes later on and reaches its full bloom in our own day when philosophers like Professor Alexander make man

[24] " Iterum cernis, quod gratia gratum faciens non est illa qua Deo placemus, sed Deus nobis placet et gratus est." Libellus de ex. eterne prædestinationis fratris Joannis de Staupitz. No. 131, cited by Janssen-Pastor.

not only the centre of *religion but even the very creator of God*.

2. A second conclusion to be drawn from this theology is that of the juxtaposition of nature and grace. The traditional position was that nature and grace were related one to the other as *perfectio perfectibile*.[25] Nature had no claim to grace as intellect had no claim to faith. But when the supernatural did come, it did not destroy nature but elevated it, there being in the natural a kind of obediential potency which makes it passively receptive for just such perfection. Nature and grace then were related as a perfection to a thing which could be perfected by a gift.

But with Luther, nature and grace ceased to be related in this way. Nature was bad to the core and irremediably so, while grace was just an imputation. One was related to the other as a cloak to our shoulders. In other words, grace and nature were *juxtaposed* one to the other; one is foreign and extrinsic to the other in every possible way.

The supernatural order is merely an imputation and not a renovation. And in this juxtaposition of the natural and the supernatural is to be found the germs of all the juxtapositions from that day on to this: juxtapositions which blossom out into such things as opposition between science and religion, faith and science, authority and experience, mysticism and logic. History is full of this unfolding of error which began with the separation of the Head

[25] i. q. 2 art. 2 ad 1.

and the Body of the Mystic Christ in which, as Mr. Chesterton has put it, " The Reformers went to pontifical man to pull off the mitre and pulled the head off with it," and from that day on to this the world has seen a body staggering down the centuries without a head, finally satisfying itself to be just a mere body made up of the brotherhood of men, forgetful that we can never call one another " brother " until we have learned to call God " Father."

While it is not to be denied that a Reformation was needed, it was a reformation of *discipline* that was needed and not a reformation of *faith*. Somewhat similar conditions presented themselves to Gregory VII, and he reformed not faith but discipline. The sixteenth century marked a double reformation, one of faith on the part of the Reformers, the other of discipline on the part of the Church in the Council of Trent.

And it will always be the wonder of those who study doctrines as well as men, how certain thinkers can point to Luther as the great apostle of progress when his initial principle — the intrinsic corruption of human nature — makes all progress impossible. It is equally strange to see how he showed the world " true and lasting union with Christ " when Christ remained something extrinsic and foreign to us, like a cloak or a covering. Such a theory does little credit to man for it makes him irremediably vitiated, and little credit to Christ for it reduces His Redemption to a mere nominal and putative one. Finally, it is rather difficult to understand why Luther should be upheld as the great apostle of reason when he so much despised it. Even Professor McGiffert, who is not at all remiss in glorifying modern theology, has this to say of Luther: "He spoke with great contempt of the human reason, and denounced both schoolmen and humanists alike because they depended upon it; and while in this he was more extreme than his associates, the depreciation of natural reason in connection with divine things was characteristic of the reformation movement as a whole." [26]

The Evolution of the Lutheran Juxtaposition.

Luther became the source of a twofold evolution of religious thinking; one current which took up nature, which he juxtaposed to grace, worked itself out by the denial of the transcendent; the other, which took up grace, which he juxtaposed to nature, worked itself out by the assertion of the immanent. From the objective side one current tends to reduce grace to nature, the other to elevate nature to grace; from the subjective side one current tends to absorb faith in reason, and the other to equate reason and faith. Religion in the successors of Luther bases itself either on a faculty of nature and develops along rationalistic lines, or else bases itself upon the individual's need of a divine power, and develops along the lines of mysticism and sentimentalism.

[26] A. C. McGiffert, "Protestant Thought before Kant," p. 113.

*Denial of the Extrinsic. The Rationalistic
Current.*[27]

It was particularly the Socinians and the Arminians who developed the rational current in Luther's
principles. The Socinians took as their formal
method the examination of religious truth in the cold
light of reason. They accepted Sacred Scripture as
the revealed word of God, but since it requires interpretation, this interpretation must be done in the
light of reason. Reason is the organ by which man
knows, receives, comprehends and judges Divine
Revelation. Certain universal axioms and common
notions (*axiomata universalia atque communes
notiones*) are set up by reason as being uncondi-
tionally true in the relation to religious doctrine;
e.g., a just person does not punish a good person in
place of an evil one; a person who is from another
is not from God.

In the light of these principles the Trinity was
rejected as being opposed to simplicity; the pre-
existence of Christ was also denied and therefore
His Divinity; consequently, His Passion and
Death were a mere example to us and a pledge of
forgiveness, but operated no redemption of the human race.

[27] A heterodox Catholic current manifested itself in Baius, for whom
the supernatural order is reduced to the natural order; in Jansenius,
for whom justification is not due to the imputation of Christ's merits
by faith (Luther), nor by obedience to the law (Baius) but in actual
help of grace which enables us to overcome what he called the terrestrial
delight or attraction; and finally in Quesnel, who combined the errors of
both. Justification for all three was something accidental and even
sentimental.

Socinianism did not last long, the political situation of Poland hastening its decline. In 1658 the Diet of Warsaw prohibited its confession under penalty of death. It found its way into England with John Biddle (1622) and into Germany with Soner of Altdorf (1612). Holland prohibited all Socinian writings in 1599. But its seed was sown and in the course of time it became one of the important harbingers of Rationalism.

What is important in the history of Socinians is the decline it effected in the belief of the supernatural. Luther believed both in the *power* and the *light* of the supernatural, i.e., grace and the Scriptures. This sect denied the power and retained the light. The " function of Christianity was reduced to the revelation of truth in order that man might know the way of life, which once known, it is in his power to follow. This estimate of Christianity prevailed more and more among the Rationalists. The Gospel ceased to mean supernatural power given from above and came to mean only supernatural light." [28]

The Arminians who followed the same train of thought reacted directly against the unnatural cold *decretum horribile* of Calvinistic predestination, under the leadership of the one from whom they have taken their name, Jacob Arminius, Professor at the University of Leyden. But there is much more in their movement than this. In *spirit* it is a continuation of a current of rationalism. " The

[28] A. C. McGiffert, " The Rise of Modern Religious Ideas," p. 20; also Hastings, *Socinianism*, " Ency. of Religion and Ethics," Vol. X, p. 652.

Arminians were infected with Socinianism. The immoral antimonianism taught by the more ignorant Calvinistic ministers in England as a direct result of Calvin's doctrine of election gave them an opportunity of appealing to mens' reason, and the appeal was made to men whose conception of the Church and the Sacraments was lower than that of Calvin and who were therefore more prepared to accept a reduced Christology." [29]

"By its underling principles of equality and freedom it was more perfectly fitted than its rival system (Calvinism) for a period of intellectual transition. Arminianism stood generally for the strengthening of the scientific temper and for the principle of moderation. . . . It strove to emancipate exegesis from the thralldom of dogmatics . . . Arminianism was a protest against the mystical interpretation of the internal world as a sufficient exponent and infallible judge of the external." [30]

The premises of Luther, the Arminians and the Socinians were the same, but their conclusions were different. Luther depreciated reason while the Socinians, and to a lesser extent, the Arminians glorified it. What was common to them all was the denial of the transcendent or what they called the extrinsic. Luther considered the Church as extrinsic, the Socinians and the Arminians considered

<hr/>

[29] Leighton Pullan, "Religion Since the Reformation," 2d ed. 1924, p. 138; A. B. D. Alexander, "Shaping Forces in Religious Thought," 1920, p. 67.

[30] Hastings, *Arminianism*, "Ency. of Religion and Ethics."

grace extrinsic, and succeeding generations marching under the banner of a revolt which ends in the absorption of grace and faith into nature and reason, denied even supernatural light, and then the Scriptures ceased to be revered as the Word of God. Luther distorted the greatest of spiritual realities, namely grace, and the Socinians and Arminians eliminated it. It now remains to develop a substitute for it.

The Assertion of the Immanent. The Philosophy of Individualism.

The separation and even the juxtaposition of nature and grace, it was said, resulted in a double evolution, one stressing nature, the other grace. The first developed into a kind of theological rationalism which we have just briefly traced. The second current starts not with reason but with the heart and develops in the direction of the spiritual and mystical rather than the rational and humanistic.

Luther sounded the keynote of the philosophy and the theology of the immanent in announcing his doctrine of the immanence of justification by faith, the personal experience of justification and the private interpretation of Sacred Scriptures. The genesis of these doctrines resulted in a kind of religious romanticism in which the individual believed himself to be in direct communication with God Who reveals Himself to man by prophecies, miracles, visions and the like.

The forms in which this individualism developed may be reduced to three:

> Dogmatic individualism
> Mystical individualism
> Moral or pietistic individualism.

Dogmatic individualism was represented chiefly by Luther as we have already indicated in treating his doctrines. In brief it was the problem of justification posited in the first person: "How am I justified?" This form of individualism is familiar to all under the form of private interpretation of Sacred Scripture.

Mystical individualism stressed the interior illumination of the soul without much emphasis on the moral or practical side. For some this communication of God is transitory and manifests itself from time to time in visions, ecstacies, and such like; for others there is a continuous real inworking of God in the human heart.[31] Dogmatic Individualism asserted the right of the individual to be his own interpreter of Sacred Scripture. Mystical Individualism, on the contrary, held not so much for private interpretation as private revelation. God is now thought of as revealing Himself to each individual. Hence the Mystical Individualists were quite out of sympathy with Sacred Scripture as a rule of faith: it was too cold and impersonal. Revelation must be personal and intimate. No one now was considered as an interpreter of the Bible, but every man was his own Bible.

[31] Pünjer-Hastie, "The Christian Philosophy of Religion from the Reformation to Kant," p. 209 ff.

The slightest acquaintance with the religious movements of this period manifests a general distrust of individual interpretation of Sacred Scriptures. But instead of returning to a mystic body, the Church, as the official guide on these matters, the later reforms had recourse to direct manifestation of God to each soul. Examples of this tendency are numerous. Melchior Hoffmann for example, (1533) and his associate Stifel believed themselves the recipients of divine visions which manifested to them that the end of the world would come at eight o'clock in the morning of the third of October, 1533. David Joris (1501–1556), one of the Anabaptists of Holland, maintained that in his early life visions and revelations taught him the speedy return of the Lord. Whenever he was asked to prove his doctrine by Sacred Scripture, he repudiated the challenge as human wisdom and philosophical curiosity, asserting that the doctrine was revealed to him immediately from heaven. Hans Niclas (1502–1577) on the same divine authority, believed the world divided into three periods: in the first, law rules under sin; in the second, Christ rules; and in the third, Hans Niclas himself rules through love, for God united Himself to him and made of him a living tabernacle in order to proclaim His works to the world. Quakerism under George Fox, Robert Barclay and William Penn believed that the "inward light" differed from the light of individual reason, and that salvation is effected through the light of Christ which does not come through creeds or dogmas or even calmly, but by a sudden seizure which is accompanied by convulsive movements of the body, whence the name Quakers.

In these individuals and sects it was not Sacred Scripture so much as revelations, visions, internal lights and ecstacies which revealed divine truth. There were other individuals who carried on a common polemic against too high an estimate of the external letter and strove above all else to delve directly into the depths of the Deity. One of the best known of this group is Michael Servetus (1511–1553), the well known physician, and geographer, who after the fashion of Nicolas of Cusa, believed that God communicated Himself to all things without which there would be no being or subsistence. The world is therefore identical with God in essence. Thomas Münzer (1490–1537) went so far in his depreciation of Sacred Scripture as to assert that " it availeth nothing even though one should eat a hundred thousand Bibles." No less opposed was Sebastian Frank (1495–1543) who declared that all death in the Church comes from a literal understanding of the Scriptures. Faith, he said, does not consist in adhering to certain beliefs as true, but in experiencing the facts of faith. Valentin Weigel (1533–1588) in his "Dialogus de Christianismo" presents to the reader a debate between a layman who expounds Wiegel's ideas, and a preacher, representative of ecclesiastical orthodoxy. Christ appears and decides in favor of the layman. The preacher, though fortified by sacraments, dies and is buried in hell, but the layman, because of his reliance on direct and personal revelation is saved. Schwenkenfeldt (1490–1562) taught that man belongs to the animal world because of his body and to the spiritual because of his soul. Hence what is external can only move the external man, whereas only God can move the spiritual, and this He does without intervention of a book or a dogma or a church. Carlstadt (1541) and von Hohenheim (1493–1541) though differing in expression yet held as a common denominator the notion that the eternal Christ takes precedence over the historical, and the Living Word over the Written Word.

Moral or Pietistic Individualism: The mere revelation or communication of God to the soul was found to be insufficient, unless it made for the improvement of the individual and the perfection of the society. As Cornhert (1522–1590), secretary of the city of Harlem, used to say: "Christianity does not consist in the lip, but in life. It is in the walk, not in the talk." Theobald Thamer (1569) soon realized after his experiences as an army chaplain that the reformation doctrines, the overflow of sentiment and gushy sentimentalism had not improved the morals of the times. Johann Arndt (1555–1621) and Joachim Betkins (1663) lamented the passing of the true imitation of Christ. Universities took up the reform for practical piety and made it their aim "rather to save one soul than make a hundred scholars." It was this craving for true piety which prepared the way for Pietism which found its best expression in Jacob Spener (1635–1705) who attributed all godlessness to the exaggeration of dogmas. Hence, in 1670, he founded *Collegia Pietatis,* that is private assemblies in his own house for pious readings and mutual edification. In answer to an attack by Lutheran theologians he wrote "*Theology of all Believing Christians and Upright Theologians*" (1680), wherein he set forth the principle that while human industry plays some part in the understanding of the Word of God, its real sense is grasped by an Illumination of the Holy Spirit; and since a requisite for such an illumination is righteous living, no unregenerate man can possess a true knowledge of God or be a good theologian.

As a constructive force Pietism bettered morals, but as a disintegrating force Pietism was twofold: "it undermined respect for dogmatic theology in general, turning men's attention from orthodoxy to life; and it reduced the traditional system to comparatively low terms by distinguishing its essential from its unessential tenets." [32]

In England the reform along practical lines centred chiefly around Puritanism. Heylyn gives the year 1565 as the actual date at which "these Zwinglian or Calvinistic factions began to be first known by the name of Puritans . . . which name has been ever since appropriate to them because of their pretending to greater purity in the service of God than was held forth unto them in the common

[32] A. C. McGiffert, "The Rise of Modern Religious Ideas," p. 10.

prayer-book. [33]   The religious principle which gov-
erned them was the inner word of the Holy Spirit
which was set above the mere external letter.   "As
if the prediction of the prophet Joel were fulfilled,
everyone appealed to the word of the Lord which he
had heard as to an immediate revelation which he
had received, or to the Spirit of God which spake in
him." [34]   For the Puritan emphasis was laid on the
fact that "it is not the head but the heart which
makes the Christian." [35]

The whole Evangelical movement in England is
also to be traced to this yearning for a more practical
piety.   Professor McGiffert in comparing the two,
writes, "Like German pietism, English evangeli-
calism was practical in its aims and methods, but
it had great influence in the sphere of religious
thought.   It is a fact of cardinal importance that
it took its rise in a period dominated not by scholasticism, but by rationalism.   It was in fact, in no
small part, a reaction against rationalism in all its
forms.   This gave it, in spite of its kinship with
German pietism a very different character in many
respects." [36]

[33] "History of the Reformation," Vol. II, p. 421.

[34] Pünjer, *op. cit.*, p. 213

[35] "History of England," Vol. 1, p. 81.   Taine writes, "His speech
stuffed with scriptural quotations, his names and the names of his children
drawn from the Bible, bore witness that his thoughts were confined to the
terrible world of the seers and ministers of divine vengeance.   Personal
asceticism grew into public tyranny.   The Puritan proscribed pleasure
as an enemy for others as well as for himself.   Ornaments, pictures and
statues were pulled down and mutilated.   The only pleasures permitted
were the singing of Psalms through the nose, the edification of long
sermons, the excitement of acrimonious controversies."   "History of
English Literature," Vol. 2, p. 323.

[36] "Protestant Thought before Kant," p. 163.

Summarizing what has been said above, Luther put an abyss between nature and grace, forever making it impossible for the latter to perfect the former. Perhaps he did not see the consequences of his principles, but his followers did. Some insisting on nature, such as the Socinians and the Arminians, rejected supernatural power or grace as extrinsic and unnecessary. Others, insisting on grace, such as those who developed mystical individualism with stress on interior illumination of the soul, and those who developed Pietistic individualism with stress on personal righteousness, treated the supernatural as natural and immanent. Luther brought the individual into prominence by asserting his rights against a mystic corporation, and by putting into his hands the Sacred Scriptures which he might interpret as he saw fit. But his followers glorified the individual still more by making the individual a kind of Scripture inspired directly by Almighty God. Though varying in form, the fact still remains that authority, Divine Light and Power more and more became immanent in man. He became free as regards a Church and free as regards a Scripture. It is this tendency to emphasize immanence in religion which constitutes the Philosophy of Individualism. A new current cuts in through this development; in fact, it was already manifest before Pietism, and that is the current of Rationalism. Its development led to the *Philosophy of Fact*.

CHAPTER V

RENÉ DESCARTES marks the beginning of a new period in the development of the contemporary idea of religion thanks to the new juxtaposition he introduced into the world of spiritual realities. As Luther juxtaposed nature and grace, so Descartes juxtaposed the intelligibile and the sensible; as Luther distorted grace by making it extrinsic to nature and not its perfection so, too, Descartes distorted intellect by making it extrinsic and independent of the sensible and not its perfection.

The origins of the Cartesian system are to be traced to two influences, one belonging to the past, the other to his own times. Descartes' relation to the past is not so marked, for he cared little for tradition or history. Nevertheless, it is true that the Protestant current did have some effect on him, for its doctrine of the immanence of spirit and experience, which was put in the place of the living word of the Mystic body on the one hand, and the authority of Sacred Scriptures on the other, naturally grew into a species of rationalism. When the inner experience grew cold it was only a matter of time when natural reason would be considered the inner light.

Then, too, there was the negative influence of a decadent Scholasticism against which he reacted, the dominant characteristics of which have been summed up by Professor De Wulf:

1. The prevalence of schools, parties and routine. The religious corporations accept the hegemony of one of their doctors. The universities flock to a standard and it is not rare to find the choice of a philosopher determined by politics or intrigue.

2. The abuse of dialectical discussion increased. The vital doctrines of scholasticism were neglected or else corrupted. In the seventeenth century manuals compared matter and form to lovers who courted, married and divorced and contracted new unions.

3. The scholastics defend themselves badly or else not at all, against the philosophers of the Renaissance.[1]

Hamelin [2] has urged that very little of the philosophy of Descartes is to be found in the past, and in support of his thesis urged the following points: the philosophers of the Renaissance were generally Pantheistic, *e.g.*, Bruno and Patritius, and Descartes was anything but a Pantheist. The physics of the Renaissance was not conducive to Cartesianism, it being for the most part, qualitative and vitalist, *e.g.*, Telesius with his twofold principles of heat and cold. Montaigne and Charron, the French skeptics, had little or no influence on Cartesian doubt except perhaps to give it a certain smack of

---

[1] "History of Mediæval Philosophy," Vol. 2, pp. 294, 5.
[2] "Le Systeme de Descartes," 2d ed., 1921.

antiquity. Mathematics offered little, for Descartes himself avows that he did not read Viete until he was thirty-one, that is at an epoch when his geometry was already well formed.

Though the past contributed little positively to his formation there was a *spirit* budding in his time which did much to mould his life and his works, and that is the scientific spirit in its experimental and its mathematical aspects. Experiment was the life of the age. Da Vinci called it the "unique interpreter" of nature; and under the inspiration of Bacon, such men as Rondelet, Visale, Aselli and Harvey used it in their quest for forms, essences and qualities. Mathematics, too, was taking new strides. Galileo has the honor of being the first to apply mathematics to physics according to the spirit of modern science. But although Galileo gave examples of the positive method he never developed the science of method, in the sense that he discussed whether one could substitute quantities for qualities in the physical world. This task remained for Descartes. Hamelin's contention is probably correct, for none of the scientists of the time exercised a direct influence on him, but certainly the spirit of the times did. His system as a system comes from within, and here we pass on to study its genesis in his own mind.

When Descartes came to study the relation between the decadent Scholasticism he had learned in Fleche and the new scientific spirit of the age, he became conscious of what he believed was a conflict between the two. In the first part of his " Discourse on Method " he tells us that the old philosophy is speculative whereas the new science is practical; the old philosophy was interested only in essences, forms and natures and qualities, while the new scientific temper concerned itself with quantities.

In the face of this opposition between philosophy and science Descartes could see only one way out,[3] and that was by a completely new approach to the subject. Having falsely identified Scholasticism with the old physics, it was only natural for him to repudiate Scholasticism in repudiating the new physics. He made war on Scholasticism from the beginning to clear the ground for his new system. Scholasticism was something to be exterminated at all costs — *ante omnia exterminanda*.[4] Once Scholasticism was out of the way he laid anew the foundations of thought. *The Aristotelian method proceeded from physics to mathematics, or more*

[3] Really there was another solution which was given by the Scholastics themselves before their philosophy degenerated, viz., to distinguish Physics or the science of pure observation from Natural Philosophy which was Physics studied in the light of metaphysical principles. The physics might change, but this in no way affected the metaphysical principles brought to bear upon it. The decadent Scholastics probably were the only ones Descartes knew well, though he did have a copy of the *Summa* with him in Holland. He forgot entirely the prudent experimental probabilism of the great Scholastics, Comm de Coelo, lib. a lect 17 (Licet enim talis) ; De Boet. de Trinitate q. 4 art. 2 ad 8 ; i q. 32 art 1 ad 2 ; Met. lib. 12 lect 10 — .

[4] " Œuvres," Adams-Tannery ed., Vol. V. p. 176. He felt dissatisfaction with it even while in school (" Discours de la Methode," Flammarion ed., 2d part, p. 13). Speaking of the philosophy which he had at Fleche, he wrote: " I should like very much to read over a little of their philosophy, something I have not done in twenty years, to see if it would not seem a little better to me now than it did then." A.-T., Vol. 3, 30 Sept. 1640, p. 185.

simply from the sensible to the intelligible. His
method was just the contrary; he proceeded from
metaphysics to physics or from the intelligible to
the sensible.

He proposed a system which would unite both
metaphysics and physics — the accord or union
of which he believed Scholasticism could no longer
effect. It is probable that this idea of a method
came to him at Neuberg on the Danube in the year
1619, where "he found leisure to enjoy the company of his own thoughts." There he dreamt of
some great universal science which would unlock all
knowledge, not only that of metaphysics, but also
that of physics and science.

The new method must be one of invention, he
argued, and this rules logic out of court for "logic
is only a dialectic which teaches the mode of ex-
pounding to others what we already know, or even
of speaking much without judgment of what we do
not know, by which means it rather corrupts than
increases good sense." [5] Logic does not invent, but
algebra and geometry do.[6] But the trouble with
algebra and geometry is that both are slaves either
to figures or to symbols. Descartes gets out of this
difficulty by *employing algebra to express geometric
relations,* and in so doing invented analytic geometry or the method of expressing by equations the
properties of geometrical figures. In this way he
found what he called: "universal mathematics, be-

[5] Preface to the *Principles; cf.* "Discours de la Methode," 2d
part, p. 13.
[6] Regulæ 10, 14, 15.

cause it contains all the elements which make of the other sciences part of mathematics." [7]

This was an important step in the history of mathematics,[8] and no less an important one in furnishing him the clue to the method he was seeking.

Since he had found that there was a generalization applicable to universal mathematics, why should there not be one applicable to the whole field of knowledge? Why should there not be a science of knowledge which would unfold truths in the same way mathematics unfolds them?

The answer to this question is " The Discourse on Method," whose purpose he tells us is to do away with the sterile logic and syllogisms of the School,[9] and to set up in their place his own method founded on mathematics "which the geometricians are wont to make use of." [10]   His first rule is "never to accept a thing as true which I do not clearly know to be such." This is what may be called the "principle of evidence." Nothing will be accepted except what is evident. But the Aristotelian categories of form, essence, the metaphysics, logic and physics of Scholasticism are not so evident — hence these are all condemned in principle.

While this method is being applied Descartes excludes certain subjects from the application of his method. [11]

[7] Regula 4.
[8] Gaston Milhaud, " Descartes Savant," 1921, p. 124 ff.
[9] " Discours de la Methode," p. 13.
[10] *Ibid.*, p. 14.   [11] *Ibid.*, p. 16.

1. Religion is not to be included in the examination of reason, for truths of religion do not fall under its jurisdiction. We must believe them, not examine them. "We must," says Descartes, "seek neither to adapt them to our reason nor to adapt our reason to them." They belong to another domain.

2. He then makes a distinction between the sphere of knowledge and of conduct. He submits to a provisional ethics which is to be replaced by definitive ethics only when the science is completed.

3. More definitely and concretely, he will not apply his method to political, ethical and social questions.

With these exceptions philosophy and science will be judged solely on the grounds of rational evidence. Anything which is not clear will be rejected. In the fourth part of his Discourse he proceeds (a) to reject anything and everything of which he has the least doubt; (b) to distrust the senses because they have sometimes deceived him; (c) to distrust reasoning, for sometimes the results of the positive sciences are erroneous. (d) It is even legitimate to suppose that an evil genius takes delight in making him err, even when he wishes to see the truth.

As a general rule, then, consent to any proposition will be withheld until it is manifestly clear.

Is there any proposition which is not affected by this doubt? There is one, and only one. My senses may deceive me, my reasonings may be false, and evil genius may delude, but there is one thing of which there can be no doubt. If I am mistaken it is because I am, and this truth *cogito, ergo sum,* is "so evident and so certain that the most extravagant doubt of skeptics is unable to shake it." This he takes as the first principle of his philosophy.

From this Descartes immediately goes on to prove the existence of God, from the idea of perfection which he has and which certainly could not have come from experience. It must therefore be a " stamp left by the workman on His work." [12]

The existence of the soul is proved in the same manner—a proof well known to those who have the slightest acquaintance with Descartes.

The Juxtaposition of the Intelligible and the Sensible.

So much for the origins, both extra-mental and mental, of the method of Descartes. But wherein does his system present characteristics which make it an epoch in the history of philosophy? What revolution did he introduce into thought which makes him one of the prophets of the modern idea of religion? Descartes distorted intellect, the second great spiritual reality, by juxtaposing it to the sensible. This is brought out clearly by recalling the various manifestations of this juxtaposition found in his system, *viz.,* his peculiar theory concerning the relation of science and philosophy, his theory of knowledge, his theory of the relation between the soul and body and, finally, his doctrines concerning the relation between Theology and Philosophy.

Descartes, it was said, failing to distinguish between sciences of observation and Natural Philos-

[12] " Discours de la Methode," p. 23.

ophy, which is the metaphysical reflection on these observed facts, fell into the error of believing Scholastic metaphysics antiquated and useless because its physics was useless. He wished to avoid that conflict between the two, and strove to bridge them in virtue of a new philosophy, which really never effected linking the two, but rather their separation. His solution was to invert the Aristotelian-Scholastic procedure of beginning with Physics as the first degree of abstraction and then working up to Metaphysics. *He chose to begin with Metaphysics* and then work down to *Physics,* in other words, to begin with the intellectual, the "clear and distinct" and only then find his way down to the sensible. In his Preface to the *Principles* he explicitly states "Philosophy is like a tree, the roots of which is Metaphysics, the trunk of which is Physics, and all the other sciences are the branches." [13] In other words, he "closed his eyes," "shut his ears," turned away from the senses, and "effaced all the images of sensible things," and thus completely upset the normal procedure of the human mind, which begins with the world of experience as the raw material for the finished products of the intellectual. After stating that his Metaphysics was a preparation for his Physics, he continues in a remarkable confession which does not say too much for his sincerity: "But you must not say so, please, for those who favor Aristotle would find great difficulty in approving it.

[13] Cf. H. Gouhier, "La Pensée Religieuse de Descartes," 1924, p. 12. E. Gilson, "L'Etudes de Philosophie Medievale," 1921, p. 115; "La Doctrine Cartèsienne de la Liberté et la Théologie, 1913.

I hope that those who read them will accustom themselves unconsciously to my principles and will recognize the truth of them without seeing that they
destroy Aristotle." [14]

In a word, Descartes hoped to attain the real
inside himself by reason, in the same way that man
finds God in himself through the infused gifts of the
Holy Spirit. Instead of using the natural procedure
of the human mind of mounting to the intellectual
through the doors of the sensible, the very way
nature intended, he used the artificial procedure of
methodic doubt, introductory to the revelation of
the Cogito, and pretended to grasp the spiritual
without the preamble of the material. He enclosed
himself in a fixed and impenetrable world, Divine
Veracity alone being the guarantee of correspondence with things — and this whole method of beginning with Metaphysics and then working down to
Physics, is the beginning of a juxtaposition of the
intelligible and the sensible which manifests itself
more clearly in his theory of knowledge.

Jacques Maritain, in a remarkable study of Descartes, [15] has developed this juxtaposition of the
intelligible and the sensible by showing that for
Descartes knowledge is intuitive as regards its
method, [16] innate as regards its origin [17] and independent of things as regards its nature. Ideas for
Descartes are only effigies of the real; what is
grasped primarily and directly is not the real but

---

[14] "Œuvres," A.–T., Vol. III, pp. 297, 298.
[15] "Les Trois Reformateurs," 1925, Chap. 2.
[16] Regula 2.   [17] A.–T., Vol. VI, p. 112.

the thought — Cogito.[18]   If the sensible is not necessary for the origin of our ideas, if the term of
knowledge is not the real but the effigy of it, then
the intellect becomes endowed with the quality of
aseity and is independent of things.   He wished to
bestow liberty on the intellect in the sense that
he desired to free it from the determination of the
sensible — and in doing so distorted knowledge.
Knowledge is like entrance into the Kingdom of
Heaven; it can be gained only by humbling ourselves.   In the true procedure knowledge humbles
itself by going down to the material for its determination and forthwith is exalted to the realms of
the spiritual.   Descartes refused to humble his
mind by going down to things, but immediately exalted it by appealing to Divine Veracity as a guarantee of the real, and for its exaltation was destined
to be humbled by locking the mind forever in the
narrow corridor of a *Cogito*.   Then and there began
the great modern problem of knowledge: how pass
from the mental to the real?   "This is the central
problem of Cartesian metaphysics, namely, the passage from thought to existence.   Thought alone is
indissolubly inherent to itself.   How then, and by
what right and in what sense can one affirm exist-
ences?"[19]   "The Cartesian reform is responsible
for that strange condition in which we see humanity
today, so powerful over nature, so informed and
skillful in dominating the physical universe, but so
weak and disorientated before intelligible realities

[18] A.-T., Vol. VII, Third Meditation, p. 160.
[19] M. Boutroux, *Revue de Metaphysique et de Morale*, Mai 1894.

to which the humility of wisdom made us formerly an heir. To fight against bodies, it is equipped as a god; to fight against the spirit, it has lost all its arms." [20]

Besides the juxtaposition of the intelligible and the sensible in all the phases just outlined, there are yet other juxtapositions among which may be mentioned that of the body and the soul, which is simply another way of putting that of the intelligible and the sensible. For Descartes, the essence of the soul was thought, and the essence of matter was extension. This necessarily brought up the problem of the relation between the two, since their natures are so diverse. It is the problem of knowledge in psychological dress. The Palatine Princess felt the difficulty — in those days princesses were philosophers — and she asked Descartes how the one could ever act on the other. Descartes finally offers excuse that he has to go to Utrecht whither he was summoned to explain something that he wrote "about one of their ministers. This compels me to end now, as I have to try to find a way of getting free of their chicaneries as soon as possible." [21]

And the problem which really was an illegitimate one from the beginning has never since been solved.

A final form of the juxtaposition of the intelligible and the sensible is to be found in his peculiar ideas concerning the relationship between theology and reason, or faith and science. Theology for Descartes is equivalent to the unintelligible. "Re-

[20] Jacques Maritain, *op. cit.*, p. 115.
[21] "Lettres de Descartes," Cousin ed., Vol. IX, p. 127.

vealed truths are above our intelligence, and I would not dare submit them to the feebleness of my reason: I believe that to undertake their examination and to succeed, it would be necessary to have some extraordinary assistance of heaven and to be something more than man." [22]

In other words, the theological is the irrational for Descartes; [23] the infinite is beyond the intelligible — all of which is implicit agnosticism. He believes that he honors God by placing Him beyond the sphere of the rational and the intelligible. In like manner he reduces to a minimum the rational preparation of faith, and the value of the proofs of rational credibility, thus proving that philosophical rationalism tends to become a kind of religious fideism. It is a remarkable thing that Descartes continually speaks of the God of the philosophers, but never the God of Love. He speaks of the world, but is brief concerning creation and when he comes to the problem of man, his origin and destiny, he is silent. [24] This juxtaposition of theology and philosophy is later on taken up by Spinoza who writes, "The end of philosophy is truth; faith is nothing but obedience and piety." [25]

The *Cogito* of Descartes thus displaced the axis of philosophy. Levy-Bruhl writes: "To the ancients and to the scholastics (theology excepted),

---

[22] " Discours," 1st part.
[23] " Principes," I, XXVI.
[24] H. Gouhier, " La Pensée Religieuse de Descartes," 1924, p. 194. Jacques Maritain, " L'Esprit de la Philosophie Moderne," *Revue des Sciences Phil. et Theol.*, t. XXIV, 1914, p. 614.
[25] Tract., Theol. Pol. cap. XIV.

the thinking mind appeared inseparable from the
universe, regarded as the object of its thought, just
as the soul itself was conceived to be the substantial
form of the living body.   According to Descartes,
on the contrary, the existence of a thinking mind,
far from being dependent on any other existing
thing, is the essential condition of every other existence conceivable to us : " for if I am certain of the
existence of anything but myself, with far better
reason am I certain that I, who have that thought,
am in existence.   The only reality I cannot possibly
question is that of my own thought." [26]

Evolution of the Cartesian Juxtaposition [27]

Descartes, in the application of his method, carefully avoided the application of his method to

[26] " Modern Philosophy in France," p. 20.

[27] A. C. McGiffert, " The Rise of Modern Religious Ideas," 1921.

A. C. McGiffert, " Protestant Thought before Kant," 1915.

Leckey, " History of the Rise and Influence of the Spirit of Rationalism in Europe," 1865.

Bernhard Pünjer, " History of the Christian Philosophy of Religion from the Reformation to Kant," trans. from the German by Robert
Flint, 1887.

Robertson, " A Short History of Free Thought, Ancient and
Modern," 2d ed., 1906.

Hunt, " Religious Thought in England in the 17th Century," 1870.

Leslie Stephen, " History of English Thought in the 18th Century,"
1876.

Mark Pattison, " Essays and Reviews," 1862, *Tendencies of Religious Thought in England*, 1688–1750.

Höffding, " History of Modern Philosophy."

A. V. G. Allen, " The Continuity of Christian Thought," 1895.

J. A. Dorner, " History of Protestant Theology," 1871.

Otto Pfliederer, " The Development of Theology," 1890.

John Cairns, " Unbelief in the 18th Century," 1881.

John Oman, " The Problem of Faith and Freedom in the Last Two
Centuries," 1906.

Faith, Morals, and Religion. But his successors were not of the same opinion. "The precaution he had taken to ' set apart' the truths of faith was not equivalent to a treaty of peace with theology, definitive and accepted on both sides. It was merely a truce and destined soon to be broken." [28]

The method of evidence and the 'clear and distinct' became the method of Rationalism. "Rationalism ultimately made its home in Protestantism rather than in the older communion, and not because the former was in principle more tolerant of divergent views, but because the divisions within the Protestant ranks made greater tolerance a necessity." [29]

Two currents flow from Descartes: (1) The denial of the extrinsic which attaches itself to the intellectual side of the Cartesian juxtaposition and ends in a rationalized Christianity — a Christianity without the supernatural. (2) The assertion of the immanent which corresponds to the sensible side of the Cartesian juxtaposition and ends in an exaltation of the *fact* of the sensible or material universe as the limit and apex of human knowledge. We do not mean to assert that Descartes was directly

---

J. Leland, " A View of the Principal Deistical Writers," 5th ed., 1837.

F. Vigoroux, " Les Livres Saints et la Critique Rationaliste," Vol. II, 1901.

Ludovic Carrau, " La Philosophie Religieuse en Angleterre," 1888.

Lechler, " Geschichte des Englischen Deismus," 1841.

[28] Lucien Levy-Bruhl, " Modern Philosophy in France," 1899, p. 109.

[29] A. C. McGiffert, " Protestant Thought before Kant," p. 187.

responsible or even the principal inspiration of Philosophy and Theology which followed him, but merely this: Descartes, for the first time in modern thought clearly expressed a principle of Rationalism. Though his followers did not all adhere to it in *principle*, they did adhere to it in *spirit*. In this sense Descartes is taken as the prophet of the Philosophy of Fact.

1. *The Denial of the Extrinsic — Rationalism:* The Cartesian method of the application of the principle of evidence to the sphere of knowledge broadened into the application of reason to all the departments of thought, both philosophical and theological. Just as Luther's denial of grace in the realm of theology ended in the denial of supernatural power with the Socinians and the Arminians, so too, Descartes' distortion of intellect in the sphere of philosophy, ends in the denial not only of supernatural *power* but also supernatural *light,* there being nothing more left to revealed religion than that which reason bestows on it or concedes to it.

Revealed religion at first was denied only indirectly by the early Deists, whose rationalism was inspired by Protestant individualism as much as by Cartesian method. Herbert of Cherbury (1583–1648), for example, began with a rationalist principle that God's perfection demands that salvation be open to all, and since this cannot be given in any particular system, which, by its nature, is not open to all, it follows that the means of salvation must be implanted in human reason whereby they will be accessible in all times, places, and circumstances. He then proceeded to draw out five propositions based on reason which constitute the norm of natural religion. Thomas Browne (1605–1682) in his "Religio Medici" anticipates Harnack in the spurious distinction between the religion of primitive Christianity and the product of its adulteration through ecclesiasticism. Charles Blount (1654–1693) with unbecoming grace turns Genesis into ridicule and in his "Oracles of Reason" adds two more propositions to the list of Cherbury, which constitute the essence of natural religion. John Locke (1632–1704), while admitting the possibility of human reason to prove the existence of God, nevertheless, in speaking of revelation sets up certain *caveats* to guard us against the too easy acceptance of pretended revelations.[30] "Whatever God has revealed is certainly true; but whether it be a divine revelation or not, reason must judge." Locke, however, had wisdom enough to see that the Deists were illogical in setting up a catalogue of fundamentals. While the method of Locke was Christian, it was empirical in its results. There is no doubt that Descartes exercised a profound influence on him. John Toland (1670–1722) rationalized revelation in his "Christianity not Mysterious," by denying there was anything above reason in it. Faith, for him, is merely a conviction based on previous knowledge and, therefore, reducible to reason. In his "Letters" to *Serena,* the

[30] "Essays on Human Understanding," Bk. 4, chap. 18, 10, 15.

Queen of Prussia, there was sufficient incredulity to attract the attention of Baron d' Holbach who translated the " Letters " into French to serve the cause of impiety in France. In this work Toland states that the doctrine of future life and the immortality of the soul are "Egyptian fictions." He wrote against Spinoza, but later became a pantheist, using the term for the first time in his " Pantheisticon." Finally, there may be mentioned among many others the Earl of Shaftesbury (1671–1713), who declared in his introduction to " Characteristics of Men, Manners, Opinions, Times," that his object is to illustrate the Stoic Principle: everything is opinion. In the name of opinion he made war on Christianity and the Sacred Scripture, but at the same time asked tolerance for all, for we can never be sure when we possess the truth.

The attack against Revelation and the supernatural became more effective when writers chose to attack its particular tenets. An important stage in the rise of rationalism is reached in Collins and Woolston who denied respectively the probative power of both prophecies and miracles. Anthony Collins (1676–1729), in his " Essay Concerning the Use of Reason in Propositions, the Evidence Whereof Depends upon Human Testimony," sought to undermine all evidence from prophecy, pointing out what he believed was a lack of correspondence between prophecy and fulfillment.

Taking as his rule, after the Cartesian fashion, the proposition that the assent to any proposition depends upon the evidence with which it presents itself to the human mind, Collins deduces *more geometrico*, two propositions concerning *Sacred Scripture*:

(a) Everything in Sacred Scripture which interpreted literally shocks our sense, should be interpreted allegorically.

(b) All expressions which are not in accord with our manner of looking upon God should be rejected as interpolations.

Collins, forgetting the distinction between what is above reason and what is contrary to reason, applied his principles and concluded that Sacred Scripture was not inspired. Thus he extinguished the one light the Socinians left burning.

In 1713 he published his "Discourse on Free Thinking Occasioned by the Rise and Growth of a Sect Called Freethinkers," which is a panegyric on the license of thought. Men have fallen in a multitude of errors; there have been false revelations; hence the best attitude to take is that of atheism, for atheism is better than superstition. His argument was very much like saying that because there is counterfeit money in the world therefore there is no good money.

Naturally these attacks in a Protestant country produced great commotion. Among those who rose up against him were Bentley, who published two volumes in 1713 under the title, "Remarks upon the Discourses of Free Thinking." Bentley treats Collins as a knave and a fool. Swift also attacked with that irony of which he possessed the secret. One of Swift's main arguments is that of misanthropy. All men are fools, therefore freethinking is an absurdity. Freethinkers are knaves as well as fools, and hence their conclusions are contemptible. "The bulk of mankind is as well qualified for flying as for thinking." [31] A contemporary said: "If any man deserved to be denied the common benefits of air and water, it is the author of the discourse of freethinking." Leslie Stephen says of him, "He was destined like his great predecessor (Newton) to illustrate the truth that a man may be an eminent mathematician and a childish theologian." [32]

Thomas Woolston (1669–1733) applied the allegorical interpretation to miracles, after the fashion of Collins, and by the same token banished them from religion. In 1705, he published "The Old Apology for the Truth of the Christian Religion against the Jews and Gentiles Revived." The Old Apology for him was the allegorical interpretation of Sacred Scripture. Why are there so many dissensions in the Christian body today? It is because up to this time Sacred Scripture has been interpreted literally instead of allegorically. Moses was purely an allegorical person; miracles in the Pentateuch are merely types; the changing of water into wine is the symbolic destruction of the Jews in a bloody war under Titus. The plague of frogs over Egypt symbolizes the Jews dispersed over the world after the fall of Jerusalem. Collins never

---

[31] Swift, 1859 ed., Vol. 2, p. 197.
[32] "History of English Thought in the 18th Century," Vol. 1, p. 212.

attempted to prove that prophecies were absurd, but merely that prophecies did not refer to the narrative. Woolston, in asserting that Christ's miracles were allegorical, was saying that *actually they did not occur.* His style is bitter and acrimonious, violent and injurious. Leslie Stephen says of him: "He is a mere buffoon jingling his cap and bells in a sacred shrine, and his strange ribaldry is painful even to those for whom the supernatural glory of the temple has long utterly faded away." [33]

No one up to the present had attacked Revelation and Sacred Scripture in its entirety. Locke had proclaimed the autonomy of reason; Toland had substituted Pantheism, and Shaftesbury, skepticism for Christianity. Collins wrote against prophecies and Woolston against miracles, but it remained for Matthew Tindal (1657–1733) to attack the Holy City from all sides. Pope says of him in his *Dunciad:* "Toland and Tindal, prompt at priests to jeer."

In 1730 Tindal published his best known work, "Christianity as Old as Creation, or the Gospel a Republication of the Religion of Nature." This work is the negation of the supernatural origin of the Bible as well as all Revelation. It can be summed up as follows: Natural religion is perfect; all other religions, Christianity included, are true religions only in the sense that they are identical with the natural religion.

He believed that Our Divine Lord promulgated a

[33] *Op. cit.* Vol. 1, p. 232.

natural religion, and for that reason, he speaks in the title of his work of the " Republication of the Law of Nature." " The Bible is not inspired; it is full of contradictions, and the story of Adam and Eve is absurd." Voltaire said of him that " he was the most intrepid supporter of natural religion." [34]

The rationalist onslaught against the supernatural was yet to be carried on by Thomas Morgan and Thomas Chubb who directed their attacks against the Old and the New Testament respectively. Four years after the death of Tindal, Morgan, his disciple, anonymously made war on the Old Testament, declaring that all revelation is the invention of theologians. It is interesting to compare some of our " new " ideas concerning God and Christ with those of Morgan. The modern idea, for example, of looking upon Jehovah as a local God of the Hebrews and an inferior kind of deity is to be traced to Thomas Morgan. He anticipated Eichhorn and Paulus in asserting that Old Testament miracles were myths, and long before the Tübingen school set forth the Petrine and Pauline parties.

Thomas Chubb (1679–1746) concentrated his attacks on the New Testament — rather an auda-

[34] In twenty years 106 refutations were written against him. The most important of all is " Scripture Vindicated," written by Daniel Waterford, which contains a fine defense of the Divinity of Christ and the inspiration of Sacred Scripture. Another remarkable work was written by J. Foster, " The Usefulness, Truth and Excellence of the Christian Revelation," 1731, in which the author proves the authenticity, credibility and integrity of the New Testament.

cious task for one who knew only English. Voltaire says of him, "He thought the religion of Jesus Christ was the religion of Thomas Chubb, but it was really the religion of Jesus Christ." Diabolical possessions were explained as natural maladies; the Bible was no more inspired than the Koran; religion is a human creation and all religions are equally true.

With the supernatural eliminated, and all religions reduced to a purely natural basis, it remained for David Hume (1711–1776) to inaugurate the idea of evolution in religion, so much a part of our modern history of religion. Polytheism was a primitive form of religion, according to Hume, and deism and theism are the fruits of the reflection of centuries. In his "Essay on Miracles" he attacked the probative value of miracles, not disproving them, nor showing their impossibility as such, but only their impossibility of serving as a guarantee of the authority of a Divine Messenger.

With Hume, deism dies and impiety takes its place. The English influence now penetrates into France and Germany. Thus England pays back its debt to France, which had given it the rationalism of Descartes. In France the reaction is one of impiety, in Germany it is one of theological rationalism. Among the French may be mentioned Peter Bayle — the "attorney general of scepticism," the author of the "Dictionary," an arsenal for much of France's rationalism; Bernard Fontenelle, who looked upon mathematics as the "universal instrument," and held the theory that the difference in peoples from one time to another is due to the necessary succession of discoveries, the theory that made Comte look upon him as the precursor of modern times; Voltaire, the scoffer whose whole life was dedicated to the destruction of Christianity, and who, in foolish pride, boasted that "it took twelve men to found that infamy (Christianity), but it will take only one to destroy it." Voltaire, at the end of his life, speaking of the dissolution of Christianity, said: "I have done more in my time than Luther and Calvin." Finally, there is Jean Jacques Rousseau, the apostle of sentiment and the exponent of romanticism.[35]

In Germany, English Deism combined with French impiety and Wolffianism to produce its theological rationalism. Among the leaders may be mentioned Charles Wolff, who sought by the mathematical method to reduce theology and philosophy to a unit; Johann Salmon Semler, with his 171 works, only one of which reached a second edition; Gotthold Ephraim Lessing, who introduced religious indifference in Germany with his theory of unlimited progress, and who published the "Fragments of Wolfenbüttel" as of an unknown author, when he knew them to have been the work of Reimarus and the gift of his daughter Elsie. Finally, there is Frederick Nicolai, the German Diderot, in the sense that he began the publication of a Uni-

[35] The influence of Rousseau upon this whole movement is quite marked, but from another point of view. *Cf.* Leon Noel, " La Philosophie Romantique," Brussels, 1927.

versal Library wherein the Bible was explained according to reason.

Thus the application of the principle of reason to revelation completed the work Luther had begun. For him, only the Church was "extrinsic," and was therefore to be denied. For his immediate followers, and for the Socinians and the Arminians, supernatural power or grace is "extrinsic" and unnecessary, and now, thanks to the principle of the rationally clear and distinct, even the supernatural light — Sacred Scripture — has gone out. All revealed religion is gone now; reason has done its work. It remains for another philosopher to show that even reason is powerless.

II. *The Assertion of the Immanent. The Philosophy of Fact.*

Another current flows from the sensible side of the Cartesian juxtaposition and ends in the assertion of the *Philosophy of Fact.*

In the "Essay on the Human Understanding" Locke proposed to approach the discussion of philosophical problems from the basis of the analysis of ideas, a psychological method. He hoped to destroy false pretensions about knowledge by showing just how ideas originate. This was a very natural problem in the light of Descartes' answer to a similar question. He immediately begins by rejecting the innate ideas of Descartes. "When men have found some general propositions that could not be doubted of as soon as understood, it was a short and very easy way to conclude them innate. This being once received, it eased the lazy from the pains of search, and stopped the inquiry of the doubtful concerning all that was once styled innate." [36]

Having disposed of innate ideas, and having proven that the mind, in the words of Aristotle, is nothing but a *tabula rasa,* he proceeds in his second book to show how ideas originate.

For Locke, the whole content of consciousness springs partly from outer experience and partly from inner experience — sensation and reflection. By means of " reflections we perceive our own mental states and activities; by means of sensation the effects of other things." [37]

Locke then argues against substance, in *denying that it is anything above the mere facts contained in experience.* He writes, " The ideas of substance

[36] Bk. 1, Chap. 24. Locke argued against innate ideas in the following manner: " For I imagine anyone will easily grant that it would be impertinent to suppose the ideas of colors innate in a creature to whom God hath given sight, and a power to receive them by the eyes from external objects; and no less unreasonable would it be to attribute several truths to the impressions of nature and innate characters, when we may observe in ourselves faculties fit to attain as easy and certain knowledge of them, as if they were originally imprinted on the mind." — Bk. 1, Chap. II, 1.   " Furthermore," argues Locke, " it is evident that all children and idiots have not the least apprehension or thought of them, but certainly they would have if they were innate." The existence of polytheism and atheism proves that the idea of God, for example, is not innate in all men, and the diversity of moral customs in various countries proves that elementary truths of moral are not universally accepted.   " Whatever we think of innate principles, it may with as much probability be said that a man hath 11 pounds sterling in his pocket, and yet denied that he hath either penny, shilling, crown or other coin out of which the sum is to be made up, as to think that certain propositions are innate, when the ideas about which they are can by no means be supposed to be so." — Bk. 1, Chap. IV, 19.

[37] Bk. 2, Chaps. 1, 2.

are such combinations of simple ideas as are taken
to represent distinct particular things subsisting
by themselves, in which the supposed or confused
idea of substance, such as it is, is always the first
and chief. Thus, if to substance be joined the
simple idea of certain dull whitish color, with certain degrees of weight, hardness, ductility, and
fusibility, we have the idea of lead." [38] *For Locke
the idea of substance is the idea of the qualities or
powers which we attribute to it.* Everything which
we attribute to substance is derived from experience. Such a notion has within it the germ of the
Philosophy of Fact which asserts that nothing is
above experience in the strict sense of the term.
Locke went so far as to say that even the idea of
God which is a substance-concept is formed by ex-
tending and elevating the ideas of spiritual qualities
taken from the inner sense.

For Hobbes, substances were only names; for
Locke a substance is a sum of qualities. Berkeley
here enters the philosophical world with his principle *esse est percipi* and concludes that there is
nothing in the world independent of mind, or in
other words, that the mind can never know material substances.[39] Berkeley retained spiritual
substances; but his successor, David Hume, denied even these. "The idea of substance is nothing
but a collection of simple ideas that are united by
the imagination, and have a particular name as-
signed to them."[40]

[38] Bk. 2, Chap. VII, 10.   [39] "Principles," Sections 35, 36.
[40] "Treatise on Human Nature," Bk. 1, Part I, 6.

Now, it is important to observe here that of the three Cartesian substances, God, matter and mind, only one remains — the first. Berkeley prepared the way for a denial of material substances, and Hume laid the ground for the denial of spiritual ones. In addition to this, Hume even denied human personality to be a substance, thus bringing man down to the realm of the material and the phenomenal.[41] It was typical of his whole philosophy; there are no substances, no *rationes,* no personalities: there are only *facts.* It is among them our mind must work, but never getting beyond them to a cause,[42] never transcending the material universe, never knowing anything beyond factors disclosed by experience. "My intention," says Hume, "is only to make the reader sensible of the truth of my hypothesis, that all our reasonings concerning causes and effects are derived from nothing but custom; and that belief is more properly an act of the sensitive rather than the cognitive part of our natures."[43] Belief is not destroyed but all its reasonable and demonstrable character is denied. God may exist, but the mind cannot rise above the *fact;* hence the ontological, cosmological and teleological arguments for God's existence are

[41] Man is "nothing but a bundle or collection of different perceptions which succeed each other with inconceivable rapidity, and are in a perpetual flux and movement." *Ibid.,* Bk. 1, Part IV, 6.

[42] "After a frequent repetition, I find that upon the appearance of one of the objects, the mind is determined by custom to consider its usual attendant, and to consider it in a stronger light on account of its relation to the first object." It is this impression, then, or determinism, which affords us the idea of necessity. *Ibid.,* Bk. 1, Part III, 14.

[43] *Ibid.,* Bk. 1, Part IV.

denied; we have no right to assume, he tells us, that there is a mind back of the universe, nor can we deduce an Infinite Creator from an imperfect world, nor a future state from the present moral order.[44]

The first forward step in the emancipation of the modern mind was the privilege of private interpretation of Sacred Scriptures. This immanence of authority, in the course of time, became the immanence of mystical revelation and pietism. Philosophically, and with Descartes, immanence of justification without the authority of a Living Word, became immanence of knowledge without the determination of the sensible. Followers of Descartes enlarged on this principle and freed the mind even from the determination of causality, necessity and transcendence. Knowledge is immanent in the *fact*, and there is no knowledge beyond it. It was once the *person* to whom the supernatural was revealed and this is the Theology of Individualism; it is now the *fact* which contains knowledge, and this is the Philosophy of Fact. Is is any wonder that Hume, who marks the peak of such a philosophy, should say of his speculations: "they appear so strained and ridiculous, that I cannot find in my heart to enter into them any further."[45]

[44] A brief but clear exposition of these philosophers finds a sympathetic treatment in "Philosophy," Bertrand Russell, p. 244 ff.

[45] "Treatise on Human Nature," Bk. 1, Part IV, 7.

CHAPTER VI

THE PHILOSOPHY OF VALUE

ONCE the idea of grace was distorted and twisted by making it extrinsic to nature, once the true function of the intellect as the crown and perfection of the sensible was denied in favor of innate ideas, there remained but one great spiritual reality untouched by the destroying hand of philosophers, and that was the will, which in traditional thought received its goal and end from the intellect. There now appears on the scene one of the best known of the world philosophers, Immanuel Kant, who, endowed with every good intention, nevertheless razed to the ground the last vestige of traditional thought by distorting the true nature of the will, the source of man's noblest aspiration.

The origins of the Kantian system, first as far as external influences are concerned, and next as regards his own mental development, merit recall. Among many others, the two principal external influences which went into the formation of his system were Pietism and Rationalism. Rationalism endangered his Pietistic leanings, and in an attempt to save the latter he worked out a system which was nothing short of revolutionary.

1. *Rationalism.* Kant announced in his "Pro-logemena " that it was the memory of David Hume that roused him from his dogmatic slumbers. Hume, it will be recalled, had limited philosophy to a knowledge of the fact, by denying necessity to ideas, the principle of causality, and the power of the mind to prove the existence of God. It was only by habit, said Hume, that we expect an effect to follow from a cause, but there is no reason for assuming the objective validity of the principle. Rationalism could sink no lower; it touched the nadir in the Philosophy of Fact. Thinkers were becoming impatient of keeping their eyes on dust. Opposition to the Aufklärung [1] in Germany, was becoming more formidable, and Wolff, who was using the rationalist method at Halle, found it more and more difficult to spread. Voltaire, in France, had already scoffed at the rationalistic optimism of Leibnitz; Klopstock and Wenckelmann in Germany, shook men's faith in rationalistic æsthetics; Lessing waged war on the canonical, the dogmas of æsthetics, poetry and theology.[2] Kant had sympathy for these forces which made war on Rationalism, and this because Hume's principles in germ made for the dissolution of Pietism which was dear to his heart. In this sense Rationalism was a negative influence on Kant.

2. *Pietism* exerted both a direct and an indirect influence on Kant. (a) " His profound sense of

[1] Ed. Zeller, " Geschichte der Deutschen Philosophie seit Leibnitz," 2nd ed., p. 69 ff.

[2] Friederic Paulsen, " Immanuel Kant," 1902, pp. 18–21.

the urgency of the moral law written in our hearts; the individualism characteristic of his ethical outlook; his conviction that not gradual improvement but a complete change of orientation is involved in the passage from a bad to a good life; his appreciation of the 'radical evil' in human nature, the corruption of the heart, which is none the less certain that it defies satisfactory explanation; not to mention his obvious familiarity with the Bible; in all these features of his mind and character we trace the result of his religious education in Pietistic surroundings." (b) "On the other hand, in his marked disposition to suspect those who indulge themselves in a supposed personal intercourse with God in prayer of a harmful and demoralizing self-illusion we may not unreasonably conjecture that we see the effects of a reaction from the atmosphere of overstrained absorption in private spiritual experience which the type of religion commonly associated with the Pietistic movement would tend to create." [3]

Kant wished to save Pietism, and in particular the belief in God, immortality and freedom of the soul. The problem therefore was, on the one hand, to secure these beliefs, and on the other, to escape the skepticism of Hume. One escape would have been to take refuge in a Fideism of the supernatural order, but this did not appeal to him for he had no inclination to the supernatural for two reasons: his revulsion for *Schwärmerei*, fanaticism

[3] C. C. Webb, "Kant's Philosophy of Religion," 1926, p. 20. H. Schmid, "Die Geschichte des Pietismus," 1863.

and spiritual intoxication, and also his unhistorical temper of mind.[4] As time went on the solution of his problem became clear and certainly one of the influences which fitted in well with his Pietism was Rousseau's assertion of the rights of feeling.

"Up until now," writes Höffding, "faithful to the principles of Enlightenment, he had sought for the essence and nobility of man in the understanding only; now he discovered a still deeper foundation, common to learned and lay, in which the simplest peasant might be equal with the profoundest thinker. And Rousseau's appeal to immediate feeling and immediate faith must have seemed all the more significant to Kant, since he was just on the point of undermining the proofs which had hitherto been supposed to support the assumptions on which the doctrine of natural religion was based."[5] The day that *Emile* appeared, Kant, much to the astonishment of his neighbors, failed to take his usual walk at the accustomed hour.

The problem for Kant was to save these beliefs which Hume destroyed by endowing them with some kind of necessity. If there was necessity in mathematics, why should there not be necessity in philosophy? Kant, in other words, sought to apply the certainty of Newtonian physics to the philosophical order. Criticizing the Leibnitzian view he asserted that progress in mathematical knowledge was not given by an analysis of purely intellectual concepts, nor by the accumulation of

[5] "History of Modern Philosophy," Vol. 2, p. 34.
[4] C. C. Webb, *op. cit.* p. 21.

sense perceptions, which was the view of Locke
and Hume, but by something midway between the
two. He never doubted for a moment that there
was an *a priori* element in mathematics and physics.
To discredit them seemed foolish. Whence comes
this necessity? The first man who demonstrated
the properties of an isosceles triangle, argued Kant,
saw a new light; his thought was creative; it con-
sisted in creating such a figure and then drawing
out of it the necessary implications of his own
thought. "He saw that he had to produce (by construction) what he had himself, according to *a
priori* concepts placed into that figure and represented in it, so that in order to know anything with
a priori certainty, he must not attribute to that
figure anything beyond what necessarily follows
from what he has himself placed into it, in accordance with the concept." In other words, unless we
approach nature with certain principles we can
never find its laws. "Even the science of physics
entirely owes the beneficial revolution in its character to the happy thought that we ought to seek
in nature whatever reason must learn from nature,
and could not know by itself, and that we must do
this in accordance with what reason itself has placed
in nature." It was a happy thought, when Copernicus, contrary to common experience, assumed
the spectator to be turning around and the stars to
be at rest. He would never have discovered the
law if he had not dared to seek it in the spectator
instead of the spectacle.

Professor Frank Thilly, in tracing out the origin of the Kantian revolution, says: "Kant believed that a new light had flashed on him. Just as Copernicus imagines the spectator moving and the stars at rest, so Kant tries the experiment in metaphysics, of presupposing that, in the perceiving of objects, it is the objects that conform to the perception, and not the perception that conforms to the objects. If experience is dependent on our minds, and something already organized by the mind, according to its laws, then we have an *a priori* knowledge of what we experience." [6]
Kant thus reached the conclusion that mathematics is necessary and universal, because it is a creation of the mind, of the perceiving and the understanding mind. Applying the conclusion to philosophy, he said that we understand space, time and causal relation because the mind relates things spatially, temporally and causally — although if there is no objective relation between the two, it is difficult to see just how the mind should relate spatially rather than temporally, or causally rather than spatially.

Such was the Kantian revolution. Up to this time it was held that ideas adapt themselves to objects; for Kant objects adapt themselves to ideas. In the constitution of knowledge the mind contributes as much as it receives. The raw material of experience is taken up and moulded to a pattern contained

[6] *Kant's Copernican Revolution* in "Immanuel Kant," Open Court Pub. Co., p. 204 ff.

within the mind itself. Time and space are no longer external to mind; they are "forms of sensibility," while the principle of causality and the categories of understanding are mental principles by whose agency our manifold experiences attain to their unity and coherence of knowledge.

For Descartes, knowledge comes from the mind or from *above* in that sense that ideas are innate; for Hume, knowledge comes from senses or from *below*, in the sense that all ideas are groupings of sensations. For Kant, knowledge comes from both above and below, both from the inside and the outside, and here he was close to the Scholastic position, but not close enough, for he failed to see a connection between the inside and the outside. Senses cannot give knowledge, for they cannot explain necessity and universality; intellect alone cannot, for its forms are empty. It needs the matter of knowledge furnished by the senses and the *forms* furnished by reason. (For the Scholastics reason does not furnish *forms*, it finds them by abstraction; hence it bridges the gap between the inside and the outside. Intellect is a light, not a mould.) For Kant, the *a priori* which is in the mind furnishes its models to chaotic data of sense experience, and thus renders science possible. It is therefore reality which is modified by mind, and not vice versa. Kant thus bore the fruit of Descartes' bad thinking. Descartes believed that the intellect attains immediately and directly its thought, the Cogito, but not the reality. It was consequently very easy for Kant to conclude that the reality behind these representations must remain forever unknown.

But up to this point we have been speaking of objects of experience. What about those objects which lie beyond experience, e.g. the existence of God, the immortality of the soul, and the freedom of the will? These, says Kant, cannot be the object of *a priori* knowledge in the same way as mathematics and physics, for the simple reason that they lie beyond experience. We can never know what lies beyond phenomena, or what exists prior to, or apart from being taken up by our mental powers. This brings up the subject of Kant's attitude toward religion, and the revolution he introduced into philosophy of religion.

Juxtaposition of Belief (Will) and the Reason of Belief (Intellect)

Kant's contribution to the evolution of the contemporary idea of religion is the juxtaposition he introduced between the intellect and the will, or belief and its rational foundation. The will, according to traditional thought, receives its object from the intellect, for the evident reason that we can never will or love or believe in a thing unless we first know it. Kant, on the contrary, said we could never have any rational knowledge of natural religious truths, and yet we were to believe in them for another reason than an intellectual one. To this extent he tore down the bridge between intellect and will, between faith and science, between belief and its intellectual justification, and thus prepared for the final exile of the last of the great spiritual realities. For purposes of brevity we will indicate this juxtaposition in the two " Critiques " of Kant and in his " Religion within the Limits of Pure Reason." The " Critiques " were not the first of Kant's works. As early as 1755, he wrote the " General History and Theory of the Heavens," which is important because it manifests the great impression the argument of design made upon him, for he confessed that the beauty and harmony of the universe made him suspect a "strange hand" behind its orderliness. Eight years afterwards, he uses another argument for the existence of God in his work: " The Only Possible Ground of Proof for a Demonstration of the Existence of God." Herein he advances not the argument of design, but a modified form of the ontological argument; something is possible and possibility supposes a real being. The implication is that a thought which is not the thought of reality is no thought at all. The concluding words of his thesis, however, cast the shadow of the " Critiques " before them: " It is necessary that one should be convinced of God's existence, but not so necessary that one should prove it." A year later he published an essay on a question propounded by the Berlin Academy, "The Clearness of the Principles of Natural Theology and Ethics," which is important inasmuch as it anticipates a later distinction between the speculative and the practical intellect, without using the term practical intellect, but rather "feeling" which he took from Hutcheson.   The last important work before his " Critiques " was the Latin dissertation, " De Mundi Sensibilis et Intelligibilis Forma et Principiis," which is generally regarded as the transition work from dogmatism to criticism.   This work does not yet make the denial that the human mind can know things as they are in themselves, apart from our perception of them, but it does speak of the senses and the forms of the understanding which figures so prominently in his later works.

It is clear that even these early works manifest the juxtaposition which was the thesis of his famous " Critiques." We are not interested in these works from the purely philosophical point of view but merely from their bearing on religion.   From this angle the Kantian doctrine and the Kantian juxtaposition of the intelligible and the credible may be enunciated as follows: " The Critique of Pure Reason " asserts that we have no rational foundation for our belief in God; the " Critique of Practical Reason " asserts that in spite of this it is necessary to believe in Him.

In his " Critique of Pure Reason," Kant denies the validity of the arguments for the existence of God, arguments which are valid enough if one would admit his revolutionary relation between thought and reality.   What is important is the conclusion he deduces from the impossibility of proving the existence of God, viz., the only theoretical use which can legitimately be made of the idea of God is the *regulative.* "Reason does not supply us with the objective validity of such a concept." [7]

The idea of God does provide us with some notion of the systematic unity of all experience; the idea is important but whether or not there is an objective reality standing behind it matters little. It still has some use.[8] The supposition, therefore, which reason makes of a Supreme Being, as the highest cause, is relative only, devised for the sake of the systematical unity in the world of sense, and a mere Something in the idea, which we have no concept of what it may be by itself." [9]

Kant even goes so far as to say that the term "Nature" might even be preferred to "God," because it suggests less knowledge of what that Being really is which lies behind phenomena.

What is true of the existence of God, is true of the immortality of the soul and all religious truths — they cannot be rationally demonstrated; at best they can serve to unite our experiences in a nominal way, but only as ideas or hypotheses, and not as objective realities.

In his next work, "The Critique of Practical Reason," he attempts to bring through the back door those truths which he had ejected through the

---

[7] Mueller's translation p. 542.

[8] "If we admit a Divine Being, we have not the slightest conception either of the internal possibility of its supreme perfection, nor of the necessity of its existence, but are able at least thus to satisfy all other questions relating to contingent things, and give the most perfect satisfaction to reason with reference to that highest unity in its empirical application that has to be investigated, but not in reference to that hypothesis itself." *Ibid.*, p. 543.

[9] P. 545.

front door. His left hand knew not what his right hand did. He shows that, while God, freedom and immortality cannot be validated by pure reason, they are nevertheless demands of moral conscious-ness. Moral consciousness postulates a universe in which the value of the spiritual experiences are con-served and supported, i.e., it must postulate a power adequate to bringing the Summum Bonum into be-ing. Practical reason is the name of human volition in the sense that it is supposed to give a reason for what is willed.

After having said that it is morally necessary to admit the existence of God, he adds that this moral necessity is *subjective,* i.e., a need — *Bedürfniss,* and not *objective,* i.e., a duty — *Pflicht,* for " it can-not be a duty to admit the existence of a thing, since that belongs wholly to the theoretical use of rea-son." [10] A few lines later he adds that the " exist-ence of a supreme intelligence, for the pure reason is only a *hypothesis,* but from the practical point of view it is an act of faith, but an act of purely rational faith." [11]

The general result of the two Critiques of Kant, from the point of view of religion is the following: the foundation of religious certitude is not to be sought in the speculative reason, for it is incom-petent, but in the imperative needs of the practical reason. Friedrich Paulsen has well expressed the juxtaposition in these words: " Kant's Critique of

[10] Kritik der Praktischen Vernunft, 1 Theil, 2 Buch, " Werke," Berlin ed., 1908, p. 125.

[11] *Ibid.,* p. 126.

Pure Reason prepared the death-blow in asserting that reality transcends the standpoint of knowledge. From this as a *consequence, religion cannot be derived from nor demonstrated by reason. Its roots are to be sought in the will."* [12]

This is precisely what we mean by the juxtaposition of belief and the reason for belief. Religious beliefs from this time on become something blind; they have no rational ground; they cannot be proved; they may be postulates of a rational faith, but we can never be certain that there are realities corresponding to them. Religious truths were transferred from the domain of knowledge to the domain of *faith,* and the problem of their validity became the problem of their value.[13] It is no wonder that Kant's fellow-countryman, Heine, called the "Critique of Practical Reason" "the farce after the tragedy," and held it as his opinion that Kant "moved by pity for the poor people and perhaps by the fear of the police, added to the first Critique the second which is in contradiction with it, and which really should have borne over it the inscription Dante placed over the gates of hell: *Lasciate ogni speranza, voi ch'entrate."*

---

[12] Immanuel Kant, 1902, pp. 18–21.

[13] "La Philosophie de la Religion de Immanuel Kant, p. 106. P. Charles, "L'Agnosticisme Kantien," *Revue Neo-Scolastique,* 1920, p. 257 ff. C. Sentroul, "La Philosophie Religieuse de Kant," *Revue des Sciences.* "Phil. et Theol.," Jan. 1910, p. 49 ff. Phillip Bridel, "La Philosophie de la Religion de Immanuel Kant," Lausanne, 1874, .p. 106. Albert Schweitzer, "Die Religions Philosophie Kant's," Frieburg, 1899. Pünjer, "Die Religionslehre Kant's," Jena, 1874. Colani, "Exposé Critique de la Philosophie de la Religion de Kant," Strasbourg, 1845.

" Religion within the limits of Pure Reason " even better shows the philosophy of value carried to its logical conclusion. This work was made up of collected essays, one of which Kant wrote against Woltersdorf, pastor of the Trinity Church, Berlin, who was a member of the Board of Censorship appointed by Frederick II, whose function it was to test the doctrines of the instructors. Two of the other essays were refused the Lutheran *imprimatur* so Kant appealed to his own university and the completed work appeared at Easter time, 1794.

What is important in this work is the application of the methods of the two Critiques. There is running throughout it the thesis that although dogmas of religion have no objective validity (the point of view of the " Critique of Pure Reason "), they have nevertheless some practical value, or else some symbolic value (point of view of the " Critique of Practical Reason "). This is illustrated first of all in his doctrine on the fall of man. He says that the fact of the fall of man, narrated in Genesis, explains very well man's propensity toward evil, but he cannot accept that explanation, for every actual sin he believes is an original sin. Adam cannot be regarded as affecting us or implicating us in his rebellion against God. He is symbolic of " Every Man "; he stands for each of us. " Mutato nomine, de te fabula narratur."

What is true of the Fall of Man is true of the Redemption. Kant is not definitely and concretely interested in whether or not Christ ever was an historical person; what is important is the subjective effect he has on the mind of the believer. This is what in recent years has been known as Modernism. "In a practical point of view," he writes, "the supernatural hypothesis (that Christ is a preternaturally begotten being) can benefit us nothing since the archetype subjected by us in thought to this phenomena is to be found in *ourselves*."[14] And as a further proof that the objective fact of Christ's historicity interests him little he avows that the "practical value of the idea of the heavenly man alone possesses moral worth, and whosoever should ask for signs and credentials would thereby proclaim his own moral unbelief."[15] Kant goes yet even further away from a rational ground for belief in Christ, by asserting that the emphasis on the miraculous origin of Christ might tend to lessen the force of His example: "the advancement of this Holy One above the weakness of human nature, so far as we can see, would rather impede than assist this idea in exciting our generous emulation to attain it."[16] In accordance with these principles Kant regarded the Virgin Birth as an idle controversy, since the doctrine has no practical value except as a symbol of humanity free from anything which hinders victorious resistance to evil. In brief, Kant substituted for the historical Christ an archetype of humanity well pleasing to God.

[14] *Die Religion Innerhalb der Grenzen der Blossen Vernunft,* "Werke," Reimer ed., Vol. 6, p. 64.
[15] *Ibid.,* p. 63.   [16] *Ibid.*

This meant the end of an historical objective religion and the beginning of the subjective.[17]

His definition of religion as "the recognition of all our duties as divine commands" was an excellent expression of his now already well developed religion of values. But whence comes the persuasion that all our duties are divine commands? If it is purely subjective, as is the Kantian contention, then religion ends in skepticism, and for what reason should we appeal to God Whose existence we can never know? If it is objective, then God has spoken in history, then Christ is historical, then the boasted autonomy of reason is only a verbal autonomy. If it is interior as the Post-Kantian said, then it is God Who speaks to me and then the revelation cannot be limited to the practical and denied to the theoretical.[18]

It is worth remarking with Professor Webb that Kant's definition of religion (1) "avoids requiring any speculative assertion, even that of the existence of God, and (2) avoids all suggestion of special duties (*Hofdienste*, court services, Kant calls them)

[17] "It may therefore perhaps be all very true that the *Person* of the Teacher of the alone true and universal valid religion is an impenetrable mystery; that His advent and departure from earth were miraculous; that His eventful life and death were likewise miracles; nay, that the very history documentarily attesting the narratives of all these wonders is again itself a miracle (*i.e.*, supernatural revelation). . . . All this, it is conceded may be done, so long as those historic documents are not perverted into elements of religion, and mankind taught that the knowing, believing and professing their contents, is in itself something whereby we can render ourselves acceptable to God." *Ibid.*, p. 85.

[18] Otto Pfleiderer, "The Development of Theology," trans. by J. F. Smith, 1923, p. 19; Gaston Rabeau, "L'Introduction a l'Etude de la Theologie," 1926, p. 51.

due to God over and above our natural duties to our
fellow men . . . Kant sees then in religion neither
an enlargement of our speculative knowledge nor
yet a collection of special duties towards God distinct from those to our neightbor, but a peculiar way
of regarding the latter." [19]

As Kant grew philosophically, it became increasingly more evident that he was bent on the denial of
the transcendent and the assertion of the immanent.
God and the intellectual justification of His existence were denied as the transcendent, and the
moral ego, the subjective self was asserted as the
immanent.

" His conception of the Creator became more and
more transcendent in the sense that the reference to
him of the order of nature became something neither
evident nor even capable of being inferred from
phenomena, but a mere 'regulative idea,' indis-
pensable perhaps, but with no claim to be taken for
metaphysical truth, although negatively valuable as
ruling out alternatives, which, in a region necessarily beyond the ken of our intelligence, would
accord less with the facts within our ken.

" On the other hand the God whose voice was
heard by Kant in the Moral Law tended to become
in his thought more and more *immanent;* for this
God could not be conceived without injury to our
moral outlook as accessible otherwise than through
the moral law . . . only on condition of seeing in
God no other than a Reason identical with our own,

[19] C. C. Webb, " Kant's Philosophy of Religion," p. 151.

as ours is with that of all rational beings, yet untrammeled by having associated with it a sensitive nature with its self-regarding appetites and peculiar point of view." [20]

It may, at first sight, seem strange to say, that Kant eliminated the will, since his *Practical Reason* was nothing else than the will, and since he saved God and immortality and freedom through belief which is of the will. It is true that Kant did retain will, but he so much distorted it as to destroy its real nature. He believed that reason and faith could not exist together: " I had to remove knowledge to make room for faith." The will, which is the seat of inclination, in belief, is never blind according to traditional philosophy. The intellect supplies its object and the reason of its belief, for nothing is willed unless it is known. It will be recalled that, for St. Thomas, the will is nobler than the intellect in those cases where the object of the will is nobler than the soul. The reason is, that the intellect drags things down to its level, but the will always goes up to meet the requirements of its love. Thus it is nobler to love God than to know all created things, for in loving God the will goes out to meet God but in knowing things it descends to the finite and the material. But suppose now that the intellect cannot know God; suppose that it cannot rise above the the transitory things of the phenomenal world; suppose that it cannot prove the existence of God, or the immortality of the soul. What then becomes of the

[20] *Ibid.,* p. 175.

objects of the will? Where will it find those spiritual objects which will elevate it? Where will it find those realities, the love of which makes the will nobler than the intellect? What will supply it with goals and ends which will be something more than ideals like pots of gold at the end of a rainbow? Here is precisely the difficulty of Kant. Since the intellect cannot know anything above the phenomenal world, as he attempts to show in his "Critique of Pure Reason," then it can never offer to the will an object nobler than itself. If the intellect does offer such objects, it is for some other reason than a rational one, and then the will is blind. It strives without a reason for striving; it yearns without any certainty that the object of its yearning is a phantom or a reality. When we have no reason for supposing there is a target before us there is not much reason for shooting at it, and if we have no real reason for the existence of God, then we have no reason for postulating Him for our moral life. Faith which has no rational ground is not faith but superstition and fancy. A will without an intellect making its postulates reasonable is not a will, but what Heine has called the "farce after the tragedy." It is in this sense that Kant eliminated the will from the philosophy of religion by distorting it and making it blind.

To this extent Kant introduced a new point of view, and in the words of Friedrich Paulsen it "may be described by means of two propositions: first, the worth of man does not depend upon his intellect,

but solely upon his will; and secondly, one's ultimate metaphysics does not rest upon the understanding, but primarily upon the will. The final
and highest truths — the truths by which and for
which a man lives and dies, do not rest upon scientific knowledge, but have their origin in the heart,
in the essential principle of the will. . . ." [21]

The Evolution of the Kantian Juxtaposition

The influence of Kant on philosophy cannot be
denied. Even in his own time it was felt that he
would change the axis of thought. Boggesen called
him a second Messias, and Stilling in a letter to
Kant in 1789, said: "You are a great, a very great
instrument in the hands of God, and I do not flat-
ter — but your philosophy will work far greater,
far more general, and far more blessed Revolution
than Luther's reform." Hölderlin, in the same
laudatory terms, called Kant the "Moses of our
nation, who is leading it from Egyptian stagnation
into the free lovely desert of his speculation and
bringing to it the dynamic law from the holy
mount."

The development of the Kantian juxtaposition
of the intellect and the will, or the belief and the
reason for the belief, was chiefly along two lines, one
negative and taking its inspiration from the " Critique of Pure Reason," the other positive and inspired by the "Critique of Practical Reason." The
first was the denial of the transcendent, or the intel-

[21] "Immanuel Kant," p. 391, 2.

lect as the foundation of belief; the second was the assertion of the immanent or the philosophy of values.

The Denial of the Extrinsic: The intellect for the traditional philosophy was the faculty of the transcendent, the power which put us in communion with being, with truth and with goodness. What the *philosophia perennis* calls transcendent, that modern philosophy calls extrinsic. The intellect is extrinsic for Kant; it cannot attain things as they are in themselves, nor reach up to a knowledge of God any more than grace, in the Lutheran conception, could intrinsically affect human nature. It can never give reasons for the faith of the will, nor for the postulates of the practical reason; and is the useless baggage in the journey toward the goal of religion.

The evolution of the Kantian opposition to intellect as the foundation of belief has been constant and unswerving. In a certain sense it has not evolved; rather it has become a fixed principle and a court of appeal. To it must be traced the present general belief that God's existence cannot be proved by reason. The favorite " argument " against the proofs for the existence of God is the " argument of authority," viz., "the fatal defects of all these have, it is almost universally conceded, been clearly expressed once for all by Kant." [22] " The bare fact that all idealists since Kant felt entitled to scant or neglect them, shows that they are not solid

[22] James Ward, " Pluralism and Theism," 2nd ed., 1920, p. 406.

enough to serve as religious all sufficient foundation." [23] "More to him than to anyone else," says
Professor W. R. Sorley, "this changed attitude toward the proofs must be traced." [24] "Through the
efforts of Kant," says Professor Taylor, "they
have been discredited [25] and have lost all their interest." [26]

Modern philosophy is now so convinced of the
uselessness of the proofs for God's existence that it
has ceased to give reasons for ignoring them. It is
in possession of a fact and the validity of its claim
does not seem to disturb its conscience. For this
reason one looks in vain in theistic literature of
the present day for a sound criticism of the proofs.
"They have long since passed the critical stage in
which critical minds find them convincing, and they
are gradually approaching the stage in which men
generally cease to find them interesting." [27]

The Inaugural Address of Philosophy at the University of Edinburgh, in 1919, which summarized
contemporary thought, bore witness to the general
opinion of the impossibility of " proving by dialectical arguments the existence of God." [28] Professor
Alexander, in his Gifford Lectures, asserted that
"no one now is convinced by the traditional arguments of the existence of God." [29] A member of the

[23] William James, "Varieties of Religious Experience," p. 437.
[24] "Moral Values and the Idea of God," p. 299.
[25] A. E. Taylor, "Elements of Metaphysics," 9th ed., 1923, p. 400.
[26] W. R. Thomson, "The Christian Idea of God," p. 177.
[27] W. R. Sorley, "Moral Values and the Idea of God," p. 299.
[28] Norman K. Smith, p. 28.
[29] "Space, Time and Deity," Vol. 2, p. 343.

Aristotelian Society has put them beyond hope:
"We cannot hope," he writes, "by intellectually
seeking to find out God." [30] The very word
"proofs" is written in quotation marks to indicate
that a value has been attributed to them which they
do not really possess.[31] No one is found " so intellectually poor to do reverence to the 'proofs' for the
existence of God." [32] "To the modern mind these
'proofs' when presented in their traditional garb,
stalk about with the unsubstantiality of ghosts.

'They were mighty, but they vanished,
Names are all they left behind them.' [33]

It is worth observing here that the Catholic
Church, which has so often been accused of being the
mortal enemy of reason, practically stands alone
today in insisting on the power of the reason to prove
God. In this sense the Church is the champion of
rationalism. The Council of the Vatican expressly
formulated and defined a canon testifying to the
power of reason to mount from the visible things of
the world to the invisible God. And this definition
gives food for thought. Our modern world boasts of
its great progress, thanks to reason. Now, whether

[30] James Ward, " Proceedings of the Aristotelian Society," Vol.
XX, 1920, p. 7. William James says they are " absolutely hopeless."
Varieties of Religious Experience, pp. 74, 171, 448, 455.

[31] W. R. Thomson, " Christian Idea of God," p. 6.

[32] Ibid.

[33] C. A. Beckwith, " The Idea of God," p. 111. Cf. R. Alfred
Hoernle, " Studies in Contemporary Metaphysics," 2nd ed., 1921, p.
302. Sir Henry Jones, " A Faith that Enquires," 1922, p. 48. George
Galloway, " Philosophy of Religion," 1914, p. 381. Pfleiderer, " The
Philosophical Development of Religion," Vol. 1, p. 137. A. N. White-
head, " Religion in the Making," 1926, p. 71.

or not one accepts the truth of the Church's teaching power, it will be admitted that her councils at various periods of history have laid bare the dominant errors of the time. She has her finger on the pulse of the world. Now if our world is progressing religiously, should not her councils in these latter days have defined intricate questions concerning the lofty and elevated problems of theology, such as the relation of Persons in the Trinity, or the Hypostatic Union? But the contrary is the fact. These were defined in the early ages, and the last general council had to define against an erring world that the *human reason can prove God*. Certainly, if there were real progress such an elementary truth should have been defined at the beginning instead of in our own day. Our thinking is in a bad plight, when we forget we have a reason! [34]

The second evidence of Kantian influence has been the repudiation of dogmas, this being merely another form of opposition to the intellectual element in religion. Dogmas to our contemporaries are "tools." "As in the case of all tools their value

[34] "Despite the frequent assertion that ours is the age of science, we are witnessing today a remarkably widespread decline of the prestige of the intellect and the reason. Though the most successful of our modern sciences, the various branches of mathematics, physics, and experimental biology, have admittedly been built up by intellectual or rational methods, "intellectualistic" and "rationalistic" are popular terms of opprobrium. Even among professed philosophers, the high priests of the sanctuary of reason, faith in rational or demonstrative science is systematically being minimized in the interests of "practical" idealism, vitalism, humanism, or intentionism and other forms of avowed anti-intellectualism." Morris R. Cohen, "The Insurgence against Reason, p. 113. Psychology and Scientific Methods, *Journal of Philosophy*, Vol. 22, 1925.

resides not in themselves but in their capacity to work shown in the consequences of their use." [35] The value of dogmas for the new-born religion resides not in their power to express an objective fact in definite terms, but in their power to influence the mind of the believer. Thus the Incarnation as a fact is not nearly so important as the subjective reaction it awakens, and consequently what is true for one worshipper is false for another.

We leave it to Professor A. C. McGiffert, who is an authority on modern religion, to summarize Kantian influence on anti-dogmatism of our day. He writes: "The criticism of Hume, and particularly of Kant, served to reveal the unsoundness of the old dogmatism, negative as well as positive. The supraphenomenal or noumenal world is quite inaccessible to the human understanding. This principle was employed by Kant to show the futility of all theoretical proofs of the divine existence, but he used it also to show with equal clearness that the existence of God could

[35] "Fear is the basis of religious dogmas." John Dewey, "Reconstruction in Philosophy," 1921, p. 145. B. Russell, "What I Believe," 1925, p. 19. E. Hershey Smith, "Shall We Have a Creed?" 1925, pp. 24–34. "The world of thought, like the world of matter, is always moving, and rigid dogmas must be left behind. One might as easily stop the earth from revolving on its axis as tie the future down to a stated creed." S. A. F. Rhys Davids, "Old Creeds and New Needs," 1923, p. 178. "Creed is the petrification of opinion." G. F. Wates, "The Religion of Wise Men," 1923, p. 90. Kirsopp Lake, "The Religion of Yesterday and Tomorrow," 1925, p. 106. S. Swisher, "Religion and the New Psychology," 1923, p. 161. C. A. Ellwood, "The Reconstruction of Religion," 1922, pp. 121, 126. G. Santayana, "Scepticism and Animal Faith," 1922, p. 10. E. S. Ames, "The New Orthodoxy," 1925, p. 117. George Wobbermin, "Wesen und Wahrheit des Christentums," 1925. A. Loisy, "L'Evangile et l'Eglise, 1902, p. 66. ff. G. Tyrell, "Through Scylla and Charybdis," p. 306.

not be proven. . . . The soundness of this position has been generally recognized since Kant's
day, and as a result agnosticism has widely
taken the place of atheism. The growth of the
scientific spirit has tended in the same direction to restrain thinking men from going beyond the
facts and asserting what cannot be proved, whether
it be by way of negation or of affirmation. Here
and there is to be found dogmatism, both religious
and anti-religious, as extreme and as intolerant
as ever, but it is decidedly exceptional in culti-
vated circles, and, as a rule, educated men vie
with one another in the modesty with which
they disclaim the right to make any positive asser-
tions touching realities lying beyond the realm of
phenomena." [36]

The Assertion of the Immanent. The Philosophy of Value.

The positive contribution Kant made to contemporary thinking far outweighs his destructive
criticism. Kant was no mere iconoclast; if he
rejected the intellectual foundation of belief it was
to substitute another for it, the basis of the practical
intellect. His followers have developed his thought
in the same vein. Professor Sorley, for example,
speaks of a Kantian substitute for the rejected intellectual system: "The theism of philosophical
research in which the idea of God is arrived at by a

[36] A. C. McGiffert, "The Rise of Modern Religious Ideas," pp.
144, 145. Cf. C. E. Moore, "Christian Thought since Kant," 1912,
pp. 1–23.

process of reflective thought must give way to the theism of religious consciousness for which God is in some way an immediate object." [37]

More definitely Kant's thought has evolved along two distinct but not unrelated lines: (1) how we know, (2) what we know. The first of these currents might be traced out according to the problem of knowledge, but that is not our present concern. Our interest is restricted to the religious problem, and here we find that the methods of knowing, inspired by the practical reason, are principally two: religious experience, and faith or hypotheses, both of which are non-rational.

Schleiermacher was the first great follower of Kant to proclaim sentiment as the proper way to know God. The faculty or religion for him is a feeling or an immediate self-consciousness of God (*Gefühl, unmittelbares Selbstbewusstsein*) " The feeling of the infinite in the finite " is the basis of our beliefs. Religion is purely a matter of the heart, and so much so that the " heart with its emotions withdraws into its own mystical depths, fearing any freezing contact with thought and purpose." In his " Second Discourse on Religion," he says: " There is no feeling which is not religious, save such as indicates an unhealthy condition of life." Dr. Wobbermin believes that Schleiermacher is the Copernicus of Theology, as Kant was the Copernicus of Philosophy, because he turned our attention from

[37] " Moral Values and the Idea of God," p. 302. S. Alexander, " Space, Time and Deity," Vol. II, p. 343.

the rational interpretation of God to the sentimental.[38]

The theories of Schleiermacher were developed by
the School of Erlagen (Hofmann, Franck) and the
School of Ritschl (Fries and Wette). Herder's
theory of emotions, Feurbach's doctrine of sentiment, Hartmann's philosophy of the unconscious-
ness, were so many manifestations of an affective
or non-rational approach to God, and so many antecedents of our contemporaries who have exalted
religious experience as the proper way to know God.
Among many others [39] we choose William James'
explanation of what is meant by religious experience. He brings out its non-intellectual character
by comparing it to a bar of iron which " without any
representative faculty whatever, might nevertheless
be strongly endowed with an inner capacity for
magnetic feeling; and as if through various arousals
of its magnetism by magnets coming and going in
its neighborhood, it might be consciously determined to different attitudes and tendencies. Such a
bar of iron, could never give you an outward
description of the agencies that had the power of
stirring it so strongly, yet of their presence and of
their significance for life, it would be intensely aware
through every fibre of its being." [40] We know God,

[38] " Die Religions Psychologische Methode." J. A. Leighton,
" Typical Modern Conceptions of God," p. 97.
[39] Otto, " Kantische Friesche Religionsphilosophie," p. 111 ff.
D. C. Mackintosh, " Theology as an Empirical Science," p. 91. D. W.
Fawcett, " Divine Imagining," p. 155. William Kingsland, " Our Infinite Life," p. 189.
[40] " Varieties of Religious Experience," p. 55.

therefore, but we do not know how we know; He is there, just as real as the thrust of a sword or an embrace.

Another form into which the practical reason of Kant has developed is that of faith or hypothesis. Faith here means a "venture; it begins with the resolution to stand or fall by the noblest hypothesis." [41] In relation to God, it may mean as it does for Hans Vaihinger in his "Philosophie des Als-Ob," that we are to live *as if* God existed [42] or it may mean as it does for Sir Henry Jones, a kind of experiment: "If there are certain forms of religious faith, certain hypotheses, which deepen the meaning of natural facts, which amplify and extend the suggestiveness of the natural sciences, and, so far from traversing their findings, accept and invite them; and if in the world of human conduct they dignify human character, and reach sanity to man's aims, construct and consolidate human society, elevate and secure the life of man and make for peace and mutual helpfulness amongst the nations . . . if, in a word, a form of religious faith or hypothesis *works*, in these ways, then indeed is the proof of its validity strong; stronger than the proof of any other hypothesis, because wider and deeper." [43]

These non-intellectual ways of knowing God, the

[41] Dean Inge, "Proceedings of Aristotelian Society," 1923, p. 180.
[42] Cf. Johannes Wegener, "Die Christliche Religion als Religion des Als Ob," 1923. H. Scholz, "Annalen der Philosophie," 3 Band, p. 2.
[43] "A Faith that Enquires," p. 104. Richard Müller, "Persönlichkeit und Weltanschauung," 1919. F. C. Schiller, "Problems of Belief." E. E. Thomas, "The Non-Rational Character of Faith."

way of religious experience, and the way of faith,
(we might also add Bergsonian intuition) are the
heirs of the Practical Reason of Kant, and it was no
exaggeration for Professor Farley to say during the
Kantian centenary that, "In a certain sense, Kant
could have a fellow-feeling with William James
when he said: 'On pragmatic principles, if the hypothesis of God works satisfactorily in the widest
sense of the word, it is true.'" [44]

We have called them examples of the *immanent*
characteristic of contemporary religion and this for
the reason that they appeal to nothing but the *self*,
either as the *subject* of the experience or as the
judge of the worth of the hypothesis. The traditional procedure, did not begin with self, but with
the world; the fulcrum of its proofs was in the open
air and reposed on the evident characteristics of the
universe which revealed God, though imperfectly,
as the painting reveals its artist.

Another, and yet more important aspect of the
Kantian philosophy of the immanent is in answer
to the problem *what do we know*. It will be recalled
that for the Kantian *speculative* reason God is
neither being nor object, but an *ideal*, in the sense
that He represents the supreme unity of a synthetic
mind. Whether or not an object corresponds to this
ideal does not matter. For the Kantian *practical*
reason God is a necessary postulate, not to establish
the bond between will and duty, but to assure the

[44] J. H. Farley, *Kant's Philosophy of Religion*, in "Immanuel
Kant," Open Court Pub. Co., 1925, p. 134.

future coincidence of duty and happiness. Schleiermacher pushed the Kantian *practical reason* to its natural conclusion — *symbolism,* by asserting that sentimental theodicy expresses only the needs of the heart and subjective dispositions. Since we cannot know God as He is in Himself, but only in relation to the needs of our practical reason, then we have "knowledge only of the being of God in us, but not the being of God external to the world or in Himself." Schleiermacher's doctrine then became not an account of what God is in Himself, but what *we* found Him to be in our religious life,[45] — a doctrine which Emerson introduced into America, in his Harvard Divinity School Address of 1838.

Feuerbach went further than Schleiermacher and said God was the *name* of the sentiment, and far from being our Creator is our work — *ens affectus.*

Ritschl, aided by Kant and Lotze, then introduced a distinction between the world of ideals and the world of facts. Beginning with sense experienced he argued that the mind appropriates sensations in a two-fold way. (1) Sensations produce feelings of pleasure or pain and so become deter-

[45] "By means of feeling applied first to himself, man finds God, for it is in ourselves that we discover the sense of the whole and then transfer it to Nature round about us. Just as man unifies nature, so he gives a soul to nature, and finds in it that which corresponds to himself. It is in others we find ourselves — . Then comes the famous Freudian passage: "Wherefore humanity and religion are closely and indissolubly united. A longing for love, ever satisfied and ever again renewed, forthwith becomes religion. Each man embraces most warmly the person in whom the world mirrors itself for him most clearly and purely; he loves most tenderly the person whom he believes combines all he lacks of complete manhood. Similarly the pious feelings are most holy that express for him existence, in the whole of humanity, whether as blessedness in attaining or of need in coming short of it." "Reden," p. 72.

mined according to their *Value* for the Ego. (2) On the other hand sensations embodied in ideas are judged in respect to their cause and their connection with other causes. These two functions make up Value-Judgments and Causal-Judgments. Ritschl introduces Value-Judgments as an aid in determining the difference between religious and theoretical knowledge. "Religion and theoretical knowledge are different functions of the spirit, which, when they deal with the same objects are not even partially coincident but are divergent throughout." [46] "In his hands," says Dr. George Galloway, "the distinction became an instrument which enabled the theologian to dispense with metaphysics and to build up a system of Christian doctrine which *claims* to be the reflection of the practical demands of the Christian conscience." [47]

It is not a long step from such doctrines, or even from the practical reason, to our modern pragmatism which attempts to prove that all proofs are worthless, and to assert that the truth of a proposition depends upon its value or utility. Once a philosopher denies the objective validity of any belief, it will not be long until its value will be the primary and unique consideration. And this was the revolution Kant effected; driving the rational element out of religion, he paved the way for what has become the dominant philosophy of our day — *the philosophy of value*. "Though he himself does not say it in so many words, we can see that

[46] "Justification and Reconciliation," pp. 193, 194.
[47] "Religion and Modern Thought," 1922, p. 78.

Kant used the idea of value to express the idea of God. . . . Implicitly, at all events, Kant made the fertile suggestion that the moral consciousness could give a valid content to the idea of God which the speculative intellect could not supply. . . . In making what amounted to a refusal to fuse into one the problems of existence and value, he opened up a line of thought which has been widely followed by a later day."[48] The transition was an easy one from God as a postulate of moral consciousness to God as a value for me.

Kant gave philosophy another ideal and philosophers another goal, besides that of truth and love of truth. If the mind could never get beyond the phenomena and the factors of experience, then it was useless to speak of religious truth. A new interest displaced it, one which brought man into greater prominence, and even made God evolve about him as his theory of knowledge made the universe revolve about mind, and this new interest was value. It was the logical outcome of a philosophy which divorced belief and the reason for belief, and left the will no greater security than a postulate; a philosophy which has so often proved its own futility, for out of a thousand that would follow Kant in his rejection of a rational ground for the existence of God, only a few would follow him in accepting God as a postulate. More and more

[48] George Galloway, " Religion and Modern Thought," 1922, p. 78. " The world of values remained in all his thinking the supreme realm of life, and devotion to it was man's chief end and glory." E. S. Ames, Religion of Immanuel Kant, in " Immanuel Kant," Open Court Pub. Co., 1925, p. 93.

philosophers tended toward an immanence, and by a gradual declension in logical consistency, the immanence at first which was only the immanence of religious experience as the source of knowledge of God (how we know) degenerated into the immanence of God in the universe in German Pantheism, then the immanence of God as identical with the feeling or experience of God, and finally the immanence of value by which each man judged for himself the reality of God by the value God had for him.   This is the contemporary idea of religion.

Conclusion

The three great spiritual realities of religion, grace, intellect and will, by which we are made to "the image and likeness of God," have in the course of the last four centuries been completely banished from religion, principally through distortions of their nature wrought by the three prophets of modern religion, Luther, Descartes and Kant.   Each of them shifted discussion from man to his psychic state, and from the total drama of all reality to the individual subject of experience.[49]   Each of them made war upon the transcendent as if it were the extrinsic, and considered as an intermediary or a barrier everything which traditional philosophy looked upon as a perfection.   Luther distorted grace by making it extrinsic to human nature and a mere imputation, and thus prepared for its final elimination; Descartes distorted the intellect by

[49] A. N. Whitehead, "Science and the Modern World," p. 201.

making it independent of the sensible world, and thus prepared for its degeneration into Rationalism; Kant distorted the will by making it blind in separating it from the intellect and thus undermined its worth and prepared the way for sentimentalism.

The denial of the transcendental realities under the guise of their being "extrinsic" has been complemented by the assertion of other and immanent principles, all of which have made for the deification of man and the humanization of God. Luther asserted the immanence of individual interpretation of Sacred Scriptures which degenerated to a mystical and spiritual individualism in which each believer felt himself the object of Divine Revelations or communications: *The Philosophy of Individualism*. Descartes asserted the immanence of philosophical "private interpretation" *viz.*, the individualism of the Cogito and the *clear and distinct*, which ultimately degenerated into a Rationalism denying material and spiritual substances and the existence of anything beyond experience: *The Philosophy of Fact*. Kant asserted the immanence of the moral law, the independence of belief in relation to a foundation for a belief, which in his followers developed into a pantheistic and psychological immanence of God in the world and in self, and the judgment of these realities not according to their objective truth, but according to their pragmatic value for the individual believer: *The Philosophy of Value.*[50]

[50] "The general development of the Modern World shows a ten-

Add to this subjectivism, this empiricism, and this pragmatism, a pinch of biology, psychology, and new physics, stir it up, bake in a pan well greased with evolution, and the finished product will be the modern God. Some call it "Space-Time" (Alexander), others "The Harmony Among Epochal Occasions" (Whitehead), others the "Perfect Process" (Jones), others an "Imaginal," (Fawcett), others "Society Divinized" (Durkheim), others a "Projected libido" (Moxon) but for those who believe that there are a thousand angles at which a philosopher may fall, and only one at which he may stand, for those who hold fast to truth rather than novelty, such gods are mere travesties, and such philosophers, sincere though they be, are hastening the advent of a new paganism and a new panic, for the day that God passes out of civilization, that day gladiators step in.

---

dency towards immanence. . . . The religious conviction of the Middle Ages regarded the other world as the true fatherland, and only in its relation to the other world did this world acquire value; the Modern World, on the other hand, began with the desire to seek the operation of the Divine more within this world. This resulted in the first place, in a pantheism as professed by the noblest spirits of Renaissance . . . . Pantheism proved overwhelmingly attractive to the German Classical Period, since it promised to bridge every antithesis and in particular to combine the broadest and freest treatment of the visible world with the open recognition of an invisible one. . . . At first the divine is brought near to our existence, then it is closely associated with it as an inspiring force, and finally it totally disappears or vanishes to an unapproachable distance. Thus religion, which was once an omnipotent power, has become, for the modern man, a thing of quite secondary importance, nay, a mere illusion, and the world of immediate experience has more and more completely absorbed his whole thought and feeling." Rudolf Eucken; "Main Currents of Modern Thought," p. 464.

PART III

Critical Appreciation of the Contemporary Idea of Religion in the Light of the Philosophy of St. Thomas Aquinas.

PART III

Critical Appreciation of the Contemporary Idea of Religion in the Light of the Philosophy of St. Thomas Aquinas

CHAPTER VII

THE FALLACY OF NOMINALISM

PASSING from historical to philosophical considerations we come into more intimate contact with the modern idea of religion. But before proceeding to the details a few general remarks concerning philosophy of religion may not be out of place.

1. Contemporary thinking is noteworthy for *an a priori denial of the supernatural* which is wholly unjustified. Man has no right to assert there is no order above him any more than the rose would have the right to assert, if it could assert, that there is no life above it. The supernatural is not destructive of the natural, but its perfection. One of the things which will always be difficult to understand is why some thinkers will believe in a blind urge pushing man on to greater and greater perfection even unto the state of deity, and yet deny the supernatural, which is such an added perfection with

this difference; viz., that in the first case the push is from below and implies the greater comes from the less, while in the latter it is a gift from above and implies that the infinite can give without exhaustion, as the ocean can send up its vapors without ever diminishing its vast content. If a plant can "supernaturalize," in the broadest sense of the term, the oxygen which it takes into its system and render it part of itself, make it live under new government, and be directed by new laws even to the extent of being organic with life itself; if the plant can be "supernaturalized" when taken into the animal, even to the extent of being one with it, so that it sees, and feels and hears because one with the animal, why should not man be capable of being supernaturalized by some power above him by which he becomes endowed with powers, natures and exigencies far surpassing his own nature and yet retaining his own personality? Biology, in leaving room for a higher kingdom, leaves room for supernaturalization. "Supernatural biology" leaves room for supernaturalization, thanks to the Kingdom of God, and to deny there is a power above man capable of elevating and ennobling him is to assert that man has Life within himself; it is completely to shut one's eyes to the truth that the very fact that man must nourish himself in order to live testifies to his dependence on some other kind of life.

2. There is a confusion of *de facto* and *de jure*, concerning the whole nature of religion. It is one

thing to say that the mind cannot prove the existence of God and another thing to say the mind has
a right, based on evidence, to make such an assertion. Kant has said that the proofs for the existence of God are worthless and from his day on
philosophers have accepted his word as final. No
less a philosopher than James Ward has said, " The
fatal defects of all these (traditional arguments)
have, it is almost universally conceded, been clearly
expressed once for all by Kant." [1]

It is quite true that Kant did assert and did give
some reasons for the invalidity of the proofs for
the existence of God, but it is quite another problem
whether or not a philosopher who effects a Copernican revolution in thought and who makes mind
the measure of reality instead of reality the measure
of mind, is entitled to pass judgment on proofs.
Kant's criticism of the proofs are valid enough provided you admit his premise that the mind can
never know the nature of things. Sometimes that
which most needs a criticism is a critique. It is
not our point here to show the fallacy of the Kantian
argument; that has been well done by others [2] but
merely to observe that there is, in modern thought,
a too general readiness to accept anything which
criticises the traditional, and too great an unwill-
ingness to judge the value of the criticism. The
general rejection of the proofs for the existence of

[1] " The bare fact that all idealists since Kant felt entitled to scant
or neglect them shows they are not solid enough to serve as religion's
all sufficient foundation." " Pluralism and Theism," 2nd ed., 1920, p.
406. W. R. Sorley, " Moral Values and the Idea of God," p. 299.

[2] Garrigou-Lagrange, " Dieu, Son Existence et Sa Nature."

God does not prove they are worthless, but merely that philosophers are willing to accept uncritically a criticism of them.

Apart from these considerations it may be said that there are three fallacies underlying the relation between God and man, as this relation is conceived by our contemporaries. These fallacies are:

    I. The Fallacy of Nominalism.
   II. The Fallacy of the Uniform Method of Science
  III. The Fallacy of Inverted Relations.

Nominalism is one of the dominant characteristics of modern thought and one responsible in large for the volatile notion of God and religion. Nominalism is opposed to realism in so far as intellectual knowledge is concerned. Realism believes that the mind is in contact with the real, and that the judgments and conclusions reached by the mind are primarily judgments of the objective world. Nominalism, on the contrary, denies this. In its philosophical form, the nominalism which has inspired the new idea of religion, may be summed up in the following propositions.

(a) The mind can never know anything beyond experience.

(b) The mind can never know the nature of reality, hence the subject, being enclosed within himself, must seek within himself, in the confines of his own conscience and heart, all the knowledge which he needs and all the beliefs he can use.

Against these tenets of Nominalism Thomism asserts their contraries.

    1. *The mind can know things beyond experience.*

Professor Whitehead was stating a tenet of Nominalism when he denied the power of the mind to know a transcendent God. " Any proof," he writes, " which commences with the consideration of the character of the actual world cannot rise above the actuality of this world. It can only discover all the factors disclosed in the world of experience." [3]

This statement of the celebrated physicist-philosopher rather proves the contrary of what he intended. In laying down the limits of knowledge he is really asserting the power of mind. That anyone can make such a demonstration is the refutation of what he demonstrates. To say we cannot know anything beyond the factors of experience is to say that we know what has already been called unknowable; to call an island a " lost island " means that at one time it must have been found.

Apart from this observation, the assertion of the philosopher would be perfectly valid provided the material universe was the total cause of all knowledge, for then we never could get beyond the " factors disclosed in the world as experienced." But such is not really the case. The sensible data and the empirical grouping of these data is not the *whole* cause of knowledge.[4] If there is a power above matter, which is not material and which is capable of working on matter, then certainly such

[3] " Religion in the Making," p. 71.

[4] Non potest dici, quod sensibilis cognitio sit totalis et perfecta causa intellectualis cognitionis, sed magis quodammodo est materia causæ. 1. q. 84 art. 6 . . . sensitiva cognitio non est tota causa intellectualis cognitionis. Et ideo non est mirum si intellectualis cognitio ultra sensitiva se extendit. *Ibid.*, ad 3.

a power is capable of producing a knowledge superior to the empirical grouping of the facts, just as marble is capable of becoming a statue of Moses given the spiritual artistry of Angelo.

The factors of experience furnish the " raw material "; the intellect, too, furnishes something and that is its abstractive power which is capable of revealing the intelligible in things. The abstracting intellect might very inadequately be compared to an X-Ray, which discloses the inner constitution of a thing which is denied to mere sense vision. Abstraction, however, does not mean the peeling off of individuating notes as we might peel an onion. It does not mean a " rough and ready method of suppressing what appears to be irrelevant details," as Professor Whitehead would have us believe.[5] The suppression of individuating notes and details in abstraction is simply a by-product of the work of the intellect and not a primitive process at all. The nature of a thing is not a core about which are grouped accidents and qualities; neither is it a skeleton. The intellect working on the factors of experience reveals the nature of these factors, or their *explanation* in terms of the intellect; it reveals their *ratio,* or even better, it reveals the *intelligibility* of empirical phenomena.

All science would be impossible were there not some power to rise above the " factors of experience." The very law of the factors, their finality, their relationship — none of these is disclosed by

[5] " Science and the Modern World," p. 77.

the factors as such. Nothing else than an intellect can perceive them, for nothing else than an intellect can perceive relation between facts; that is why man is the only being in the universe that can laugh. He has the faculty of seeing relations and deducing from suggestions. There is nothing in this world quite so boring as an ambitiously funny story the point of which is disclosed too soon in the telling. Equally true there is no philosophy quite so pessimistic as a nominalism whose conclusions are on the same level with its empirical premises. The inability to transcend the factors of experience is the foundation of all pessimism; it is a philosophy with its eyes on the ground like a mole, not on the heavens like an eagle.

But how does the intellect rise above this world? Even though it be granted that the intellect can know the nature of things, does it still follow that it can know beings which do not directly and immediately fall under its experience? The position of St. Thomas and the whole tradition of common sense is that the intellect can know beings which do not fall under the senses, and that it can even know God. A parenthesis of Thomistic metaphysics here becomes necessary.

Every faculty, according to St. Thomas, has an object to which it is ordained by nature. In the *order of generation* a very definite color is the object of vision, and a definite sound the object of hearing. But in the order of the *formal object* the object of vision is not a particular color, green for example, but all colors. The *ratio* under which vision seizes its object is color, and the *ratio* under which hearing grasps its object is sound, for unless a thing is sound it can never be heard.

But the intellectual knowledge is of a superior kind to sensible knowledge. Consequently, it must have its own proper and superior object. There must be some *ratio* under which all knowledge is grasped, just as there is a *common ratio* under which the eye sees its object.

What is the common ratio of the intellect? It is *Being* in all its latitude. This is its formal object. "That which is first apprehended is *being,* the knowledge of which is included in all things that the intellect apprehends." "Without being there can be no knowledge." "It is that which the mind first conceives as most known, and it is that into which all its other conceptions are resolved." [6]

But if *being* is the common *ratio* under which everything is known, it would seem that the object of the intellect is only *being which is common to the nature of material things*. How can we know a being which is beyond that which is common to all sensible experience? How can we know God? Can His Being be embraced under such a restricted object, namely, the being common to material things? It would seem that Professor Whitehead's contention is justified; namely, that we can know nothing except what is disclosed by the facts as experienced and can never know anything beyond these facts.

[6] 1–2 q. 94 art. 2; 3. q. 10 art. 3; De Veritate, q. 1 art. 1.

The answer of St. Thomas to this difficulty is as follows: Every faculty has a double object: a motivating object and a terminating object. This is true of the sense as well as the intellect. The motivating object of the eye, for example, is the red house. The terminating object of the eye is color. In the intellectual order the motivating object is the nature of material things, or the "factors disclosed in the actual world as experienced."[7] Quite naturally the motivating or the proportionate object of the intellect will be greater than that of the senses for the reason that the sensible is not the total cause of the intellectual knowledge but only the matter of the cause.[8]

Let it be noted that the motivating object never adequates the capacity of a faculty. Green does not exhaust the potentialities of vision, for the eye can see other colors besides green. So neither does the essence of material things exhaust the potentialities of the human intellect. The terminating object far surpasses its motivating object, for under the former consideration its object is *being in all its latitude*.

But why is not the intellect adequated by the being which is common to material things? Why is not its object the intelligible being of the material universe instead of being in all its latitude? Here it is necessary to recall the basic principle of the

[7] 1. q. 17 art. 3; De Veritate, q. 1 art. 12; C. G. lib. 3 cap. 56. The motivating object has also been called the proportionate object. John of St. Thomas, Phil. Naturalis, t. 3. p. 3. q. 10 art. 3.

[8] 1. q. 84 art. 6.

Thomistic theory of knowledge, namely the greater
the spirituality of a thing, the greater is its power
for knowing. Knowability increases with separa-
bility from matter. Knowledge increases with
separation from matter.[9] But the intellect is a
spiritual faculty. Being spiritual it can be actuated spiritually, *and the more spiritual the object
the more adequate it is for the intellect,* and the less
spiritual it is the less adequate. The only adequate
object of the human intellect then must be *being in
all its latitude.*[10] Due proportion being guarded
the human intellect shares the same adequate object as the angelic and the Divine Intellect.

	PORPORTIONATE OBJECT	ADEQUATE OBJECT
Human Intellect	material essence	
Angelic Intellect	angelic essence	Being
Divine Intellect	Divine essence	

The object then of the intellect is being, which
embraces everything from prime matter which is
pure potency on to the *Actus Purus* which is God.

Since the adequate object of the intellect is *being
in all its latitude,* just as the adequate object of
vision is color in all its latitude, it follows that any
judgment or reasoning process built on *being* will
be valid for the whole range of being.

Abstracting now from the psychological and the
chronological origin of judgments, what will be one
of the first judgments in the ontological order?

---

[9] John of St. Thomas, Logica, t. 1 p. 2. q. 27 art 1; Philosophia
Naturalis t. 3. p. 3. q. 10 art 2.

[10] 1. q. 79 rat. 2 ad 3; C. G. lib. 2. c. 98.

The first judgment will be one of affirmation. In other words it will be Being = Being, or the principle of identity. Now this principle is not an equation for an equation is merely a conditional identity; e.g., $3x = 6$ is true on condition that $x = 2$. There is nothing conditional in the affirmation that being = being, or in the sense that the same is the same. Rather it means everything is its own nature. Expressed negatively this judgment is that it is impossible that a thing be itself and another thing at the same time and under the same formal consideration. This is the principle of contradiction.

This is what is known as the first principle of thought, and corresponds perfectly to the three conditions which Aristotle laid down in his metaphysics: (1) The first principle ought to be one about which it is impossible to be mistaken. (2) It should not be a supposition. (3) It should be naturally known — that is to say, it must not be reached by demonstration.[11]

The principle of causality attaches itself to the principle of identity and the principle of contradiction and is an unfolding of both; it can never be demonstrated directly, but merely indirectly by an appeal to the foregoing propositions. To deny the important principle of causality is to assert that that which has not in itself the reason of its being, *has* within itself the reason of its being — a manifest violation of the principle of contradiction. The

[11] Fourth Book Cf. St. Thomas, Commen. lect. 6.

Principle of Causality then is not the statement of a mere succession of events, nor is it empirical, nor is it the psychological expression of will-activity. It is intellectuality rooted to being.[12]

What is generally called an effect is that which has passed from non-being to being. This transition cannot be traced to the being which has already come into existence, otherwise it would have to have been before it was. Here there would be violation of the principle of identity and the principle of contradiction. Nothingness can never be the cause of being. If something exists, there must have been some being distinct from it which brought it into existence, or which produced the transition. It is in this sense that there never can be an effect without a cause.

The next act of the mind in the ontological order is reasoning. Reasoning is not merely taking things out of a container. The relation between the major and the conclusion is one of act and potency. The syllogism is showing to the mind, by its mean term the reason of the identity of the extremes, and thus necessitates the mind to see this identity in the light of the premises.[13]

Every concept is in answer to the question, "What is it?" Every judgment is in answer to the question, "Is it?" Every reasoning process is in answer to the question, "On account of what is it?" Thus nothing is intelligible except in func-

[12] Cf. "God and Intelligence" for a development of these points. p. 159 ff.
[13] In Lib. Periherminias. lib. 1. c. VII. lect. 10.

tion of being. Being is the soul of every concept, judgment and syllogism. Not even the possible is knowable except through it, for the possible is that which is capable of being.[14]

Now can the mind whose object is being in all its latitude, whose principles are transcendental and necessary, rise up to a knowledge of what is beyond the factors disclosed by experience? First of all, there is nothing impossible about such knowledge, for all that *is* is capable of being known by the mind. Secondly, since the principles of reason are not empirical but necessary, they are capable of leading us out of the morass of a spatial-temporal universe into the realm of causes, finalities and even God.

St. Thomas gives five ways in which the existence of God can be proved, based upon five notes of the universe: three dynamic notes, two static. The dynamic notes are — movement, dependency and contingency; the static notes are — composition and multiplicity.

It is not our present concern here to elaborate the proofs of the existence of God but merely to indicate its broad outlines.[15] Very simply these five arguments reduced to the fundamental one of Being, can be stated in some such way as this. All things in this world are composed of the determined and the undetermined, the conditioned and the unconditioned, act and potency, essence and existence. In virtue of this composition they change,

[14] In Meta. lib. 5. lect. 14.
[15] Garrigou-Lagrange's "Dieu, Son Existence et Sa Nature" is the finest presentation of the Thomistic proofs.

or evolve or die — evolution without composition
is impossible. If I seek the reason of this participation I am driven back necessarily to something
distinct from the composed elements and which
has grouped or united them together.[16] Thus one
mounts up to God in Whom there is no composition, but Whose very essence it is to exist, and in
this He differs from creatures whose existence is
not their essence. And to ask the cause of God,
Whose essence it is to exist, is to ask that that which
has existence as its essence be explained as that
which has it not, or that that which is First Cause
be at the same time a second cause, or that God
shall be at the same time cause and effect.

But grant that God is known as Being, does it
follow that we can designate Him properly or know
anything about His character? There are some
thinkers who wish to designate God in function of
evolution, the needs of the age, and in relation to
our emotions and our democratic form of government. This is not good metaphysics. There are
certain predicates which in themselves imply no
imperfection, and these can be applied to God.
Such ideas are those of being, goodness, truth and
the like. Being free from imperfection in their
formal aspect, these notions can be applied ana-
logically both to God and creatures, thus solving
the difficulty that there is no proportion between
the finite and the infinite. "If there is no proportion between the finite and the infinite, it does not

[16] 1. q. 44 art. 1. ad 1.

follow that there is no proportionality, since what the finite is to the finite, the infinite is to the infinite, and thus it is that the similitude of God and creatures must be understood; namely, that God is in the same relation to that which concerns Himself as the creature is in relation to that which concerns itself." [17] Take the word " good " for example. I can apply it to a book, to a tree, to a dog, to a man, and in each case it designates the object. In each case it is applied according to the nature of each of these things; a book is " good " according to its nature; a tree is " good " according to its nature; a man is " good " according to his nature. But God is Infinite, therefore Goodness will be applied to Him in an infinite degree.[18] The same is true of the other concepts.

The intellect then, thanks to its abstractive power and its capacity for a knowledge of *being* as *being* can rise to the conquest of truths quite beyond the mere factors of experience; it can even rise to a knowledge of God as First Cause, and in doing so is not dealing with a mere symbol but with the objective and the real. This leads us to the second tenet of Thomistic realism.

II. *The Intellect can know the nature of the real.* Nominalism contends that ideas are mere rubrics or words under which facts are grouped. God, then, through the application of this principle, is merely a symbol for the " ideal tendency in things," or anything else quite equally vague. It is the contention

[17] De Veritate, q. 23. art. 7 ad 9.
[18] Sheen, " God and Intelligence," p. 175 ff.

of St. Thomas, on the contrary, that the mind knows things before it knows the ideas of things; what is known immediately by the mind is the thing itself and not its effigy or its image.[19] "The stone is that which is known and not the idea of the stone, except indirectly by the act of reflection when the intellect turns back upon itself."[20] The idea then is neither a portrait nor an instrumental sign like a model which is first known before making known. It is a *sign*, the like of which does not exist in the material world, i.e., a *formal sign*, the nature of which is to signify and make known before being itself known by the act of reflection. Ideas then are the ideas of reality; we know cause, before we know the idea of a cause; we know God, before we know the idea of God.

St. Thomas enumerates two conclusions which would follow a denial that the idea gives the real: (1) Every science would then be concerned, not with the objects outside the mind, but only with the ideas in it. In other words, science would be mental and would have no basis in the real. It is rather a strange fact that Thomistic and Mediæval philosophy which is said to be so unscientific, should be the very one to uphold the very reality of science; while our modern philosophy which is said to be born of science and nourished by it, denies it a real right to existence, in denying that its ideas are ideas of the real and objective world. (2) If the ideas were merely effigies of the real and not the

[19] De Veritate, q. 1. art. 9; q. 5 art. 2.   [20] 1. q. 76 art. 2 ad 4.

real, then the mind would be forced into a degenerate pragmatism which maintains that whatever seems is true. As the Angelic Doctor has no sympathy for those who deny the reality of science, neither has he sympathy for those who are content to rest in a mere-seeming truth. He fears individual interpretation brought to the facts of nature, in which each man would determine for himself what is true and what is best.[21]

Ideas then are primarily ideas of the real; and judgments built upon them are also judgments of the real.[22] The thinking subject is not enclosed within himself; therefore he must not seek within himself or the confines of his own conscience and heart all the knowledge which he needs and all the beliefs he can use. Not only that: since the mind can know things above experience and know them as real and objective, there is no necessity for the mock humility of nominalism. That is why the mere Will-to-Believe, the Als-Ob Philosophy, and Faith Philosophy must always be unsatisfying: they are based upon an acknowledged inability to grasp things as they really are. Since the mind can rise above the factors of experience, since it can know God objectively and not as a mere symbol, there is no necessity for an hypothesis or " Will-to-believe."

[21] 1. q. 85 art. 2.

[22] To reduce the ontological judgments of being to a purely subjective law, as all Nominalism would do, is to identify two notions which are manifestly distinct, namely, the impossible (or the irrealizable) and the inconceivable. It also means to doubt the extra-mental reality of the absurd. He who doubts the ontological value of the notion of being ought to say: a squared circle is inconceivable, but it is not irrealizable outside the mind.

These tentatives might do very well if philosophy had to despair of acquiring a knowledge of transcendental objects, but why delight in faint gleams of light through latticed windows when one can enjoy the sunlight?   These prescriptions force us to believe without any intellectual justification for such a belief. As Flint so well remarks: "A 'will' virtually identified with our own non-intellectual or 'passional nature' is not real will, not will either in its proper psychological acceptation, and its relationship to belief must be on the whole very different from that of will, properly understood, to belief. There is no such act of the mind possible as willing to believe what does not seem to be true or promise to give pleasure, or in other words, which seems destitute of any reason or evidence for being deemed true or good. There is no mere 'will to believe'; a merely willed belief is a sham belief; it is no real belief. . . . The part which willing has in the game is this: the mind can either will to follow along the paths on which the true light shines, and in which alone therefore right belief can be attained, or will to deviate from them, and so wander into the regions of darkness and delusion." [23]

The same is true of the "wish to believe." "If," writes Archbishop Whateley, "a mode of effectual and speedy cure be proposed to a sick man, he cannot but wish that the result of his inquiries concerning it may be a well-founded conviction of the safety

[23] "Agnosticism," p. 451 ff.

and the efficacy of the remedy prescribed. It would be no mark of wisdom to be indifferent to the restoration of health, but if his wishes should lead him to put implicit confidence in the remedy without any just grounds for it, he would deservedly be taxed with folly. In like manner, a good man will indeed wish to find the evidence of the Christian religion satisfactory, but will weigh the evidence more carefully on account of the importance of the question."

" I cannot agree with those philosophers," writes L. P. Jacks, " who maintain that religion is based on the will to believe. The two are clearly connected, but it would be truer to say that the will to believe is based on religion . . . God is not a product, but the author and living principle of the will to believe." [24]

Hence these philosophers who tell us: " believe what is in line of your needs," " believe that life is worth living," " believe that the universe still has values " — but all this advice about believing does not create the fact. It is a kind of mental hypnotism. No belief without a sound basis can produce good.

" The argument that we should believe certain things because they are helpful to what we have assumed to be practical interests, is a wilful confusion between what may be pleasant for the time being and what is determined by the weight of rational evidence. Theoretic reason in the form of logical science is the effort to determine the weight

[24] " Religious Perplexities," 1923, p. 35.

of things. To tip the scales by the will to believe is childish foolishness since things will generally continue to weigh what they do despite this tipping." [25]

The *Als-Ob*, another non-intellectual substitute offered by Professor Hans Vaihinger [26] is a fiction and in the all important question of deciding religious beliefs it is not only not serviceable but positively harmful. Living as if we had money will never keep us out of the poor house, but would be the quickest way of getting us in. Living as if he were well fed will never keep a hungry man from starving. The sailor cast on the salty waters of the sea might live as if the waters were not salty, but he would never slake his thirst. The *Als-Ob* philosophy is the philosophy of hypocrisy; it means pulling the wool over your own eyes and living as if there really was a God. Certainly, such a foundation for religion is no foundation at all.

The reason for living " as if " there was a God rather than as if there were not, must have either a mental or a real foundation. If it is only mental, then there is no reason for choosing " as if there was a God " rather than " as if there were not," any more than there is for living as if there were, or as if there were no ghosts. If the foundation is real, then we are not free to live " as if there were not "; only one alternative is possible, just as if my hand is really burnt, I am not free to live as if it were not burnt.

[25] Morris R. Cohen, " The Insurgence against Reason," *Journal of Philosophy and Scientific Methods*, Vol. 2, 1925, p. 126.

[26] " Die Philosophie des Als-Ob," 1911.

Living " as if " there was a God is not the same as living as if there were centaurs. The world can plod along without centaurs, but the world cannot be a world without God. God is the principle of all that is, and without Him there is nothing that is. It is easier to go through life " as if " there was food, yet without taking it, than to go through life " as if " there was no God.

Furthermore, God's existence does not hinge upon His utility for me, any more than air begins to exist because of its utility for my lungs. God does not exist, because He is useful; He is useful, if you will, because He exists. If His existence depended upon His usefulness, then He would exist for Mr. A. who finds Him useful and would not exist for Mr. B. who believes He can get along without Him. God would then twinkle in and out of existence like a star, depending upon the individual need and utility.

What has been said about the will-to-believe applies equally to Professor Perry's rather disconsolate attempt to bring in a hypothetic God as the ground of values. This distinguished Harvard Professor argues that whether or not God *actually* exists does not alter the fact that He can affect the manner of our living, for an unrealized proposition (a man ten feet tall) may be true and affect a present judgment (such a man would be taller than any living man).[27]

It is very well to say that an unrealized truth may

[27] " General Theory of Value," p. 687.

affect the truth of a present proposition, but to pass from the logical to the real order is quite another matter, and this is the error Professor Perry commits. Where there is no causal dependence between a future unrealized truth and a present one, then the latter may stand without the first, but where there is dependence, then the other truth must be realized and actualized, otherwise the second one would be meaningless. Such is the case with God and us. We are like the rays of the sun which disappear with the setting of the sun. We depend on God, and we cannot consider our existence apart from His. Considering God as hypothetical would be more absurd than considering all the food we will need between now and the end of our lives as hypothetical and yet not affecting our present existence. We need the food for our physical life and we need God for our very existence.

Nominalism has shifted the emphasis on the reality and objectivity of God and religion to a subjective outlook on the universe. As Professor W. Selbie so well says: " The net result of this type of reasoning is that these psychologists would tie us down to a purely subjective view of religion. It is no more than an outcome of human activity. They confuse God with the idea of God and make it a projection of man's hopes, fears and ideals. In other words, God is but a phantasy which has a certain value for man's moral and spiritual development. The worship of God is a form of infantilism and survives because it meets a certain elementary need and satisfies the sense of dependence which man never altogether loses. So conscience becomes an emotion and sin is merely moral disease, the result of expressed or unsatisfied instincts, and to be explained in terms of the complex. Now we have here an extraordinary mixture of truth and falsehood, of legitimate and illegitimate reasoning. It is an attempt to explain religion, which really explains it away, and the air of scientific assurance with which it is done makes it very convincing to untutored minds. The real question at issue is not merely, How does the human mind work in relation to religion and the idea of God? but, *Is there a God, and have religious ideas any objective reality?* [28]

Either the idea of God and all other spiritual concepts ultimately correspond to some objective reality or they do not; if they do correspond to something objective, then it is nonsense to speak of the " changed conception of God "; or " a new notion of religion "; if they do not correspond to anything objective, then the idea of God and religion is only a mental nightmare and the stuff that dreams are made of, and we are dreamers instead of philosophers. It is often said, in full accordance with the nominalist doctrine, that what is right in one age is wrong in another; and that God as Supreme Being must give way to our modern conception of God as " creative power "; that miracles as a Divine intervention in nature must now be understood as a " novelty " in the process of evolution; that original sin must no longer be understood as

[28] W. Selbie, " Psychology of Religion," p. 297.

the loss of original justice, but as a "fall in the evolutionary process"; that revelation is no longer God speaking to man in confirmation of doctrine, but God immanent in all nature and one with it, for all earth is crammed with heaven " and every common bush aflame with God "; that Christ is no longer to be understood as a Redeemer, but, in accordance with modern ideals, as a great moral teacher to be ranked with Buddha and Confucius; that Redemption is not a purchase of divine life for sinners, but merely an inspiration for the believer to convince him of the love of God; that the Church is not the continuation of Christ as the *Totus Christus* or mystic body, but an organization standing between us and God; that religion is no longer the ordination of man to God by knowledge, love and service, but only " faith in the conservation of values "; that religion has no need of God, but only a conviction that we should live *as if* God existed; that God is not a reality but only a " mental projection "; that God is not supreme Truth, Love and Goodness, but only " society divinized "; that God is not the Providence which rules this world, but merely a name to symbolize the trust that we can put into the universe; that God is not a Being on whom we are dependent, for " in all things it is well to exalt the dignity of Man, by freeing him as far as possible from the tyranny of the non-human power "; [29] that God is not personal for " it would be difficult to estimate the harm

[29] Bertrand Russell, " Free Man's Worship in Mysticism and Logic," 1925, p. 46 ff.

done by the conviction that for its ethical improvement society is dependent on a personal God; [30] that God is not a reality but only " the name, not of the whole of things, God forbid, but only of the ideal tendency of things "; [31] that God, in accordance with new physics and the quantum theory is no longer transcendent but the " ideal harmony of the universe." [32]

And all this is perfectly logical, if God is only a name and has no objective reality. But if God really is, then it is absurd to say that He is one thing in the fifteenth century and another in the twentieth. This is equivalent to saying that a thing is true at three o'clock but false at half-past four, and that two apples plus two apples make four apples on Monday but not on Friday. That all this should be called progress is a mystery, as if there could be

[30] James Leuba, "Psychology of Religious Mysticism," p. 329.

[31] " Letters of William James," Vol. 2, p. 269.

[32] A sample of nominalism carried to its limits is to be found in " The Rise of Modern Religious Ideas " by McGiffert, p. 241, in which he writes: " In the mediæval conception of God's character. . . . God was thought of as the avenger of sin, and, at the same time as a merciful being, providing men with a way of escape from the consequences of their transgression. . . . Gradually, with the spread of the idea of the ability and worth of the natural man, traditional notions of God began to change. . . . The opposition was greatly strengthened, particularly in the eighteenth century, by the rapid spread of the idea of human equality, and the doctrine of equal rights for all. . . . As the rights of men over against each other and over against their rules grew, their rights over against God received fuller recognition. . . . As democratic ideals crowded out the aristocratic and authoritarian ideals of an earlier day, of course the character of God appeared in a different perspective. His absoluteness and his responsibility only to his own character gave way to the notion of relativity and responsibility to man. They, too, have rights and God is bound to respect them." Thus within five hundred years God has changed from the King of Kings to the " President of the Commonwealth," and men are no longer His subjects, but He is subject to men!

progress without a fixed term. If we deny the substance of things and the reality of things, and dis-
solve entities into environment, then we can never
have a goal for progress. If we are going to make
God just a whirling vortex of Space-Time then we
are no longer free to speak of God, just as an artist
is no longer free to draw a giraffe if he draws it with
a short neck. If God is Fixed, Abiding and Immutable, then there is room for progress, but if God is
progressing from a king to a president, then we do
not know whether we are progressing or not. The
one thing in the world that never progresses is the
idea of progress. " If the standard changes, how
can there be improvement which implies a standard? If women, say, desire to be elegant, it may
be that they are improved at one time by growing
fatter and at another time by growing thinner. But
you cannot say that they are improved by ceasing
to wish to be elegant and beginning to wish to be
oblong. Nietzsche started a nonsensical idea that
men had once sought as good what we now call evil ;
if it were so, we could not talk of surpassing or even
falling short of them. How can you overcome
Jones if you walk in the other direction? You
cannot discuss whether one people has succeeded
more in being miserable than another succeeded
in being happy. It would be like discussing whether
Milton was more puritanical than a pig is fat." [33]
If God is only a name then there is little to choose
between the old idolatry and the new, the ancient

[33] G. K. Chesterton, " Orthodoxy," p. 62.

idols being fashioned by hands, and the modern idols being fashioned by mind. Isaias speaks of the old as follows: "The carpenter hath stretched out his rule, he hath formed it with a plane; he hath made it with corners, and hath fashioned it round with the compass; and he hath made the image of man, as it were a beautiful man dwelling in a house. He hath cut down cedars, taken the holm, and the oak that stood among the trees of the forest; he hath planted the pine tree, which the rain hath nourished . . . he made a god and adored it; he hath made a graven thing, and bowed down before it." [34]

The modern idol maker goes not to the forest but to the laboratory, and there, with the help of scientific concepts moulds the kind of God he will adore. Such is the penalty of a philosophy which no longer speaks of God but the "idea of God"— and herein lies the difference between much of contemporary philosophy of religion and that of Scholasticism. Professor James B. Pratt, so conspicuous in the philosophical world for his sane thinking, reminds his fellow workers that it is bad psychology to confine ourselves solely to pragmatic factors in the God-idea because "it neglects altogether certain real elements in the religious consciousness, whether found in philosopher, priest, or humble worshipper — men who through all the ages have truly meant by 'God' something more than 'the idea of God,' something genuinely tran-

[34] Isaias, XLIV 13 ff.

scendent. It is bad epistemology because based
ultimately upon a viciously subjective view of
meaning, a view which would identify our objects
with our ideas of our objects, and which, carried to
its logical conclusion would result in solipsism." [35]

It is God, then, and not the "idea of God" with
which philosophy is concerned and which men worship. We cannot make God to our image and
likeness for God has first made us to His image and
likeness. When philosophy reaches a point where
it insists that we need a new idea of God, it is time
for it to make a philosophical examination of conscience. If there is any fitting to be done, it is we
who ought to fit ourselves to God, and not God to
ourselves. [36] To speak of God and mean only "a
principle of concretion"; to speak of Deity and
mean only "quality"; to speak of the Divine and
mean only the "harmony among epochal occasions"; to speak of religion and mean only "a
projection into the roaring loom of time of a concentrated unified complex of psychical values" is to
adopt a license of language and thought which can
only lead to a confusion worse confounded. It is to
turn back the hands of the clock and yet to speak
with a voice which we would have never known
unless the clock had long since advanced. It is
to strip God and religion of all spiritual content and
yet to use these words that have mirrored for ages

[35] "Religious Consciousness," p. 209.

[36] "Veritas quæ est in anima causatur a rebus non sequitur
æstimationem animæ, sed existentia rerum." De Veritate, q. 1 art. 2
2 ad 3.

the highest associations that are unintelligible apart from it. If we are only to have a "mental projection" or an "epochal occasion" then let us say so, and we will know what we are about. Let us not cheat ourselves with phantoms and effigies of God and religion, when we have emptied heaven of all its reality and left nothing for the starving heart but empty names. Why should we force upon theology the terms of physics, psychology and a spatio-temporal continuum when these can mean little more than sounding brass and tinkling cymbal? If God is nothing more than a "name for the ideal tendency in things" then philosophy, history, and art are cheated. And certainly, if God were only a name it would be much more preferable to look upon Him rather as a King than a "nisus." It is incomprehensible to a thinking mind to see how philosophy and civilization are enriched by ceasing to think of God as God and beginning to think of Him as a blind and whirling space-time configuration dancing dizzily in an Einsteinian universe, plunging forward along a path of which He is ignorant, toward a goal of which He knows nothing whatever. At the present time God is *really* denied; but *nominally* asserted. The next step will be to eliminate even the name. That will be the extinction of daylight; then we shall be marching to the music of ghosts and not the voice of reason.

CHAPTER VIII

THE FALLACY OF THE UNIFORM METHOD OF SCIENCE

THERE is one predominating argument advanced for the new notion of God and religion, and that is the necessity of harmonizing it with the latest discoveries of science. The necessity of accommodating religion to the new physics, it will be recalled, constitutes the burden of Professor A. N. Whitehead's "Religion in the Making," as well as Professor Alexander's "Space, Time and Deity." It is even the progress of science to which appeal is made by psychologists and sociologists who would give us a God born of their science and their method. Professor H. W. Carr, in a "metaphysical meditation" on "Changing Background in Religion and Ethics" writes, "We of the scientific age have lost interest in the theological cosmologies not alone on the ground of their naïve anthropomorphism and anthropocentrism, but because being the reflection of a pre-scientific age they no longer express our attitude to the world problem.[1] . . . The problem of religion and ethics in modern thought is not, as I conceive it, to harmonize natural science with the old religious concepts, but to reform our concept of God in accordance with

[1] p. 20.

224

our progress in interpreting our knowledge of the physical world."[2] There is modern philosophy of religion in a nutshell; our concept of God must be reformed to meet requirements of modern science.

A critical appreciation of this view does not mean taking sides on the so-called conflict of religion and science. Indeed the two are not and can never be in conflict, for God is the source of both. The philosopher is right in saying that there must be harmony between the two. Only when he asserts that the concept of God must be revised to match the color of science does the problem begin. In other words, the problem is, how far can science go in its demand for a new kind of God, and of what value is the God born of science and nurtured by its laboratories. Put in question form the problem involves these three aspects:

1. What is the Value of Empirical Science?
2. What is the Value of a Philosophy of Nature built on empirical science?
3. What application of these conclusions can be made to religion?

I. *What is the Value of Empirical Science?*

To ask this question not only of the modern philosophers of science but also of the great luminary, Thomas Aquinas, is both interesting and important. The Angelic Doctor, following Aristotle, distinguishes between *deductive* sciences,

[2] p. 6.

which reveal the intelligent necessities inherent in things, and the *inductive* sciences, which reveal the reason of being of things through a general observation of their effects or manifestations. The first are sciences of *explanation*, or sciences of the *propter quid;* the second are sciences of *observation* or the sciences of the *quia*. The first are outside of time because they are concerned with natures apart from their concrete existence; e.g., whether or not a concrete triangle ever existed, it would still be true that all the angles of a Euclidean triangle are equal to two right angles. The second are not wholly outside time because they study natures in their material condition.

Inductive sciences at the present day are commonly called empirical sciences, or more simply *Science*. Now, what is the value of Empirical Science, and what necessity does it bring with it? St. Thomas holds that all sciences of observation and description, such as physics, biology, geology, are only *probable* in their conclusions. He reasons as follows: Such sciences deal with the nature of certain things in their material existence; e.g., the biologist studies life by studying *this* life either under a microscope or with a scalpel. But the nature of a thing, thanks to matter, is capable of indefinite multiplication; the nature of man, for example, is not confined to a hundred possible men, but has been realized in millions in the past, and will continue to be realized in millions in the future. Peter is not Paul, and yet both are men. They are the same in nature, but differ, thanks to material configurations which constitute the principle of individuation.[3]

Since matter is capable of multiplying natures indefinitely, it follows that there is no limit to the possible singular instances which science may study. But the possibility of error increases with the multiplication of particulars. Consequently, so long as there is wanting a verification in every possible instance, there can be no absolute certainty in science.[4]

Sciences of pure observation then are probable in their conclusions because of the variability of the particular instances which they study. This does not mean to assert there is no certainty in such

---

[3] Incertitudo causatur propter transmutabilitatem materiæ sensibilis Post. Analy. lib. 1 lect. 14 Infinitum congruit materiæ quæ est individuationis principium. . . . Quanto magis procedetur versus particularia, tanto magis itur versus infinitum. *Ibid.*, Contingentia in rebus sensibilibus est conditio consequens materiam individuantem sensibilia. Cajetan in 1. q. 86, art. 4 X. In order to conclude to a universal and necessary conclusion, the enumeration of singular instances should be complete. " Oportet supponere quod accepta sint omnia quæ continentur sub aliquo communi; alioquin nec inducens poterit ex singularibus acceptis concludere universale. . . . Patet igitur quod inducens, facta inductione quod Socrates currat et Plato et Cicero, non potest ex necessitate concludere quod omnis homo currat, nisi detur sibi a respondente quod nihil aluid contineatur sub homine quam ista quæ inducta sunt. Post Analy. lib. 2. lect. 4: n. 4.

Cf. John of St. Thomas, Cursus phil. Thomisticus. Logica. 1 Pars. Illustrationes q. 8 art. 2.

[4] " Ex hoc vero quod ejus consideratio est circa res mobiles, et quæ non uniformiter se habent, ejus cognitio est minus firma, quia ejus demonstrationes, ut in majori parte sunt ex hoc quod contigit aliquando aliter se habere: et ideo quanto aliqua scientia magis appropinquat ad singularia, sicut scientiæ operativæ, ut medicina, alchimia et moralis, minus possunt habere de certitudine propter multitudinem eorum quæ consideranda sunt in talibus scientiis, quo quodlibet si omittatur, frequenter erratur, propter eorum variabilitatem." In De Trinitate Boetii, q. 6 art. 1.

sciences. Scientists do affirm, as a matter of fact, a necessary bond between subject and predicate when they enunciate a scientific conclusion, but this enunciation always supposes the concrete existence of the subjects studied, and here there is limitation.

After enunciating the principle that empirical sciences lack absolute certainty because possibility of error increases with particular manifestations, St. Thomas proceeds to carry the principle into practice. There is no reason, he says, why the Ptolemaic system of the universe should be the true one. Later on, when scientific methods are improved and scientific instruments perfected, it may be that a new theory will be propounded which will be more in accord with facts.[5] St. Thomas reminds us also that Aristotle did not accept all the scientific conclusions of his day, and in doing so was perfectly within reason for they were only problematic and by no means absolutely certain.[6] The Angelic Doctor himself is not certain that the astronomical theories of his own day explain the heavens and the

[5] Licet enim talibus suppositionibus factis appareant solvere non tamen oportet dicere has suppositiones esse veras, quia forte secundum aliquem alium modum nondum ab hominibus comprehensum apparentia circa stellas salvantur. In Com. De Coelo. lib. 2. lect. 17 n. 2.

[6] Dicendum quod Aristoteles non fuit hujus opinionis, sed existimavit quod omnes motus coelestium corporum sunt circa centrum terræ . . . postmodum autem Hypparchus et Ptolemæus adinvenerunt motus eccentricorum et epicyclorum ad salvandum ea quæ apparent sensibus in corporibus coelestibus, unde hoc non est demonstratum, sed suppositio quædam. De Coelo. lib. 1 lect. 3. . . . Ad octavum dicendum, quod opinio Ptolemæi de epicyclis et eccentricis non videtur consonare principiis naturalibus, quæ Aristotelis ponit, et ideo illa opinio sectatoribus Aristotelis non placet. In De Trinitate Boetii, q. 4 art. 3 ad 8; Cf. Metaphysics lib. 12, lect. 10. De Coelo, lib. 1, lect. 3. n. 7.

movement of the sun and stars for "some other theory might explain them."[7]

Now, it is quite a remarkable fact that modern philosophers of science are in agreement with St. Thomas on the question of the value of empirical sciences. St. Thomas holds that inasmuch as they are based on incomplete induction, they can give only probable certitude. Our contemporaries hold that scientific conclusions are only provisory approximations of reality, and not its adequate representation. Such scientists as P. Duhem,[8] H. Poincaré,[9] G. Milhaud,[10] E. Boutroux,[11] E. Meyerson,[12] Hugo Dingler,[13] O. W. Richardson[14] and

---

[7] 1. q. 32 art. 1 ad 2, Cf. In Job. XXXVIII, lect. 2, where St. Thomas shows a connection between scientific theories and "debilitas cognitionis humanæ." Also, De Cœlo, lib. 2 lect. 17, n. 1 and 8; The sole ambition, says St. Thomas, that one can have concerning the explanation of the comets is to arrive at a "possible solution." The reason is because in this matter sensible knowledge can teach us so little. Meteor. lib. 1. lect. 11, n. 1. The same is true of the study of earthquakes; only a truth, "aliquid modo" is possible. Meteor. lib. 1. lect. 1. n. 7 and n. 9 Physics and the scientiæ mediæ because they treat sensible and particular things are less certain than mathematics. Post Anal. lib. 1. lect. 41. n. 3; lect. 42. n. 3; Meta. lib. 1 lect. 2; lib. XI, lect. 7; in De Trinitate Boetii, q. 6 art. 1.

[8] "La Theorie Physique," Paris, 2nd ed., 1914, pp. 53–76.

[9] "La Valeur de la Science," 28th ed., Paris, 1920. "La Science et l'Hypothèse," 36th ed., Paris, 1920. "Dernières Pensees," Paris, 1924.

[10] Essai sur les Conditions et les Limites de la Certitude Logique, 2nd ed., Paris, 1898.

[11] "Science and Religion," New York, 1905.

[12] "De l'Explication dans les Sciences," Vol. 2, Paris, 1921; Vol. I, pp. 14, 15. An excellent survey of the principal theories of the present day is to be found in an article by Dr. M. F. Renoirte, "La Theorie Physique," in the Revue Neo-Scolastique of Louvain, 1923, pp. 349–375.

[13] "Physik und Hypothese," Leipzig, 1921; "Grundlagen der Physik," Berlin, 1923, p. 172.

[14] "The state of physics at the present time is not unlike the

others may differ in the detailed treatment they give to the problem, but at bottom all are in perfect agreement. Science does not penetrate into the essence or nature of physical things; this it leaves to the metaphysician. It is content to summarize in the most complete and commodious fashion data revealed by experience, describing rather than explaining. "Modern experimental science," writes E. Boutroux, "just because it is based solely upon experience, appears as limited in its range, whether on the side of theory or on the side of practice. . . . Science has in reality occupied herself with the search and the discovery of hypothetical definitions which enable her to interrogate nature. . . . I call science, the hypothesis of constant relations between phenomena." [15]

Professor Gilbert N. Lewis, in his Silliman Memorial Lectures in Yale University, developed the same idea concerning the contingent character of science: "The scientist is a practical man and his are practical aims. He does not seek the *ultimate*, but the *proximate*. He does not speak of the last analysis, but rather the next approximation." [16]

It is not to our present purpose to discuss these opinions critically or to distinguish between laws of

political and economic condition of the globe." "Problems of Modern Science," 1922, p. 79.

[15] "Ainsi nous ne pouvons nourrir l'illusion que les lois que nous decouvrons soient veritablement des ' lois de la nature.' . . . Ce ne sont que des lois de la nature en ses rapports avec notre sensation et notre intelligence." "Science and Religion," pp. 242–244. E. Meyerson, *op. cit.* Vol. 1, p. 17.

[16] "Anatomy of Science," 1926, p. 6.

nature and scientific descriptions of these laws;[17] neither is it to our purpose to examine whether or not the foundations for the Thomistic and the modern conclusions are the same.

We are only stating that modern scientists (not the popularizers of science) and St. Thomas are in accord concerning the value of empirical science; viz., its conclusions are only provisional and problematic. They are generalizations based on experience and often expressed for the sake of easy handling in algebraic terms, but new experiences and new discoveries may overthrow them and relegate them to the limbo of obsolete theories. The rock-sureness of " Science " does not exist in the mind of the scientists themselves, though it does live and throb in the minds of publicists and propagandists. Scientists themselves disclaim they possess ultimate truth; rather they look upon it as a horizon toward which they are proceeding. Modern science, as testified by its greatest masters, concerns itself only with the relations of concomitance and succession among the phenomena, in the measure that its instruments and methods permit. It may and does seek the antecedent phenomena, but never the cause in a metaphysical sense. This does not mean to say that science is agnostic; agnosticism is a philosophical doctrine, and empirical science is distinct from philosophy by the specialization imposed on its methods. One cannot reproach the

[17] Cf. F. X. Pfeifer, "Widerstreiten die Wunder den Naturgezetzen, der Werden Letztere durch die Ersteren Aufgehoben? " *Phil. Jahrbuch,* 1893, pp. 287, 288.

scientific method for not attaining realities which it does not assume to consider.

Science may be different in its methods in the thirteenth and in the twentieth century; new theories of the heavens may have supplanted the old, but when one descends to the rock bottom, the twentieth century is repeating or echoing the thirteenth in asserting the probability and approximative character of the conclusions of empirical sciences.

II. *What is the Value of a Philosophy of Nature built on Empirical Science?*

Two elements go into the make-up of every empirical science: *observation of facts* and *interpretation of these facts*. Observation takes its point of departure in the sensible world.[18] The steps in this cognitive process are the following: the conservation of the action of particular instances by the memory, then the repetition of these instances which constitutes what is known as the experiment.[19]

Observation is a very simple matter. A cat walking through a laboratory may see exactly the same thing in a test-tube that the chemist sees, and may even see it better in the dark, but the cat is not a scientist. What differentiates the two is the second element; viz., the reflection which the scientist brings to this phenomena, or the application of intel-

[18] Post. Analy. lib. 1. lect. 30, n. 4–7.
[19] lib. 2 c. 76 and 83.

lectual principles to the data before him.[20]   Experiments alone do not make knowledge, for so far as the experiments are concerned we are no wiser after the hundredth than we were after the first.   To affirm a constant character of a common subject is mere repetition.   There is arithmetical universality; there is a multiplication of facts; experience abounds but there is no knowledge.   There is merely a plurality of objects accidentally juxtaposed.   The only way in which knowledge can be gained from these facts is to reduce them to unity by intellectual abstraction which alone makes laws possible.

Now we may ask this question: Is the science of the twentieth century better than the science of the thirteenth century?   First, as regards observation of phenomena there can be no doubt that our science is superior.   We have better instruments, better methods and better technique.   Inventions such as the microscope, the X-Ray and the telescope have permitted a study and penetration of detail of which our predecessors were wholly ignorant.   Professor Whitehead is the authority for the statement that "in science, the most important thing that has happened during the last forty years is the advance in instrumental design."[21]   But though our observation of nature is far better developed than that of the ancients, it does not follow that our interpretation is necessarily better.   Better instruments do not

[20] Ex sensibus fiunt in nobis memoriæ ex quibus experimenta de rebus accipimus, per quæ ad comprehendum universalia scientiarum et artrium principia pervenimus.   C. G. lib. 2 cap. 83.   Post. Analy. lib. 2 lect. 20 n. 11.

[21] "Science and the Modern World," 1925, p. 166.

insure a better philosophy of science any more than a perfect violin insures good music irrespective of who plays on it. Professor Whitehead leans favorably to such a conclusion when he says " the reason why we are on a higher imaginative level is not because we have a finer imagination but because we have better instruments." [22] There seems to be little doubt that the interpretation of the facts of nature by a realist like St. Thomas who admits that reality exists independently of the mind's knowing it, would lead to a truer science than the interpretation of nature by a Kantist for whom space and time are purely subjective moulds which unify experience. An Hegelian interpretation of the atom in terms of thesis, antithesis and synthesis is apt to carry one into an unreal world much more quickly than the interpretation of an Albert the Great. It seems hardly open to dispute that a philosophy which interprets observed facts in the light of common sense, a philosophy which believes that there is such a thing as truth and that science is useful in just the proportion that it is true and in correspondence with the objective reality, is far nobler and better suited to guide us scientifically and humanly than a philosophy which makes the true the useful, or which makes the mind the measure of reality, and which refuses to look upon the laws of nature as anything else than mere mental configurations and endowments of a blind weaver working at his loom.

These preliminaries discussed, it now becomes

[22] " Science and the Modern World," 1925, p. 166.

apropos to ask what value has a Philosophy of Nature built upon an Empirical Science? A Philosophy of Nature is a combination of the twofold method of science, observation and interpretation, except on a far larger scale. In a Philosophy of Nature the observed facts now become the empirical science, and the reflection on a consequently larger scale becomes philosophy.

In order to understand the value attributed to a Philosophy of Nature by St. Thomas and the Scholastics it is necessary to recall their outlook on its constitution. Being complex, i.e., a union of Nature and Philosophy, the particular relation of one to the other is all-important. There are three supreme sciences according to Aristotle and St. Thomas based on three degrees of abstraction — Physics, Mathematics, and Philosophy. In an admirable passage in " De Trinitate Boetii," the Angelic Doctor enumerates the reason for this hierarchy of sciences.

Physics is concerned with matter inasmuch as it is moveable, sensible and clothed with certain qualities and properties which are experimentally observable; it considers things in their concrete and material reality, making abstraction only from the fact that a thing is singular. This is the first degree of abstraction.

Mathematics considers material things just as physics, but it makes abstraction from all their sensible properties such as light, heat, color, and considers only quantity, number, or extent by itself.

The object of thought cannot *exist* without sensible matter, but it can be *conceived* without it, for nothing sensible or experimental or tangible enters into the definition of a line or a cube root. This is the second degree of abstraction.

Finally, the human mind can concern itself with things, not merely inasmuch as they are in movement, or inasmuch as they are quantitative, but simply inasmuch as they *are* or have *being*. There are certain objects of thought which can not only be *conceived* without matter, but which can also *exist* without matter, such as God, Justice, Fortitude, Beauty and Goodness. This science which concerns itself with *being* as being is Metaphysics and belongs to the third degree of abstraction.[23]

Philosophy of Nature for St. Thomas was a combination of the first and third degrees of abstraction,

[23] "Quædam igitur sunt speculabilium quæ dependent a materia secundum esse, quia non nisi in materia esse possunt et hæc distinguntur, quia dependent quædam a materia secundum esse et intellectum, sicut, illa in quorum diffinitione ponitur materia sensibilis: unde sine materia sensibili intelligi non possunt, ut in diffinitione hominis oportet accipere carnem et ossa, et de his est physica sive scientia naturalis. Quædam vero quamvis dependeant a materia secundum esse, non tamen secundum intellectum, quia in eorum diffinitionibus non ponitur materia sensibilis, ut linea et numerus, et de his est mathematica. Quædam vero sunt speculabilia quæ non dependent a materia secundum esse, quia sine materia esse possunt, sive numquam sint in materia, sicut Deus et angelus, sive in quibusdam sint in materia et in quibusdam non, ut substantia, qualitas et actus unum et multa, et hujusmodi, de quibus omnibus est theologia, id est divina scientia, quia præcipium cognitorum in ea est Deus.

Alio nomine dicitur metaphysica, id set transphysica, quia post physicam discenda occurrit nobis, quibus ex sensibilibus competit in insensibilia devenire. Dicitur etiam philosophia prima in quantum scientiæ aliæ ab ea principia sua accipientes eam sequuntur." lib. Boet. de Trinitate, q. 5 art. 5 ad 1.

i.e., a combination of the science of the contingent, and the science of the necessary.[24]

There is a hierarchy among the sciences as there is between the various orders of creation. The nobler must always rule the less noble, the inferior must be attracted by the superior. Now since the noblest science is metaphysics — Aristotle called it the " divine science " — because of the transcendence of its object, it follows that it must let its light shine upon other sciences with more limited objects. It is metaphysics or philosophy which justifies and defends the principles of other sciences. The axiom of geometry, for example, viz., two quantities equal to a third are equal to each other, is a particularization of the metaphysical axiom that two things identical to a third are equal to each other. It is philosophy also which furnishes physics and chemistry and all other sciences with the basic principles of experiment — the laws of the uniformity of nature, causality, end and determination.

What was the Philosophy of Nature for St. Thomas? It was the application of the principles of metaphysics or philosophy (the third degree of abstraction) to the purely inductive sciences or sciences of observation, e.g., Physics (the first degree of abstraction). The phenomenal world furnished the *matter,* and Philosophy or Metaphysics the

[24] 1. q. 86 art. 3. Philosophy of Nature was the combination of Physics and Metaphysics in the sense that while Physics alone studied *ens sensibile,* or was a science of observation, Philosophy of Nature put the accent on the *ens* and attempted to discover the reasons of being of the object.

form, thus making Philosophy of Nature an inductive-deductive science.

Two important conclusions can be drawn from this conception of the Philosophy of Nature, one having reference to the effect of a new scientific discovery on the Philosophy of Nature, the other having reference to a new Philosophy of Nature which has so recently come into being.

What effect would an entirely new Physics have upon Philosophy of Nature? As a matter of fact there is a new Physics developing today, so new in its conception that it has brought about one of the most astounding crises in scientific thought since the days of Copernicus, Kepler and Galileo. The Newtonian physics has been found inadequate to translate the world of concrete fact in a way suitable to the intellect, and the physics of the last three centuries has been founded on what Professor Whitehead has called "the Fallacy of Misplaced Concreteness."

It is not for philosophers to dispute this statement. Professor Whitehead and Mr. Bertrand Russell are no mean authorities in the field of science, and their conclusions cannot be waived aside by the gesture of a hand. Taking due account of their statements that the Physics of the present day is "biological" rather than mechanistic, a query naturally arises concerning its effect on the Philosophy of Nature.

According to the Thomistic conception of science, the new Physics means only a *new Physics*, but *not a new Philosophy.* Since the principles of philosophy were not based on the old physics they do not fall with it, and since the principles of philosophy are not based on the new physics they do not rise with it. The principle of identity, the principles of causality and finality, the transcendental properties of being, the value of ideas, all of these remain what they are, independent of a new scientific construction. Physics is not the foundation of Philosophy but only a particularization of some of its principles — a particularization which is apt to be wrong because of the incomplete induction upon which it is based. That is why St. Thomas could repeat over and over again, in the texts we have quoted, that some day there might be a new physics and a new astronomy which would upset the old, but knowing this, he never concluded that philosophy must be revised for that very reason. Philosophy of Nature was the application of the principles of metaphysics to observed facts and phenomena of the universe; these facts might be wrong, they might be proved false, but that did not mean the metaphysics was wrong; it only meant that metaphysics had to *be applied to a new set of observed facts.* Two and two still make four, though I observe two drops of water and two drops of water fuse into one. No one ever thought of plucking out his eye because he saw a stick bent in water.

Why is it then that Professor Whitehead and others are so insistent that our whole Philosophy of Nature must be revamped because of the new

Physics? If a new Physics does not necessarily mean a new Philosophy, why is it so often stated among the leaders of this new scientific group that a new philosophy is necessary? Why is it that the recognized leaders of science are expressing dissatisfaction not only with the old physics but even with the old philosophy? Why is it that they are no longer swinging from one extreme of the scientific pendulum to the other, but are questioning the very corner-stone of philosophy? Why, in their mind, does a new physics demand a new philosophy?

It may seem paradoxical at very sight to say that the demands of the new science for a new philosophy are perfectly within the bounds of reason since we have already said that a new physics, in the Thomistic conception, does not demand a new philosophy. But there is no contradiction, for the *philosophy against which the new science is reacting is the Cartesian tradition of modern philosophy and not the Scholastic tradition of the philosophia perennis.* What is the difference between the Thomistic conception of science and the Cartesian? The difference is this: *In St. Thomas the third degree of abstraction is applied to the first, i.e., metaphysics to observed facts of nature,* in *Descartes the combination was between the first and second degrees of abstraction, namely a mathematical physics, a science materially physical but formally mathematical.* The new science of Descartes was something introduced between Natural Philosophy and Phys-

ics. Still continuing to concern itself with bodies of
the material world, still continuing to adhere to
objects furnished by the first degree of abstraction,
it no longer regarded these things from the point of
view of *being* (*ens mobile*) but from the point of
view of mathematical quantity. The sound, established transcendental principles of the mind no
longer illumine the observed facts of the laboratory
or the microscope so as to give us a philosophy of
nature; all that we have now is merely a physico-
mathematical knowledge of nature. It is the imperfect light of mathematical intelligibility and not
the pure light of metaphysical intelligibility which
illumines experimental physics. Hence it is that
the great ideal of the modern philosopher is merely
to translate the observed facts of nature and science
in terms of algebraic and mathematical symbols.
Witness in Einstein the transportation of *time*
which properly belongs to physics, to the domain of
mathematics where it does not properly belong.
The mathematicization of time which he effected
does tell us what the universe is in terms of *mathematical relations,* but not what the universe is in
terms of its causes.[25]

[25] This does not mean to say that there is no place for mathematical
physics. St. Thomas speaks of mathematical physics in the following
lines: "Quanto scientia aliqua abstractiora et simpliciora considerat,
tanto eius principia sunt magis applicabilia aliis scientiis; unde principia
mathematicæ sunt applicabilia naturalibus, non autem e converso, propter
quod physica est ex suppositione mathematicæ sed non e converso, ut
patet in III Cœlo. In Lib. Bœt. De Trinitate, q. 5 art. 3. ad 5.
ad 6. Thus St. Thomas admits applying mathematics to physics, but
not physics to mathematics, for this is a subversion of the order and
hierarchy of sciences and right reason. Making time mathematical

Now it follows that the reason Professor Whitehead is desirous of scrapping Philosophy of Nature
is because by Philosophy of Nature he understands
a Mathematical Physics, and since the mathematical physics of the present day is entirely different
from the day of Descartes, it follows that our philosophy likewise must be different. For Descartes
the objective world was made up of spatial matter
with simple location in space and time and subjected
to very definite rules as to its locomotion. For our
living scientists, substance and quality, "simple
location" and the like are antiquated notions. The
latest thing in physics is the introduction of biological categories into physics, which has given rise
to Professor Whitehead's peculiar theory that nature is organic rather than mechanistic. Here we
are not deciding the merits of the mechanistic and
organic view of nature; suffice it to say that Professor Whitehead's system has the merit of reintroduc-
ing finality into the universe, and in the words of
Professor Taylor: "takes us back in a very striking
way to the ideas of the great men of the Christian
Middle Ages and the great Greeks who lay behind
them."[26]   Our point merely is that Professor
Whitehead's dissatisfaction with philosophy to the
present time is a protest against the Cartesian tradition and not against the Thomistic or the tradi-

---

is an example of such a subversion. Cf. Jacques Maritain, "Philosophie
Scolastique et Physique Mathematique," *Revue Thomiste*, 1918–1919,
Vols. 23 and 24, p. 164 ff. Also "Philosophie et Science Experimentale,"
Revue de Philosophie, Vol. 26, No. 4, 1926, p. 342 ff.

[26] "Dr. Whitehead's Philosophy of Religion," *Dublin Review*,
July 1927, p. 28.

tional;[27] and that he is asking for another Mathematical Physics, or Biologico-Mathematical Physics, and not a new Philosophy. The Metaphysics of Aristotle and the Schoolmen is sound; new Physics does not affect even in the least its principles. If Philosophy of Nature at the present day were built on Thomistic lines, and the supreme truths of the intellectual order were the guides and the light which illumined the observed facts of nature, there would be no demand for a new Philosophy of Nature. If there is such a demand today it is because our thinkers are content with a mathematical or symbolic expression of nature's laws instead of a metaphysical explanation, and because they are satisfied with a description in terms of algebra rather than an explanation in terms of causes.

III. *Application of These Conclusions to Religion.*

Empirical science, because it deals with matter, which is capable of a kind of infinite multiplication, must always be content to draw conclusions based on incomplete induction. Empirical science, on the admission of the leading scientists themselves is merely an approximation of truth, for science does not aim to explain, but merely to describe. Now if scientific constructions are tentative because they explain the facts today and probably not tomorrow, why overthrow the certain, the fixed and the established principles of natural reason and natural relig-

[27] "Science and the Modern World," pp. 71-82, 209, 210.

ion out of tribute to these budding theories? It might well be asked whether the new physics is a stable and permanent foundation upon which to build the whole fabric of philosophy and religion. What guarantee have we that a philosophy built upon the theories of our day is likely to be more permanent than constructions built upon the scientific constructions of Descartes, Galileo and Kepler? We do not wish to be understood as asserting that the new theories are unsound (many would say they are), we are merely suggesting the idea that since scientists claim for their theories nothing more than a mere approximation of truth, there is always the danger that a philosophy built on something so insecure is more likely to be found on examination to possess no greater stability than the foundations upon which it has been constructed.

The whole appeal of the new idea of religion is that it is in perfect accord with the latest findings of science. Professor Whitehead, so deservedly recognized as a great scientist, has recently come forward in his " Religion in the Making " to construct a religion on the new theories of science. If a theory quite as fragile as relativity is dubious for science, the field where it properly belongs, it does not seem reasonable to make it serve as religion's all-sufficient foundation. There can be no doubt that it is the novelty in the application, and not the truth which appeals. It is not by bread alone that the modern philosopher of religion lives, but principally by catchwords. As a German writer puts it: " We are very resourceful in coining marketable and attractive formulæ, but idle in creating fully developed systems and views of the world." [28] Professor Perry, bemoaning the same spirit in modern philosophy writes: "We suffer from a new kind of credulity. It was once complained that men are too easily inclined to believe what their fathers believed; that men lacked originality, independence. But there is now reason to fear that men may too easily believe what no one else has ever believed before. Men with settled convictions may become as rare as were freethinkers in an earlier time. And the consequences must be scarcely less detrimental to social welfare than the consequences of the earlier complacency and narrow-mindedness." [29]

There is humility and there is prudence in the caution of scientists when they speak of their theories as hypotheses, but there is no humility and no prudence in the recklessness with which philosophers of religion apply these hypotheses to religion. Religion is not to be made the proving ground of every scientific hypothesis any more than the soul is to be made the puppet of every demand of the body. It is not wisdom, it is not common sense to overthrow the established relations between God and man, because of certain hypothetical relations between space and time. It is not good science, it is not good philosophy, it is positively bad philosophy of religion, to make approximations, and uncer-

[28] Ludwig Stern, "Die Philosophiscen Stromungen der Gegenwart," p. 7.   [29] "Present Philosophical Tendencies," p. 20.

tain explanations of the universe the reason for overthrowing the abiding and eternal relation of Sovereignty and Paternity which are the bonds uniting man to God.

Up to this point we have assumed with the modern scientists themselves that their theories are only theories, that they are approaches to the truth rather than truth itself. Here we go a step further and grant that their theories are laws, and their hypotheses established truths. Would it then still follow that religion is to be constructed and interpreted in the light of these laws and these principles? The answer must be clearly in the negative, for what is certain in the empirical sciences is derived from the illumination afforded by the intellectual principles of metaphysics. Physics, biology, and sociology are not the ground and foundation of metaphysics; otherwise the science with a more restricted object would rule the science with a more general object. That is why St. Thomas asserts that a changed conception of empirical science does not involve a change in the metaphysics which ruled that science. Philosophy is independent of science, but independent does not mean contrary to science, nor necessarily separated from science; the independence is founded on the difference of the *how* and the *why*, description in terms of mathematics and explanation in terms of causes. The difference is founded on an abstraction which reveals the *reason of being* of the juxtaposed phenomenal qualities. That is why the Angelic Doctrine contends that there is no uniform method in science, viz., because the various sciences are separated by different abstractions, and each has its own material object and its own formal object. To overflow one into the other so as to confuse abstractions and objects would be the ruination of science.[30] — *et propter hoc peccant qui uniformiter in tribus speculativæ partibus procedere nituntur.*

St. Thomas calls that tendency to make all sciences uniform in method and content a " sin," and if there be a general academic " sin " today it is precisely that. Here we call it the " Fallacy of the Uniform Method of Science " — the fallacy of taking one science as the norm, and making it the measure, the guide, the interpreter, and the inspiration of every other science. The history of philosophy bears witness that our own generation is not the first to build a metaphysics and a religion on the data of a science to the exclusion of all other possible foundations. There is a fashion in sciences as there is in clothes. Each generation seems to have its own science which is supreme for the moment. Auguste Comte gave to the world the sociological method which was genuinely scientific so long as it was confined to society. But the lyricizers of science would not keep it restricted to its material object; they overflowed it and applied the sociologi-

---

[30] In divinis neque ad sensum, neque ad imaginationem debemus deduci; in mathematicis autem et imaginationem et non ad sensum; in naturalibus autem etiam ad sensum. Et propter hoc peccant, qui uniformiter in tribus speculativæ partibus procedere nituntur. De Trinitate Bœtii, q. 6 art. 2.

cal method to religion and to God with the result that we have today the ingenious sociological interpretation of God as "society divinized." Another generation saw the popularity of another science, viz., biology, which Darwin carried to new heights and new revelations of the development of the organic world. Biology is a perfectly legitimate and necessary science so long as it remains biology and confines itself to the study of living beings, but Darwin and all the other biologists could not hold lyricizers in check, and soon biology was applied not only to philosophy as in the case of Herbert Spencer, but even to God, with the result that certain modern theologians look upon God as "the God of evolution," or the "God who advances from life to life" as in the case of Sir Henry Jones. Then came the new fashion — psychology. James and Meyers, confining themselves to a study of the subconscious mind, gave to the scientific world many interesting and important conclusions concerning the effect of sublimated ideas on our waking life. But the fallacy of the uniform method of science got the better of some psychologists who refused to make psychology a study of the mind and its states, but insisted on making religion and philosophy dance to its tune. Psychology then became identified with theology and conversion was explained as an eruption of a subsconscious state, sin was explained as a "complex," and God as a "mental projection" as in the case of Professor Leuba, or as a "sublimated libido" as in the case of the Freudian theologians.

At the present time the fashionable science is not sociology, not biology, not psychology, but physics. It is fashionable because the most important scientific theories in the world today are coming from that field. Intellectual giants in that field like Duhem, Whitehead, Einstein, Poincaré and Meyerson, have given to the world new interpretations of the physical universe which do seem to fit the facts better than the older theories. The thinking world welcomes these intellectual advances, but it cannot help but frown upon any attempt to interpret everything else in this world in terms of physics, a spatio-temporal continuum, and relativity. Professor Whitehead, although the deepest thinker among the physicists themselves, is also their greatest offender and their greatest lyricizer. After writing such a delightful scientific work as "Science and the Modern World," he follows it with a venture into theology in his "Religion in the Making," wherein he is destined to be set forth before the world as a sorry example of the truth that a man may be a really great scientist and a lamentably poor theologian.

It is worth repeating here that we are not opposing science but lyricism of science, not scientific methods, but a uniform scientific method for all departments of knowledge, not physics, but physics-religion.

But there is a danger that this Thomistic or common-sense point of view — the two are synonymous — may be open to the charge of obscurantism.

This is because there is current in the world today
the notion that religion is a controversial question,
and that science is not. To dispute the extension
of physics to the domain of religion is to be " unscientific," and yet to dispute the sacredness of established principles of religion is to be "broad" and
"tolerant." Disagreeing with science is considered
as vicious as disagreeing with the multiplication
table, but to disagree about religious fundamentals
is like disagreeing with the World Court. The
Thomistic point of view is not that science is unscientific, but merely that religion is " unscientific " in
the sense that physics is not the science which best
studies it. It is true, and may be said without
offense, that as theologians, some of the modern
lyricists of science are good physicists.

The three principal sciences which have been lyricized into religion are psychology, sociology and
physics, the latter being the most generally applied
today. All modern philosophers have not fallen into
this pit. We are glad to quote Professors Rashdall,
Leighton, Thouless, among others who protest particularly against psychology dominating religion.
" The business of psychology is to tell us what actually goes on in the mind. It cannot possibly tell us
whether the beliefs are true or false — a man cannot
be satisfied as to the truth of his beliefs simply by
being told that the beliefs are actually there." [31]
" The idea of religion which is merely based upon
psychology and involves nothing else is a delu-

[31] R. H. Rashdall, " Philosophy and Religion," 1909, pp. 111, 112.

sion." [32] "A religion which does not tie the soul
of man up with some permanent reality beyond the
shows of sense is no religion. The denatured definition of religion without a God-idea, which various
writers have offered as a way out of the difficulties
in squaring religion with materialism, does not
correspond to any historical or actual working religion." [33] "Psychology must supply us with the facts
about the human mind and its experiences. . . . It
is then the task of the theologian to explain what
kind of universe it is in which such experiences
occur, i.e., in the end to ask what God is like. But
science must not beg the question before it asks
theology to answer it because to begin to know how
things are done, we cannot assume that God doesn't
do them." [34]

One of the difficulties which will always confront
the sociologist who attempts to interpret God in
terms of social-science, will be the rebellion of a
human heart against making a religion out of an
irreligious humanity. If the individuals who make
up society are God-less how can the combination of
them produce the sacred object of religion, or even
a God? Ten thousand imperfect men do not make
a saint, and neither can ten thousand God-denying
individuals constitute a God Who is their collective
ideation. The sociological explanation of religion
will always be extrinsic to religion itself, will de-

[32] H. Thouless, " Introduction to the Psychology of Religion,"
1923, pp. 261, 262. Cf. W. Selbie, " Psychology of Religion," p. 297.
[33] J. A. Leighton, " Man and the Cosmos," p. 537.
[34] F. R. Barry, " Christianity and Psychology," 1923, p. 172.

scribe it when it has been cooled off and poured into moulds, but never as a life which it really is.

And even if the sociological method were capable of being applied uniformly to theology, its satisfaction would still be doubtful. As Mr. Chesterton has so well said: "Man is maimed as well as limited by arresting those upward gestures that are so natural to him. Even if mankind could become such a mutual admiration society men would in fact find each other less admirable. A self-contained and self-centred humanity would chill as in the same way as a self-contained and self-centred individual. For the spiritual hungers of humanity are never merely hungers for humanity. In other words it is impossible to turn all the eyes of that mutual society inward." [35]

Furthermore, it will always be dubious as to how influential humanitarian religion really is. "Did any man or woman — it may be asked with no intention of flippancy — ever worship God in spirit and in truth for the sake of providing the children of the poor with pasteurized milk, or in order to found homes for orphans? Did any man or woman indeed ever worship God in spirit and truth for the sake of making his neighbors across the street or next door more honest? A plain answer to this question puts the matter in a clear light. To anyone who has known religion even at a distance the question will seem perhaps more than absurd. The

[35] *Introduction*, O. Dudley's "Will Men Be Like Gods?" 1925, p. VI.

truth is that a religious person may particularly express or give outward result to his religion through good works, even of an organized kind. He may thus, for instance, help to support 'fresh air homes' for city children, or more questionably, he may see to it that his neighbors do not disobey the prohibition law or falsify their income-tax returns. But others may do the same thing from quite another motive, from simple good will or benevolence, from devotion to efficiency, from the itch which allows no rest to the meddlesome busybody. Good works then are not even certain evidence of religion, and are by so much the less religion itself. . . . This means essentially that religion is not social activity at all, and that moreover, the very entrance way to religion is a deep conviction of the relative emptiness of the mutable things of this outward world. . . . Nothing worth having can be got through palpable misuse of words; and religion is a word whose right meaning has long since been definitely fixed. Self-deception is in fact the most innocent name one can give to attempts at the transference of a creditable name to secular activities however meritorious." [36]

The method and content of one science is not the method of every other science; just as the subject or predicate of one sentence cannot be rashly transferred to another sentence, so neither can the categories of one science be transferred without correction to the categories of another science.

[36] Robert Shafer, "Progress and Science," Yale Press, 1922, pp. 25, 26.

"The roses are red" is one sentence; "the sphinx is silent" is another. The predicate "red" cannot be applied to the subject "sphinx" without doing violence both to facts and language. In like manner, the method of astronomy cannot be the method of biology, nor can the categories of chemistry be transferred to sociology. Oxygen and hydrogen cannot be studied in the same way as Justice and Fortitude. It is one thing to be a relativist in physics and another thing to be a relativist in theology. There is a danger that a scientific ideal, like relativity, if it is isolated, is apt to go to one's head. As an angry man sees everything "red," so even a physicist may see everything "relativized."

This lyricism has been carried so far that now we are content to take our religion from anyone whether or not he be religious-minded. We would never call in a plumber because we had broken our finger-joint, nor would we call in a piano-tuner to fix the key of our door, nor a florist to heal a burn on the palm of our hand, but we will hear and hearken to anyone when the most important and the only important question in the world is asked: namely, man's relation to God. Professor A. E. Taylor, speaking in the same vein, says: "No one would think of regarding the verdict of an archæologist or a chemist on a moot point of law as deriving any particular value from the eminence of the archæologist or the chemist in his known subject; no one would attach any weight to a Lord Chancellor's opinion about the genuineness of an alleged Rembrandt, or a disputed fragment of Simonides, because the opinion was that of the best Lord Chancellor the country has ever possessed. We all understand that the sort of consensus of 'authorities' which makes it proper for the man who is not an 'authority' to dispense with his own private judgment is the consensus of 'authorities' in a particular subject, who derive their claim to authority from a native aptitude and long training. But we ought to be equally ready to recognize that in the same way the only consensus which is of weight on matters of religion is the consensus of deeply religious men. Religion is not shown to be an 'illusion' because worldly-minded men who have never felt the sense of personal sin or the need of adoration can see nothing in it any more than, for example, the Theory of Relativity is shown to be 'moonshine' because it seems unintelligible to the type of man of whom R. L. S. used to speak as the 'common banker,' or disinterested devotion to be an illusion, because a clever cynical diplomatist assures one that he has never felt such devotion himself and sees no evidence of it in the behaviour of others. . . . It is as though one should say there can be no gold in a certain district because I, who know little or nothing of the signs of the presence of this metal, and care less, have traversed the district from end to end without discovering what I had made no attempt to find." [37]

The sciences are valid within their own sphere but only there, for a science is not the whole of all

[37] *The Vindication of Religion*, in "Essays Catholic and Critical," edited by E. G. Selwyn, 1926, pp. 40, 41.

knowledge but only a special kind of knowledge which makes up for its one-sidedness by the precision of its vision. The scientists themselves can tell us about the human brain, but always about the human brain as it is for the physiological or anatomical observer, who is looking at it from the outside. "So long as we keep strictly to the method of the natural sciences we never penetrate, so to say, within our own skins. . . . But in truth the thought and deeds of men are not mere 'events' but something more: they are personal acts. Hence, I submit, the information of the psychologist and the anthropologist is true and valuable so far as it goes, but it does not go far enough." [38]

Why, too, it may be asked, should the physics of relativity enjoy the exclusive privilege of re-interpreting God and religion? Have our ideas of God and religion been so closely built on a world of "simple location" and "point" and "atom" and "event" that the overthrow of these ideas means the overthrow of God? Because time and space are found to be physical ultimates, does it follow that God is Space-Time, or that Space is His Body and Time is His Soul as Professor Alexander would have us believe? Because the physical universe can be better interpreted in terms of the organism rather than that of mechanism, and in terms of "events" rather than location, does it follow that therefore God is the "Harmony of these events," as Professor

[38] *The Vindication of Religion*, in " Essays Catholic and Critical," edited by E. G. Selwyn, 1926, p. 43.

Whitehead would have it? Why should it be the kingly privilege of the new physics, any more than medicine or engineering, to interpret God in terms of its categories? Why should not the medical profession be entitled to revise the concept of God to be in better keeping with insulin than with the quinine-stage of medicine? Why should not the Egyptologist be entitled, by the same logic, to revise our concept of God, to be more in keeping with the discovery of the tomb of Tutankhamen? Because life evolves does it follow that God evolves? Are the laws and hypotheses and categories of one science transferable indefinitely to other sciences? If the laws of psychology are not applicable to astronomy, and the laws of music not transferable to law, and the predicates of an amœba not applicable to a Pantheon, why should the categories of physics, psychology and sociology be applicable to God? There is far more reason, it is true, for applying biology to God than there is for applying chemistry or mineralogy, for the laws of biology are more universal than those of chemistry, because life is more universal than chemical elements. But the laws of organisms are no more applicable to the spirit than the laws of the chemical to the non-chemical, or the laws of the flesh to the spirit, or the laws of a protoplasm to God.[39] Briefly there is danger that the uniform method will be carried too far. Relativity is valid within its own order perhaps, but it becomes laughable when it states that we have six toes on one foot

[39] Sheen, "God in Evolution," *Thought*, March 1927, p. 581.

counted one way, and four on the other counted the
other way. The temporal and the spatial are not
the best approaches to the non-temporal and the
non-spatial. There is much necessity of us heark-
ening back to the wisdom of Aquinas, to learn all
over again that Metaphysics and not Physics is the
science which properly studies God: " Quædam vero
sunt specuabilia quæ non dependent a materia secundum esse . . . id est, divina scientia vel metaphysica." [40]   The standpoint of religion and
metaphysics is more inclusive than the merely physical one as being is more extensive than space-time.
Man is greater than all his standpoints, and the real
problem, as St. Thomas so well says, is to find the
standpoint of the whole man and the whole universe from which to judge the validity of all partial
and subordinate views. On the contrary, there is
something tragic in our modern philosophy of religion. Much of it is intoxicated by modern physics;
space-time has gone to its head; whole cosmic
streams of flux have swept it away from its moor-
ings. Space-time has become a cult and Time a God
and Physics a Revelation. Philosophers of religion
breathlessly await the latest decree of space-time
physics as industrialists await the latest design in
machinery. And what food for thought! Sacred
Scripture says " *There will be no more time.*" Philosophers of religion today have constructed the universe out of it — and even God!

[40] In De Trinitate Boetii, q. 5 art. 1.

CHAPTER IX

THE FALLACY OF INVERTED RELATIONS

THE third fallacy of the contemporary idea of religion is the fallacy of inverted relations. By this is meant that obtuse mental tendency to invert and turn upside down the natural relation existing between *knowledge and reality on the one hand, and God and man on the other*. The two are correlative, and since knowledge is the pathway to God it follows that a wrong conception concerning knowledge entails eventually a wrong conception concerning God. The path that leads to Rome does not pass by Babylon.

Traditional thought asserts first, that the human intellect is a thing measured not a measure, and the relation between the intellect and reality is that of a determinable thing to its determinant; secondly, the Divine Intellect is a measure, not a thing measured, and the relation between God and things which are not God and distinct from Him, is one of dependence. The first principle asserts the proper relation between mind and things, the second between God and man.[1]

---

[1] Intellectus divinus est mensurans non mensuratus; res autem naturalis, mensurans et mensuratus; set intellectus noster est mensuratus, non mensurans quidem res naturales, sed artificiales tantum. De Veritate, q. 1 art. 2. In sentiendo et sciendo mensuramur per res quæ extra nos sunt. In Met. lib. 10. lect. 2; 1. q. 21 art. 2; q. 16 art. 1; 1–2 q. 93 art. 1 ad 3.

I. *Relation Between Things and the Human Intellect*

The human intellect is a determined or measured thing, not a measure, — such is the Scholastic position. No faculty completely determines its object. The eye, for example, does not create color; the ear does not create sounds nor impose sound on what it hears; the sense of touch does not communicate sensation to the object, it cannot make thorns feel like roses. The same is true of the intellect; it does not determine reality or create it by imposing space and time forms on sensible experience, or intellectual knowledge. Rather, it is determined by reality and in this sense is measured by it. Reality does not need to enter into a finite mind in order to exist or to find its true being. Hence there is no real relation between reality and mind. Concepts are not true on account of the intellect, but because they conform to reality. The intellect does not endow things with being, nor goodness, nor truth — it discovers them. It is only in the case of artistic creation that man is a measure; the sculptor, for example, determines the statue he chisels. To this extent man resembles God as Creator.

This conception of the relation between mind and reality has the great advantage of corresponding to common sense. Kant, it is true, effected a Copernican revolution in philosophy by making reality revolve about mind, instead of mind about reality. What Kant really did was to apply the principle of independence and freedom from the "extrinsic," introduced in the sixteenth century, to the realm of philosophy. He asserted the liberty or license of the mind against reality in the same way that others before him asserted the liberty of conscience against the mystic Christ. Traditional thought began by humbly acknowledging the mind's primitive poverty and asserting the necessity of something extrinsic to measure and determine it. Once it humbled itself it became exalted, "for he that humbleth himself shall be exalted," and thanks to the spiritual power of the soul it rose above matter to a knowledge of supra-sensible things.

Contemporary thinking, on the contrary, denies this relation between intellect and things. It inverts the relation and asserts that *the human intellect is a measure and not a thing measured*. It is a measure, because it determines and is, to some extent, the source of the great metaphysical transcendentals, — being, truth, goodness, and we may add, beauty.

The Human Mind as the Measure of Being: Contemporary thought whether idealistic or empirical agrees on the Kantian revolution that reality is in some way the work of the mind.[2] The mind measures being either by creating *a priori* forms native to the mind — and this is the Idealist's answer; or by practical forms arising from need and utility —

---

[2] A happy reaction is to be found in Neo-Realism of the present day. It is unfortunate however that this philosophy has not been more metaphysical. Cf. R. Kremer, "Neo-Realisme Americain," Louvain, 1921.

and this is the Empiricist's answer. One is the modern interpretation of the First Critique of Kant, the other of the Second Critique.[3]

The Human Mind as the Measure of Truth: Its source is not something transcendent to man; it *becomes* as man *becomes*. There is no such thing as a Truth "with a big 'T.'" [4] Truths "make themselves as we go." They are "so many new creations that add themselves as fast as history proceeds." Instead of being an "antecedent principle" that animates a process, truth is but an abstract name for its results.[5] Being devices, the measure of truth will be its utility — its utility to us in handling the facts of experience. Subjective interests, our needs, our desires will be at every step the measures of these "truths." [6] The measure will not be something objective, it will be that which satisfies us, or that which is expedient in the way of our thinking. If an idea "works" then it is true. "If theological ideas prove to have a value for concrete life, they will be true for pragmatism in the sense that they are good for so much." [7] "If the hypothesis of God works satisfactorily in the widest sense of the word — experience shows that it certainly does work — it is true." [8]

The Human Mind as the Measure of Goodness:

---

[3] Leslie Walker, "Theories of Knowledge." A fuller treatment of this point is found in "God and Intelligence."

[4] James, "Pragmatism," p. 242.

[5] *Ibid.*

[6] F. C. S. Schiller, "Humanism," p. 11.

[7] "Pragmatism," p. 73.

[8] *Ibid.*, p. 299.

The common-sense Philosophy takes as a more or less proximate guide of morality the conformity with the ultimate natural end of man. St. Thomas commenting on Aristotle's Ethics tells us " the rectitude of the appetite in respect to the end is the measure of truth in the practical order." [9] Every man by his nature is equipped with a norm for his actions. This measure is naturally known and in demonstrable first principles which are the seeds of moral virtues.[10] They form the major proposition in judging the morality of an act, the particular act under consideration constituting its minor.

But these first principles which are the measure of morality have a source by which they are measured. Their ultimate source is outside man since every measure must be extrinsic to the thing measured. That ultimate source is God, "Who enlightens every man coming into the world." [11] The first principles of the practical reason are sufficient to explain the moral acts of man, but they are not sufficient to explain themselves. There is nothing either in man as an individual or in man as a social animal which will give the final answer to question. Their source is without; it is God.

Contemporary thought, on the contrary, has seen fit to reject this interpretation of the ultimate source of the *bonum*. The basis of morality is to

[9] Rectitudo appetitus per respectum ad finem est mensura veritatis in ratione practica. Ethicorum Lib. VI, lect. 2.

[10] In Eth. Lib. V, lect. 12, De Veritate, q. 16 art. 1. Summa 1–2 q. 63 art. 1.

[11] Commentary on the Gospel of St. John Chap. 1, verse: " Erat lux vera."

be sought ultimately within man himself. There
is no need of God standing outside and apart from
man. There are no fixed and indemonstrable first
principles which are the "seeds" of morality.
Morality is a growth; it is an evolving thing. Evolution accounts for it. Its source is man. The
source of the moral is the non-moral; the source
of the ethical is the non-ethical.

For the general purpose of simply indicating the
spirit of modern thought it suffices to divide the
modern notions of the goodness into two great
divisions:

1. Those which seek the origin and the measure of morality in the individual.
2. Those which seek the origin and measure of morality
in society, implying that society is a source distinct from
man as an individual.

According to the first conception, morality is
the result of association. In the course of the biological evolution of man, certain stability has at-
tached itself to certain feelings of pleasure or pain.
Those actions which gave pleasure became associated with the good and those actions which gave
pain became associated with the bad. There were
no "seeds" of morality in the mind of man; if there
were any "seeds" of morality at all, they were in
his body. The study of biological and psychological development would reveal the moral development.

This theory soon passes into the theory of the
Sociological Origin of Morality. Man being a

member of society it is only natural to relate his acts to it. The Sociological School of Durkheim-Levy Bruhl is the popular exponent of the notion that society is the measure of morality. Society is considered as a distinct and totally different reality from the individuals which compose it. It is *sui generis,* and is not merely a different mode of being from the individuals who compose it. The measure of morality, this school argues, cannot come from the individuals, for no individual can measure himself; it cannot come from God, for this is an unscientific hypothesis. It must therefore come from society.[12] And Society is God, " Je ne vois dans la divinité que la societé transfigurée et pensée symboliquement." [13]

Another manifestation of the anthropometric attitude of modern thought is to be found in its theories of æsthetics. Its conception of what constitutes beauty is in complete variance with that of traditional thought on the subject. For the latter Beauty is essentially a Divine thing; it belongs to God. In creating He gave it in a measured way to His creatures. The Beauty of creatures is nothing else than the Divine Beauty participated by things. St. Thomas thus carries his theory of Æsthetics to a point which no other theory has even remotely approached. He places Beauty in the very Trinity itself — in the Son Who is the image

---

[12] Cf. Simon Deploige, "Le Conflit de la Morale et de la Sociologie," for an exposé and criticism of this theory.

[13] E. Durkheim, *Bulletin de la Societé Française de Philosophie,* T. VI, p. 129, quoted in Deploige.

and splendor of the Father.[14] As Creation measures
the beauty in nature by the Word, so does the
artist, another creator, as it were, measure the
beauty of his work. Beauty then is really *outside*
him as well as inside.

The modern æstheticians on the contrary are
inclined to exaggerate the role of impression in art
and eventually to deny the necessity of an *other* by
which Beauty is measured.

(a) The Symbolic Sympathy Theory made current by Basch and Lalo[15] maintains that Beauty is
not in the work; it is not something inherent in the
object and measured by a mind which conceives
beauty. Rather, it is the state of consciousness
which is beautiful. We project our sentimental
states into the objects which surround us; by some
mysterious extension of our sentimental states we
project our emotions in the things outside us.
Once this endowment has taken place there
arises a sympathetic fusion and the notion of
beauty rises. The source of beauty is lifted from
the domain of the intellect and lowered to the field
of the sensibilities. Its ultimate source is not therefore something by which man is measured. Man is
its source inasmuch as he has lived through a certain sentimental state and projected that state outside himself.

(b) A second form of anthropometric æsthetics
is a development of the anthropometric sociology.

[14] Summa 1. q. 39 art. 8.
[15] Basch, "Les Grands Courants de l'Esthetique Allemande Con-
temporaine," *Revue Philosophique,* 1912. C. Lalo, "Les Sentiments
Esthetiques," 1910.

According to this theory moral values come from society. The development of this man-as-source philosophy in the field of æsthetics gives rise to the theory that beauty too has but a social value. M. Lalo[16] in exposing this notion declares that a work of art is beautiful only in proportion as it is recognized as such by society. With this theory, as with the previous one, man is the source of beauty, but man considered from the point of view of sociology and not from the point of view of psychology.

(c) Pragmatic Æsthetics is a particular aspect of a pragmatic philosophy. According to this philosophy, truth is subject to the fluctuations of human valuations. In like manner beauty is delivered over to the non-intellectual valuations and appreciations of man, and beauty becomes synonymous with a pleasurable reaction which it engenders within me.[17]

The Measure of Beauty then is wholly from *within*. Man is the measure of Beauty in its entirety; all that which might justly be considered as a measure of his art, is considered by him as a limitation and an attempt to crush out all individuality and originality.[18]

---

[16] *Revue Philosophique*, July 1914, p. 47.

[17] These systems are given in detail in "L'Oeuvre d'Art et la Beauté," Maurice De Wulf, 1922.

[18] Jacques Maritain, "L'Art et Scholastique," Chap. 2. Cf. "Belphegor" Julien Benda, Paris, 1919, p. 26. "La volonté de la peinture moderne de repousser tout element intellectuel se traduit encore dans une autre series de doctrines, dont l'intention, à travers les milles gloses qu'on en donne peut se resumer d'un mot; susciter l'impression que nous recevons des choses *hors de la signification que* notre esprit leur donnes.

The result has been a glorification of the subjective states of the artist and the birth of the cult of the indistinct. The indistinct is not a mere negative term. It has a positive signification for them. Bergson has written on the " Idea of Disorder " in his Creative Evolution. The painter, the musician, seeks not to describe a burning house either on canvas or in sounds but rather to describe how *he felt* in seeing the house burn. There can therefore be no measure of beauty other than the subjective state itself. It is a sensation taken for a perception and every sensation is incommunicable. Only ideas are communicable. In a certain sense therefore it is true to say that every public recital of "subjective music" and every public exhibition of a modernist picture is a refutation of the philosophy behind it. It seeks to communicate to others what is, *ex-hypothesi* incommunicable — viz., the subjective state.

In making man or the human mind the measure of being, truth, goodness and beauty, contemporary thought has attributed to the human mind precisely what St. Thomas and his followers have attributed to the Divine Mind.[19]   Dr. James H. Ryan has more clearly expressed this thought in these words: "Kant at least never confused human with divine psychology. But his successors, including the leading neo-idealists of the present day, Croce and Gentile, did and have continued to do so. The effect of this confusion of thought upon epistemol-

[19] De Veritate, q. 1 art. 2.

ogy has been marked, for it has resulted in the substitution of a theory of Absolute Mind and its knowledge for that of the human mind and its knowledge. Epistemology has thus become a theory of knowledge in utter abstraction from our ordinary modes of thought." [20] God is the Source, the Measure, of all Being, Truth, Goodness and Beauty according to traditional thought. To make man the source is to *divinize man*. The Thomistic conception tended to the *elevation* of the material universe through man's spiritual soul which ennobled things by knowing them. The present day conception is not concerned with the elevation of the material but with the *divinization* of man.

A metaphysical revolution which makes man a tyrant over nature instead of its benefactor may not seem to the superficial observer to have any religious implications; but really it has, for the divinization of man implies necessarily the humanization of God, and ultimately the humanization of all religion. There is a necessary connection between the exaltation of man and the humiliation of God. This alteration is not in the objective order, it is true, any more than there is an alteration in a public dignitary when an insane mind imagines himself to be such. God is God, though Baal call himself God. But subjectively there is a profound relation between the two. Just as two material bodies cannot occupy the same space at the same time, neither

---

[20] "The Approach to the Problem of Knowledge," *New Scholasticism*, Vol. 2, No. 1, Jan. 1927, p. 27.

can magnified finitude exist with dwarfed infinity.
"I must decrease; He must increase" expresses a
relative truth which extends quite beyond the confines of the Jordan as a place and the first century
as a time. The bigger a philosopher thinks he is,
the less he thinks God is. The psychology of
sainthood brings out this truth. The closer souls
mount to God the less assured they are of their own
importance, and the more certain they are of their
own imperfection and nothingness.[21] The reason
for this is that as we get near the perfect and the
infinite, the more clearly the defects of imperfect
and the finite show forth, just as the closer we bring
an object to the light the more its imperfections and
defects are revealed. The contrary is equally true:
the more a man exalts himself, the less God seems to
him in comparison. The good man is never sure he
is good because he measures himself by the Perfect;
the evil man is quite sure he is good because he
measures himself by himself. A mole hill may look
like a mountain to an ant, but it looks like a mole
hill to man. Humility — philosophical humility
— is the condition of wonder and the one fact
which makes fairy tales interesting. As Jack could
never have delighted in the bean-stalk unless Jack
was smaller than the bean-stalk, so neither can
philosophers enjoy this universe if they are bigger
than the universe, neither can they enjoy God if
they are bigger than God.

[21] Quanto enim aliquis magis afficitur ad Deum et ipsum cognoscit,
tanto videt eum majorem; et se minorem immo prope nihil in comparatione ad Deum. In Ephes. 5 lect. 7.

II. *Relation Between Man and God*

An error in the relation between mind and reality involves an error in the relation between man and God. The inversion of the due order of the one leads to an inversion of the due order of the other. But what is the due order between man and his Maker? First of all there is some kind of relation; that much is implied in the very question. Relation signifies some kind of dependence between terms.[22] In the ultimate analysis there may be three kinds of relations accordingly as the terms are: both logical, or both real, or mixed, that is logical and real. The relation between a genus and a species is an example of a logical relation; the relation between a father and a son is an example of a real relation which implies a distinct substance and a real dependence on that substance.[23] But there is yet another kind of relation which is not wholly logical, nor wholly real, but mixed; that is when one of the terms is real and the other is logical. The real relation is to be placed in the dependent term. For example, the right side of a pillar is, properly speaking, not in the pillar itself, but in its relation to man. The right or the left side of a pillar depends on man and not on the pillar, hence the real relation is to be placed in the man and not in the pillar.[24]

[22] C. G. lib. 2. c. 12; De Veritate, q. 21 art. 1; De Potentia q. 7 art. 1 ad 9.

[23] 1. q. 13 a. 7. Cf. E. A. Pace, The Idea of Order, *New Scholasticism*, Jan. 1928.

[24] Quandocumque aliqua duo sic habent ad invicem, quod unum

The relation between knowledge and reality, or intellect and things, belongs to this third class, for one of its terms is real, the other logical. The reality of things does not depend upon a finite knowing mind, but the knowledge of reality does depend upon reality. The relation between knowledge and the real external world is real, for without the raw materials of the sense world we would never know; but the relation between the external world and human knowledge is logical, for the external world would continue to exist whether or not a finite mind ever knew it. We do not endow it with existence, we do not make it real, any more than geology makes the strata of the earth.[25]

This opens up the heart of the question. St. Thomas asserts that there is the same relation between man and God as there is between knowledge and reality. That means that the relation is real

---

dependet ab altero, sed non e converse, in eo quod dependet ab altero, est realis relatio; sed in eo a quo dependet, non est relatio nisi rationis tantum; prout, scilicet, non potest intelligi aliquid referri ad alterum quin intelligatur etiam respectus oppositus ex parte alterius. De Veritate, q. 4 art. 6. Unde Philosophus dicit in 5 Meta., quod non dicuntur relative, eo quod ipsa referantur ad alia, sed quia alia referuntur ad ipsa. 1. q. 13 art. 7; 1. q. 28 art. 1 and art. 2; d. 20 art. 1; d. 26 q. 2 art. 1; De Veritate, q. 1 art. 5 ad 16.

25 Sicut scibile relative dicitur ad scientiam, non quia ad ipsum referatur, sed quia scientia refertur ad ipsum. 1 q. 6 art. 2 ad 1; 1 q. 13 art. 7; 3. q. 35 art. 5 ad 3; 1 d. 8 q. 4 art. 1 ad 3; 1 d. 20 q. 1; 1 d. 26 q. 2 art. 1; 1 d. 30 q. 1 art. 2 and q. 3 art. 3; 1 d. 40 q. 1 art. 1 ad 2; C. G. lib. 2 c. 12; De Veritate, q. 1 art. 5 ad 15; q. 4 art. 5; in Meta. lib. 5 lect. 17; in Meta. lib. 10. lect. 8; in Phy. lib. 5 lect. 3.; Relatio enim scientiæ ad scibile consequitur actionem scientis, non autem actionem scibilis; scibile enim eodem modo se habet quantum in se est, et quando intelligitur et quando non intelligitur; et ideo relatio in sciente realiter est, in scibili autem secundum intellectum tantum; dicitur enim quod intelligitur scibile ad scientiam relative, ex eo quod scientia refertur ad ipsum C. G. lib. 4. c. 14.

in us but logical in God, just as the relation in knowledge is real in the human mind but logical in things.[26]

"Since God is outside the whole order of creation and since all creatures are ordained to Him and not conversely, it is manifest that creatures are really related to God Himself."[27] This is the doctrine of Aquinas and the doctrine of all who have followed the tradition of common sense. It is founded on the elementary truth that since nothing can come from nothing, there must be some Being to account for the participated being which is common to all things in this universe.[28] If there was ever a moment when there was nothing, then nothing would ever be. Things have not the plenitude of being; the very fact that they change, that they share this being with others, that they die, proves that their existence is but a borrowed thing and not their own. Just as the rays of the setting sun cease with the setting of the sun, so too would the imperfect rays of being in this world cease to exist unless there was a Being Who sustained and Who gave them existence. This relation between man and God is not the same as between the architect and the house; the house can continue to exist long after the architect has passed away, for the architect is only the cause of the *becoming* of the house and not its *being*. Without a Supreme Being as the Ground and the Cause of im-

---

[26] Comparatur igitur Deus ad alia entia sicut scibile ad scientiam nostram quod ejus mensura est. C. G. lib. 2. c. 12.

[27] 1. q. 13 art. 7.   [28] C. G. lib. 2 c. 15.

perfect being in this world, the human mind would necessarily be driven to the absurd conclusion that that which has not within itself the reason of its own existence, *has* within itself the reason of its existence — a manifest denial of the principle of contradiction. And it is into this absurdity that everyone must fall who denies the principle of causality, for causality is not founded on an addition of experiences, nor upon reflection on voluntary movements, nor is it a postulate; it is founded on being and is related to the first principles of thought — the principle of identity and the principle of contradiction.

Modern philosophy of religion considers the world as *given*, without any reason for its being *given*. Certainly if it is given, it must have been given by someone. To say it is eternal does not do away with the necessity of accounting for a Creator, for the chronological problem has nothing whatever to do with the ontological one. There is too often a confusion between spatially imagining creation and intelligibly understanding it. The understanding of creation depends on a knowledge of such distinctness between imagination and intellect. The universe may be running a Marathon as far as the clock is concerned, but even though it did exist from all eternity (which we know from Revelation is not the case) it would still be eternally insufficient to account for its own existence. In other words, it would be eternally dependent on God. *The intellectual attitude in the face of the universe is not:*

the world began, therefore some one made it; but rather, the world exists, and since it has not within itself the reason for its existence it must be dependent on a Being Who made it. " We cannot possibly conceive a passage from not-being to being, as the Greeks phrased it, or from potential to actual existence, except through the operation of some energy which is already actual, before the process in question begins, and adequate to produce every result in which such a process may ultimately issue. We can conceive actual being giving rise to contingent being, however unable we are to trace the mode of the occurrence. But to reverse the process, and to speak as if the totality of actual being had been gradually evolved, is to use words that convey no shadow of meaning, it is literally to talk nonsense. If, therefore, we employ the term universe to signify the sum-total of all being, we can conceive development within the universe but never of the universe. And this does not mean that such a process may have taken place, though we cannot picture it; but that, if the laws of human thought are valid, such a process cannot possibly have taken place." [29]

A second subterfuge to escape the real relation between man and the universe and God is that of evolution. The fault here is that evolution is taken as an *explanation*, whereas it is only a *description*. Evolution is a perfectly sound hypothesis to account for the *how* of things, providing it does not ask us to believe that the greater comes from the less. But

[29] J. R. Illingworth, "The Doctrine of the Trinity," 1909, p. 8.

the *how* things happen is quite a distinct problem from the *why* they happen. To describe a watch as machine made or to describe it as hand made, would explain the *how* of the process, but there would still be room for the question, Who made it? So too with the universe. " Evolution involves no fundamental issue. It clashes with no theology or philosophy. . . . Evolution simply means continuous growth; a tree growing from a seedling is an example of evolution; growth is the universal phenomenon apparent in ourselves and all organic life around us, and to discover it generalized is no shock, but rather an extension of the obvious." [30] Evolution is one of the possible methods of creation. The problem of the evolution or the antiquity of the world has nothing to do with its origin. Some philosophers believe that. Evolution is a problem of the before and after; creation is a problem of the above. Evolution is concerned with relations in a circle; creation is a tangential problem. If there is evolution, there is then a double reason for the existence of God, because God must be postulated, first as the Source of being as being (God, Creator); secondly, as Source of being inasmuch as it is in evolution (God, First Mover); and thirdly, as Cause of the order according to which the world evolves — that is the intelligibility which it expresses and the ends which it realizes (God, Word; God, Alpha and Omega; God, Beginning and End). The problems of evolution, then, or the antiquity

[30] Hilaire Belloc, " A Companion to H. G. Wells' 'Outline of History,' " 1926, p. 12.

of the world has nothing to do with its origin. Some believe that to speak in terms of millions of years gives them a right to dispense with a Creator. This is much like saying that if the crank of an automobile is long enough it will be a self-starter. An old race horse does not cease to be an old race horse because it runs slow, neither does the universe cease to be a dependent universe because it has taken centuries to unfold itself. And this opens up the problem of God and the dependence of man and the universe on God from Whom they hold their being.

Creation is not the sum of two moments, one of labor, the next of rest. Creation is not a *change;* it is a *relation.* St. Thomas on this point says: "Creation is not change, except according to a mode of understanding. For change means that something should be different now from what it was previously. But in creation, by which the whole substance of the thing is produced, the same thing can be taken as different now and before only according to our way of understanding, so that a thing is understood first as not existing at all, and afterwards as existing. But as act and potency coincide as to the substance of motion and differ only according to diverse relations (Phys. iii., text. 20, 21) it must follow that when motion is withdrawn only diverse relations remain in the Creator and in the creature." [31]

[31] 1. q. 45 art. 2 ad 2 and ad 3. Inter esse autem, et non esse quæ sunt quasi extrema creationis, non potest esse aliquod medium; igitur non est ibi aliqua successio. C. G. lib. 2 c. 19. Creatis nihil est aliud

" Since therefore God is outside the whole order of creation, and all creatures are ordained to Him, and not conversely, it is manifest that creatures are really related to God Himself; whereas in God there is no real relation to creatures but a relation only in the idea, inasmuch as creatures are referred to Him." [32]   In other words there is the same mental relation existing between God and man as there is between reality and mind, or between an object and its science.[33]   Reality can exist independently of its entrance into a finite mind.   The existence of the trees, the flowers and the birds does not wait upon my knowledge of them; chemicals do not depend for their existence upon the science of chemistry — indeed, if they did, they would not have come into existence before Lavoisier; plants can exist independently of the science of botany; animals can exist without the science of zoölogy; the earth can exist without geology; so too can God exist without man.   No cause is dependent on its effect; the potter does not depend for his being on the clay, nor the sculptor on his marble.   Creation added nothing to God.   Therefore there could be no dependence on created things as far as He is concerned.   Suppose there were only one man in the world who possessed knowledge.   Knowledge would then be qualitatively and quantitatively one.   Now suppose other beings came into existence, so that this learned man could

---

quam relatis quædam ad Deum cum novitate essendi.   De Pot. q. 3 art. 4.

   [32] I. q. 13 art. 7.

   [33] Comparatur igitur Deus ad alia entia sicut scibile ad scientiam nostram quod ejus mensura est. C. G. lib. 2 c. 12.

communicate his knowledge. What would be the result? Knowledge would increase quantitatively, and instead of there being only one man who knows, there would be thousands. But qualitatively the knowledge would remain the same; there would be no more knowledge, qualitatively speaking, in the world than before. So too in Creation, there was an increase of being *extensively,* but not *intensively.* God was no richer after it than before. There were more beings in the world after creation than before, but there was no more Being; there were more beautiful things but no more Beauty; there were more true things, but no more Truth; there were more good things, but no more Goodness. Before creation there was no such thing as " having; " there was only Being, creation introducing that word " have " into the world to denote participation. God gained nothing, for He is Gain; God lost nothing, for He no more communicated His substance to this world in making it than a hand communicates its substance to the wax when it leaves its impression therein.

But this conception of the relation between Creator and creature is rejected in up-to-date philosophy of religion. Once the true relation between reality and mind is distorted, it is but a short step to the distortion of the relation between God and man. What Kant effected in the criteriological order his successors have accomplished in the theological order. In other words the *present day religious attitude inverts the due order of things, and asserts there is only a logical relation between man and God,* but *a real relation between God and man. This is what is meant by the Fallacy of Inverted Relations.*

Minds that have been used to thinking in a common-sense fashion will always find it difficult to understand how a philosopher can say that God depends on man or man's universe. But the difficulty does not alter the fact that such is contemporary teaching. God depends on man and man's universe — such in simple terms is the new religion as advocated by some of its exponents. The explanation given in favor of such an inversion is generally three-fold: philosophical, psychological, and sociological; [34] philosopical inasmuch as God is a " budding off of the evolving universe "; psychological, inasmuch as God is a "mental projection"; sociological, inasmuch as God is "society divinized." A few quotations from contemporary philosophies of religion attest the prevalence of the view that God depends on us either individually or collectively:

"We also help to maintain and sustain the nature of God and are not merely his subjects. . . . God himself is involved in our acts and their issues, or as was put above, not only does he matter to us, but we matter to him. . . . He is in the strictest sense not a creator but a creature." " Deity owes its being to pre-existing finites with their empirical qualities and is their outcome." [35]

[34] See Chap. 1.
[35] S. Alexander, " Space, Time and Deity," Vol. 2, pp. 388, 398, 399.

" He began to be with the slow coalescence of the superior sentients of a world system." [36] " And since God is a society of finite sentients and finite sentients are each and all evolved, the evolution of God is seen to be the compensation for that corruption of eternity in which the world process began." [37] " He buds off from the Divine Imaginal." [38]

God is " developing through the co-operative contributions (conscious and unconscious) of all creatures." [39]

" Apart from the actual world with its creativity there would be no ideal vision which constitutes God." [40]

" God Himself, in short, may draw vital strength and increase of very being from our fidelity." [41]

Note too that in the majority of definitions of religion it is not God, but the universe with which man is in relation.[42] Religion no longer means an ordination to a Creator, but an outlook on creatures; it no longer implies friendliness with God but friendliness with the cosmos: " Is the cosmos friendly to my ideals? "

There are others who believe that God is not the product of an evolving universe, in which case God depends on the universe, but rather that God is the

[36] D. W. Fawcett, " Divine Imagining," p. 223.
[37] *Ibid.*, p. 22.
[38] D. W. Fawcett, " Imaginism and the World's Process," *Mind,* April 1922, p. 168.
[39] H. A. Overstreet, God and the Common Will, *Hibbert Journal,* Vol. XIII, No. 1, p. 155.
[40] A. N. Whitehead, " Religion in the Making," p. 150.
[41] W. James, " Is Life Worth Living? " pp. 24–28.
[42] Chap. 1.

product of the human mind — in other words, its fiction. This was the import of the psychological explanations of religion, e.g., that of Professor Leuba, who believes " it difficult to estimate the harm done by the conviction that for its ethical improvement society is dependent upon a personal God." [43]

Finally, God is dependent on man, not psychologically, but socially. To speak of a God Who is Supreme irritates, and in the words of one of the exponents of the sociological origin of God, " it smacks of the adoration or flattery, such as was formerly given to tyrants and despots." [44] The same sentiments are expressed by Professor Charles A. Ellwood for whom God means nothing more than Man. " And since service of God is in reality service of man, there will be sin in this new religion of democracy; it will be a failure to serve mankind." [45] Professor Overstreet puts it still more boldly and lets it be known that " God is ourselves." [46]

Whatever be the particular presentation the common ground of all seems to be that God is man, and man is God. The very false connotation given to words with fixed meanings, such as " God " and " religion," is sufficient to condemn such theories. Certainly if " God " means anything, He does not mean either a " quality " or a " creature."

[43] " Psychology of Religious Mysticism," p. 329.
[44] E. S. Ames, " The New Orthodoxy," 1925, p. 117.
[45] " The Reconstruction of Religion," pp. 139, 143.
[46] " The Democratic Conception of God," *Hibbert Journal*, Vol. XI, p. 140.

But this is not the sole reason for expressing discontent with such novelties. The very systems which give birth to these are themselves self-refuting. Take for example the Italian school for whom religion is nothing more than man contemplating his own spirit idealized, or admiring himself in the mirror of his own reflective acts. God then becomes the object taken apart from its relation to the subject, i.e., the subject's self-annihilation. Such is the theory of Croce. Gentile's theory on the contrary believes Religion to be the subject's affirmation of the object as infinite and absolute.

The different expressions matter little; in the ultimate analysis God and religion are constructions of the human mind, not objective, but subjective. God, on such a theory, depends on our knowing Him. If religion is nothing more than the moment of absolute objectivity in the eternal cycle of the spirit's activity, then we are face to face with an inexorable dilemma. Either the subject really and completely denies himself and loses himself in the object (and in such a case there cannot be for him any resurrection, and human history should have come to an end long ago) or the subject survives and consequently survives as knowing the object and capable of knowing any number of objects. In the latter case the idea of God as Absolute and Infinite object which according to this theory comes only through the subject's self-annihilation, could never arise at all. Such a system has been rightly called by one who understands it, " the apotheosis of self-assertion." [47]

Professor Otto, in his work " The Holy " is not nearly so guilty of the Fallacy of Inverted Relations. There is nothing in his work which directly asserts that God is a mental projection, but there is much suggestion that God is nothing distinct from man's " sense of the holy." Nowhere has he made clear the distinction between mere stimuli of the faculty of divination and the veritable manifestation of the numinous. The most he will say is that " the numinous is *felt* as objective and outside self." [48] This comes very close to identifying the feeling of the Holy with the Holy, and the feeling of Overpoweringness with Power. Certainly, since he excludes the rational element entirely, there is left no criterion for judging between feelings. To exclude the rational is to exclude ground for objectivity, for feelings by themselves are essentially incommunicable. I can communicate a truth but not a toothache. It is this tendency to make the non-rational fundamental which exposes Professor Otto to identifying God with the sentiment of God. It is one thing to say that the universe justifies us in speaking of God; it is another thing to say God is the non-rational element in reality Who cannot be the object of rational thought. [49]

[47] Angelo Crispi, " Actual Idealism," *Hibbert Journal*, Vol. XXIV, No. 2, p. 259. Cf. Angelo Crispi, " Contemporary Thought of Italy," 1926, *passim*.

[48] P. 11.

[49] Leonard Hodgson, " The Place of Reason in Christian Apologetics," 1925, p. 20.

The system of Professor S. Alexander, in which God is a "quality" emerging from an evolving universe, is also subject to rather embarrassing objections. His system opens not with the Johannine evangel, "In the beginning was the Word," but rather with the tidings of new physics: "In the beginning was Space-Time." These two standing in close relation to each other is all he has to begin with. One props up the other, thus making a very insecure foundation for a universe. Professor J. S. Mackenzie [50] says: "It looks as if we began with pure emptiness." But Professor Alexander contends that time is not empty, since it contains space; and space is not empty since it contains time. This reminds one too much of the famous islanders who earned a precarious living by taking in one another's washing. It would seem that the real filling of the spatio-temporal system is supplied by the *qualities* that occur in them and that evolve from the most simple to the most complex types. But if we start from pure space-time it is hard to see where all these admirable qualities are to come from. Here we are reminded somewhat forcibly of Carlyle's remark that the making of the universe raises the same sort of question as that which one of the Georges found in the making of a dumpling — "how the apples got in." Professor Alexander indeed says quite frankly that "quality is the great mystery," but as qualities appear to be the only concrete things that exist within his scheme a theory

[50] "Ultimate Values," 1926, p. 34.

that leaves their existence a mystery can hardly be accounted very satisfactory.

Professor Alexander's whole system depends on the rejection of two elementary facts of experience, viz., there can never be a movement without a thing that moves, and secondly, the greater can never come from the less. Denying the first he imagines a motion without a mover as the source of things, from which motion Space-Time is analyzed. By the denial of the second he imagines that Space-Time will go on producing higher and higher qualities from something lower and lacking these qualities.

Finally, what must be said of a system in which "Deity owes its being to pre-existing finites" and in which God is a creature? And what is said here may be applied equally to all "God-producing philosophies." Either such a God is greater or less than man. If He is greater than man then the greater comes from the less, which is absurd; if He is less than man, then He is not a God but a puppet and a travesty on a name.

Language loses its meaning when we call black white; religion a libido; God a creature; and man a creator. A material civilization does not confuse dollars with cents, pounds with shillings; on these matters it is intolerant. Two dollars and two dollars make four dollars and not three, and no amount of pleading for monetary tolerance could change the truth. But, on the all important matter of the Ultimate Ground of the Universe, the Final End of Man, the meaning of God and religion, there is a

tolerance stretched to the point of the absurd. Ultimately the confusion of dollars and cents will not
affect mankind so vitally, will not make for his weal
or woe so potently and quickly, as a confusion of the
due relations between God and man. And if our
intellectual vision were keen enough we would realize that it is not debits and credits, budgets and
armaments, balances of trade and elevation of guns
that make this world a fit place to live in, but rather
a humble and profound knowledge that God is our
Master, our Lord and our all. "Unless the Lord
build the city they labor in vain who build it."

To make God the outcome of the cosmic forces,
the projection of a mind, or the symbol of society,
in a word, to make God dependent on things is
to build a religion without God. *It means to proceed from religion to God, instead of from God to
religion*. Such is the fundamental difference between the *philosophia perennis* and the new spirit
of the day. And this is but one of the many phases
of the fallacy of inverted relations. In the domain of
revealed religion, the modern procedure is to go
from faith to Christ, instead of from Christ to faith.
It is Christ Who is the Ground of faith and God Who
is the Reason of religion, and to invert this order
is to create a situation as difficult to imagine as a
circumference without an equi-distant relation from
a centre. To say that God is the product of religion,
and not its Ground or Reason, is equivalent to saying that matter is a product of physics; that life is
the product of biology and that without science life

could not exist; that man is the product of anthropology; that animals are begotten of zoölogy, and plants of botany, and the insane of pathology. What rare wisdom there was in Aquinas to insist that a misunderstanding of the relation of an object to its science, entails a misunderstanding in the relation of God to man! As a mind cannot create reality, as the stomach cannot create its food, so neither can man make God.

"Ye will be like unto God" is a prophecy from Eden that is being fulfilled in so much contemporary thinking. It is no longer man who is made to the image and likeness of God, but God Who is made to the image and likeness of man. *There are two ways of denying God: One is to say with the atheist: "There is no God"; the other is to say: "I believe in God," but God is "creature," or "Space-Time."* "Any philosophy which misrepresents God, which demonstrates Him as other than He is, which positively denies Him those things which are proper to Him, or positively affirms of Him that which cannot stand with His nature, may, in a very true and real sense, be said to abolish God, and to exclude the notion of God from the realm of truth wherein philosophers are at home." [51] The denial of God either explicitly or implicitly, the denial of the primacy of the spiritual, is to contradict the epitome of individual and historical experience, namely, we are not "God-makers" but "God-made." It may have the appearance of a novelty which so often solicits a

[51] J. Leycester King, "Reason, Not Sentiment," *Month*, May, 1927, p. 385.

generation that cares little for truth; it may have the ring of sincerity, and the gait of a seeker of truth, but such a teaching by no stretch of imagination can be called a doctrine. The denial of God is no more a doctrine than is the denial of the sun — it is a *cry of wrath*. Negation is disguised hate; it is only in his heart and not in his mind that the fool denies — *Dixit insipiens in corde suo*. Thus the Scriptures remind us that if we would not have softening of the heart we will sooner or later have softening of the brain.

Let us suppose for a moment that God did not exist, suppose He belonged, as atheists claim to the mere realm of fiction and fairy-tale. In that case what is the difference between Don Quixote battling a windmill which he mistook for an enemy, and an atheistical Don Quixote battling a God Whom he takes as a fancy? What is the difference between an insane man swinging his arm as wings, because he believes the pads in his cell are clouds, and an atheist swinging his arms in fury because God is only a make-believe? There is no difference if there be no God for both are fighting a figment of the imagination and that is what makes a man insane; viz., the projection of a fancy.

There is one fact that must be forever kept in mind and to the eternal credit of the atheist. The atheist at his desk is not the same as the crazy man in his cell: society incarcerates one but not the other, locks up one and lets the other loose — and why? Because the object the atheist is fighting is

real, and the object the insane man is fighting is
not. In other words what saves the atheist from
the stigma of insanity is the fact that God is real,
not like a dream but like an enemy at his door.
Foch was not insane when he took grey uniforms
to be the uniforms of an enemy; Washington was
not a crazy man when he took the red coats to be
English soldiers. They were real — real like the
thrust of a sword or an embrace; and simply because
God is real, because the enemy is a real and not a
fictitious one, atheists must never be classed as mad
men. It is the reality and objectivity of their enemy
which makes them sane and sound. That is why
one may speak of the Theism of Atheism.

The energy of atheists, their tireless propaganda,
their spirited discourses, testify to a belief in God
which puts to shame mere lip-worshippers. They
are always thinking of God. Do men pour out
such propaganda, flood the country with letters,
the press with copy, and the air with speeches in
protest against halitosis, fallen arches, the general-
ship of Napoleon, the meekness of Moses, the intelligence of the Piltdown man, the belief in ghosts,
faith in centaurs? How account for the fact that
a hatred of God excites men much more than a
hatred of an enemy at our doors; how account for
that fact that no man has ever dedicated himself to
a negation, as such, except the negation of God?
How account for such hatred merely on the grounds
of negation? Does not a negative imply a positive?
Would there be prohibition unless there was some-

thing to prohibit; would there be atheism if there was nothing to " atheate "? Men do not gather figs from thorns nor grapes from thistles, neither do they gather hate from a negation. Hate proves the reality of the object hated, and since God is the only Being Who is infinitely hated and infinitely loved, I must conclude not only that He is, but that He is Infinite. And that always makes me feel doubly sorry for the atheist: he never can say Good-Bye (God be with you) to his friends.

CHAPTER X

RELIGION AND VALUES

L ITTLE or no attention is paid by the majority of philosophers to the traditional concept of God. Directly or indirectly the existence of God is denied, either by making Him a mere projection or a symbol of something which is not Himself, by equating Him with a so-called nisus or by conceiving Him as the conceptual harmonization of the universe. No two philosophers are quite agreed on what constitutes the nature of God. It seems that there are as many gods as there are philosophers, that a modern museum which would contain them all would have to be something of a philosophers' pantheon. Yet, in order that they might possess a common cause and a common banner under which to march forth to war on the traditional, our contemporaries regard a philosophy of values as the ground or basis of all religion. Historically, the source of this value-philosophy is to be traced to the Kantian tradition which denies the power of the speculative reason to transcend human experience. Man must content himself with the value which his beliefs may have for the practical reason.

From the metaphysical point of view a philosophy of value bases itself on two negative principles, which, although they rarely come to the surface in the discussion of value itself, are nevertheless to be recognized as fundamental to its nature. These principles are: (a) the impossibility of ever knowing truth, and (b) the denial of substance.

A system of philosophy which acknowledges the existence of a real objective order and the capacity of the intellect to attain to that order by and through an act of knowledge will perforce seek truth as its unique object. Since truth is regarded as objective in such a system, it is not made by the knowing intellect. Even though every human intellect were blotted out, there would still be truth, for the Divine Intellect, which is Ultimate Truth, would still exist. Our intellects do not make the truth; they attain it; they discover it. Moreover, truth is what it is despite any wish on our part that it be otherwise. But suppose for a moment that the mind's capacity to get outside itself is denied, and suppose that the first thing known by us is the idea and not an object, then, as St. Thomas says,[1] there is no refuge left for the thinker but a pragmatism which asserts the seeming to be true. Pragmatism is the logical consequence of a denial of the objectivity of truth. It may glory in the fact that as an epistemology it can be said to correspond to human needs, yet it still remains true that one of the greatest of human needs is to be something more than a pragmatist.

If the mind can never attain truth, philosophy has but one resource left, and that is to be interested in the value which things have for us. As Professor

[1] I. q. 85 art. 2.

Mackenzie expresses it : " One statement is not truer than another, but only more convenient for certain practical purposes, and in that sense more correct — just as we commonly say that certain modes of behaviour are more correct than others. In other words, according to this view, *truth is essentially a mode of value and nothing more.*" [2] Hence James and his followers can say : " If God has a value for you, He exists for you; if He has no value for you, then He does not exist for you." It is, therefore, the value for our thinking and our living that, in the last analysis, determines God's existence. A philosophy which surrenders truth as its supreme goal may still have an objective, though a less satisfactory one — value.

The second negative principle which underlies the philosophy of value is the denial of substance. It was Bergson who revived Heraclitus and his philosophy of becoming, and in his own lucid style gave to the world the doctrine that there can be movement without a thing that moves; that there are no things, only a *devenir;* that substance, things, or anything which is supposed to be abiding is really a mere solidification of the flux of life effected by the intellect which by nature is the faculty of the static. More recently a philosophy built upon a lyricized science has asserted that the universe is but a spatio-temporal continuum. From the physical point of view this seems at present to be a more or less fair description of what the universe is, but that it

[2] J. S. Mackenzie, " Ultimate Values," pp. 57, 58.

is a good philosophical description of the world is
quite another matter. The interesting feature about
such a philosophy, from our point of view, is that it
marks a culmination of the gradual elimination of
substance from the realm of philosophy. Descartes, writing under the influence of certain decadent
Scholastics, misunderstood totally the idea of substance and reduced all substances to three: matter,
mind, and God. Spinoza believed in but one absolute substance. Leibnitz fell back on a multiplicity
of substances. Berkeley alleged that the conception
of substance had been arrived at illegitimately, and
that to deny the existence of material substance is
not absurd. Hume attempted to show there was no
thinking substance. Thus, after a century of speculation concerning the nature of substance, only one
of the Cartesian substances survived for philosophy, namely, God. Now, when substance went out
of philosophy, causality went with it. Everyone
knows of the futile attempts which Kant made to
revive this idea. At the present day philosophy has
recognized the logic of the premises upon which it
is founded and denies the category of substance altogether, even the substance of God. Thus Professor Alexander, in his " Space, Time and Deity,"
has succeeded in eliminating Deity. For him the
spatio-temporal system of the universe is alone necessary. All forms, categories, and predicaments
can be deduced from it. The world system is thus
to be regarded as four-dimensional, three of which
are spatial, the other temporal, and all are infinite

in extent. Within and from this great Space-Time matrix, not things nor substances emerge, for there are no substances, but only qualities which may be said to develop into more and more complex forms, which forms ultimately lead up to God Who possesses the quality of Deity.

With substance eliminated, philosophy, if it is to have any interest in things human or material, must rest in the consideration of qualities, and the one quality which best fits in with the anti-intellectualist temper of modern thought is naturally the quality of value. Admittedly it would be a queer grammar which concentrated on predicates and ignored or denied subjects, but it would be no less queer than a philosophy which denies the existence of substance and admits the existence of qualities. But facts are what they are. Contemporary thinkers refuse to accept substance; this tenet commits them to a philosophy of qualities, and, more particularly, to a philosophy of value.[3]

All of which brings us to the question to be discussed: Is religion also to be understood in terms of value? Or is religion, after the most generally accepted definition, to be understood as " faith in the conservation of values " ?

First of all, it may be pointed out that religion, from the natural and the philosophical point of view,

---

[3] J. S. Mackenzie confirms our statement that the philosophy of value has arisen from a denial of substance. " It already has been noted," he writes, " as one of the general characteristics of the thought of our time that the old conception of substance has tended to decay or to be subordinated to other conceptions." *Ibid.*, pp. 27 ff.

is not faith in anything, in the sense that faith is an hypothesis, an *als-ob*, a leap in the dark, an accumulation of possibilities, a hope, a wish to believe, or "an organic response, the psychological presupposition of which is a system of reflex arcs so integrated that some given assertion may be responded to positively." [4] We can never begin with faith as we cannot begin with authority. For faith is not primitive; it presupposes a reason for the faith that is in one. If we have no legitimate grounds for believing in an authority, or reposing our trust and confidence in a thing or a person, then such faith is vain and illusory. Granted that religion is not faith in its primitive and natural meaning, is it true that religion may still be interpreted in terms of value? This question brings us to the second aspect of the contemporary conception of religion which looks upon religion as "the conservation of values." Now, we believe such an idea to be altogether unacceptable and for the following reasons: (a) Value implies some relation to human consciousness, and this feature of value makes man not God the centre of religion. (b) Values are inexplicable without God. This criticism applies to those who neglect God and hold to purely human values. (c) Even for those thinkers who acknowledge God as the ground of value, the expression "conservation of values" falls short of real religion.

(a) It may be well at the beginning of this discussion to say a few words about value as understood

[4] Wesley R. Wells, "Biological Foundations of Belief," p. 71.

in the Scholastic philosophy. Value, for the Scholastic, means a form or kind of " good," and a thing is good, in a general way, when it is desirable.[5] Now there are three kinds of good: the useful, the pleasurable, and the absolute good.[6] The useful good is that which leads to an ulterior good. The pleasurable good is the subjective enjoyment which accompanies the pursuit or the attainment of some end. The absolute good, or the good in itself, is that which is desirable in itself apart from the pleasure it may give or the use it may have.

The modern term value may be related either to the *bonum delectabile* or the *bonum utile* of the Scholastics, but has nothing in common with the *bonum in se*, for the reason that value introduces something into the concept of good which is contrary to its nature, namely, a real relation to the one possessing it. Things indeed have value; and they have a value because they are related to a person or a thing which can use or take pleasure in them. But this is the very contrary of the *bonum in se*, which existentially is independent of any value it may have for either a person or a thing. The fact that our contemporaries protest against the use of the term " good " (as *bonum in se*) as being " too suggestive of something absolute and unquestionable " proves that it has not for them the same meaning as the term " value."[7] That the *bonum in se* and value

<hr>

[5] Ratio enim boni in hoc consistit quod aliquid sit appetibile. 1. q. 5 art. 6.

[6] I. q. 5 art. 6; 1–2. q. 99 art. 5.

[7] J. S. Mackenzie, " Ultimate Values," p. 93.

are not identical is further borne out by an examination of the more important modern theories of value which may be reduced to two, namely, the relational theory and the harmony theory. The relational theory maintains that value is not in the object alone, but the object as standing in relation to the satisfaction of some desire. When the object, whatsoever it may be, is conceived as existing out of that relation, then its value disappears.[8] The harmony theory of value, on the other hand, asserts that not the individual interest but the social intelligence determines values.[9] Thus, for the first theory, value is a matter of quantity, for the second a matter of degree of adjustment, but in either case value is unintelligible apart from a consciousness either human or social. Even for those who bring God into their system of value, "the centre of value lies in the subject and in the way it reacts on the object, rather than in the character of the object. The essence of value lies in the experient subject, and we cannot transfer it to a system which somehow transcends the subject."[10]

The point to be insisted upon here is that value and good (*bonum in se*) are not the same. The relation between the good and the experiencing subject is a purely logical one; things are good independently of our attitude toward them. But the relation between value and the experiencing

[8] R. B. Perry, "A Definition of Value," *Journal of Philosophy*, II, 1905, p. 141.
[9] D. S. Robinson, "The God of the Liberal Christian," p. 82.
[10] Galloway, "Philosophy of Religion," p. 356.

subject is real; " the essence of values lies in the experient subject." We endow things with value; but we do not endow things with goodness.[11] Now, to centre religion on that which by its very nature is dependent on a sentient subject is to ground religion in man and not in God. Religion would then be but the sum of God's duties to man, instead of the sum of man's service to God. Such a view perverts the order of nature and makes the potter the servant of his clay. Such a system, too, proceeds on the false assumption that God is Value because things are valuable, whereas the truth is that things are good because God is good.[12] Goodness implies no real relation in man, and hence implies no real dependence of God on man, but value must be said to imply such a dependence on the admission of contemporary philosophers themselves. By all this we do not mean to say that values have no place in religion, nor that God is not the ground or foundation of all values. The point we are insisting on is simply this: religion is not to be defined primarily in terms of value.

(b) Now, the philosopher who defines religion as conservation of values is faced by a serious dilemma. Either he denies the existence of God or he admits God as the ground of value. But if he deny the existence of God, the conservation of values is inexplicable. How is it possible to conserve values without God? Without the abiding,

[11] The term good is much preferable to " intrinsic value " for the reason that it admits of no confusion concerning objectivity.

[12] " Hebdom.," lib. 4. c. 5.

without the Perfect, without God, so-called "permanent and conserved values" can only mean their preservation by the successive generations of human society on this earth. "This means in the first place, that every human person is a means to the experience of value in other persons; every generation a means to the experience of value in later generations; that every human being is a means only; none is an end in himself . . . it makes every generation a bonfire to warm the hands of the next, which in turn is fuel for its successor. The tragedy is that no one remains to be warmed without being destroyed; and add to this the probability that the whole bonfire itself will doubtless some day be extinguished. Such permanence of values is no true permanence." [13]   As Professor Hocking has so well said: "Values, human values, can survive only if, reaching out toward a metaphysical condition which their dream shapes foreshadow, they *find* it. They really need reality to climb on; they need a reality they *can* climb on. They want an independent source of standards, a mooring outside nature. Their own *poussée vitale* droops, half-grown, unless it meets an equivalent *attrait vital* streaming into its environment from some pole outside itself." [14]

(c) Even if one postulates God as the ground of

---

[13] E. S. Brightman, "Religious Values," p. 120.

[14] "Human Nature and Its Remaking," p. 412. "To identify religion with the service of unrealized and purely human values, while denying to these values a cosmic foundation, is a confusion of thought." Joseph A. Leighton, "Man and the Cosmos," p. 537.

James Lindsay, "Great Philosophical Problems," p. 1.

value the definition "conservation of values" still falls short of the real significance of religion. If there be no God, as we have said, then how conserve even the best values? And if there is a God, why rest in the *conservation* of the imperfect? Why not seek its *transcendence* in the realm of the Infinite and the Perfect? A religion which reaches the depths of the human heart and satisfies the spiritual longings of the immortal soul can never and will never be dedicated to the mere conservation of values, for religion at its best is a transcendence of values. How strange it is that those who most loudly decry sanctions of reward and punishment as unworthy of true virtue are those very thinkers who most eloquently plead for the conservation of their own values! To talk about our values, to seek the safeguarding of them, to fumble with our highest interests, and, at the same time, to talk of God as the Ground of these values, is to separate the existence of God from the value He has for us. There is no distinction in God between the metaphysical and the moral attributes; He is. Religion then can rightly be understood only in terms of existence and not in terms of value. That is why St. Thomas speaks of religion only after he has finished discussing values. Religion begins where values leave off and it is the transcendence of values which marks the beginning of true commerce with God. In his most complete treatise on values, the whole of Question II in the Prima Secundæ of the *Summa,* St. Thomas con-

siders singly those values which present-day thinkers would like to conserve, earthly values of riches,
worldly values of fame, glory and power, physical
values of pleasure, intellectual values such as the
knowledge of the good, the true and the beautiful,
and, finally, all created values, and in none of these
does he find the proper object of religion. The
religious objective is something quite beyond,
transcendental to these values, surpassing them
as the light of the sun surpasses that of the faint-
est star. It is God Who is man's ultimate end, not
values.

Although the philosophy of value has a suspi-
cious family history and a bar sinister in its es-
cutcheon, it is still a legitimate problem of philosophy, but only secondarily a problem in religion.
Values can never be the primary consideration for
religion, for God is not a value, and to look upon
Him as nothing higher than the Ground of values,
and the Conserver of our best and highest interests,
is to shift the centre of reference in religion toward
man and away from God. Fundamentally, religion
is intelligible only in terms of God and Existence,
and secondarily, in terms of value. For that reason
we prefer to follow the ultra-modern St. Thomas
rather than the modern philosopher of value, and
to discuss religion in its secondary consideration
not so much as "the conservation of values" but
as the *transcendence of values through the sacra-
mentalization of the universe.* And be it noted that
the sacramental philosophy of St. Thomas accepts

what is best in value-philosophy, without being burdened by any of its serious defects. It is here offered not as a criticism of the system of value so much as its very perfection and crown.

What, we may ask, is the great ideal of contemporary religion? Is it not to bring man into greater prominence in the general scheme of things? How often do we not hear it stated that " man must have a vote in the cosmic councils of the world "; that " man is not a mere puppet in the hands of God "; that " the seat of authority has been shifted from heaven to earth "; that " man must now take his share in the governing of the universe "; that " God as a monarch is passing out of existence," and that " man is gradually freeing himself from the other-worldly pull of divine theologies "? For many thinkers the philosophy of values satisfies this desire of the modern man to be the important element in religion. But let us remark also that it brings man into prominence only at the expense of God. Either the existence of God as a Supreme Being is denied outright, or His existence is reduced to the unknowable, or He is made identical with an evolving universe or the ideals of the human family.

It is our contention that the sacramental philosophy of St. Thomas satisfies the best in the ideals of modern thought, namely, to bring man into prominence, without in the least sacrificing either the truth of the existence, nature, or dignity of God, or making man the measure and the maker of his Maker. In other words, the sacramental philosophy of Aquinas makes man the center of this universe, but does not fall into the error of making man the only thing in the universe incapable of being perfected.

What is meant by the term "sacramental philosophy"? A sacrament is any material thing used by us as a means of spiritual sanctification. In the strict theological sense of the term, there are seven sacraments, each and every one of them being a sign instituted by Christ for the conferring of Divine Life on the souls of men. But in the broad meaning of the term, everything in this world may be regarded as a sacrament in the sense that every material thing is a means, an instrument, a stepping-stone, a scaffolding, a ladder to the spiritual, the infinite, the eternal. Now, the whole sacramental character of this philosophy can be reduced to the following proposition: everything in the universe centres about man and was made for man, but man was made for God.[15] Hence, everything in this world has a value for man inasmuch as it is a means to the attainment of His ultimate end Who is God. Because things have values and are not permanent abiding goods in an Eternal City, they are but earthly sacraments leading us on to absolute perfection.

Everything on this earth has been made for man. As the servant serves the master, so in the great hierarchy of creation that which is lower serves that

[15] I. q. 21 art. 1 ad 3; q. 47 art. 3; q. 103 art. 2 ad 3. C. G., Lib. 1. c. 78; lib. 3. c. 98; 1 d. 44 q. 2; De Veritate, q. 5 art. 1 ad 3; De Potentia, q. 5 art. 4 ad 2; q. 7 art. 9.

which is higher.[16] The various elements, hydrogen, oxygen, and the like, serve plant life. If the clouds refuse to send down their benediction of rain, if the sun would rebel against serving the plants with its light, it would not be long until plant life would perish from the earth. Just as chemical elements serve plants and are necessary for their life, so do plants serve animals, and animals serve men. And these lower things serve man not only as ministering to his needs, as affording subsistence for his life, but even as offering him the raw material of knowledge, and the starting-point for a study of great spiritual realities.[17]

The universe thus presents the spectacle of a great pyramid at the base of which are minerals and chemicals, and at the peak of which is man. Life grows in intensity and in immanence as the pyramid mounts up through the kingdom of plants and animals until finally it is crowned with the superior life of man, a life which is not merely vegetative or sensitive but intellectual.[18] It is in virtue of this superior kind of life that man exercises dominion over all lower creatures. For man is not guilty of murder when he plucks up the plant for his food, nor when he serves the flesh of an animal at table,

[16] Creaturæ ignobiliores sunt propter nobiliores sicut creaturæ, quæ sunt infra hominem, sunt propter hominem. I. q. 65 art. 2; C. G., lib. 2. c. 42; De Veritate, q. 27 art. 7 ad 4; 1. q. 21 art. 1 ad 3.

[17] Vel ad intellectus perfectionem, quas in eis veritatem speculatur; vel ad suæ virtutis executionem; et scientiæ explicationem ad modum, quo artifex explicat artis suæ conceptionem in materia corporali; vel etiam ad corporis sustentationem, quod est unitum animæ intellectuali. C. G., lib. 3. c. 112.

[18] C. G., lib. 4. c. 11.

though it can be said of him that he is destroying life. He is the master of these lower creatures. They were made for him, are necessary for his existence, and he may use them as he sees fit.

The progress of man, and, in a certain sense, the very progress of this universe consists in the gradual domination of all things by man. Uncontrolled and unharnessed natural forces never make for progress any more than uncontrolled social forces make for peace. Domination consists in the unification of forces, and the more man succeeds in conquering and domesticating the wild untamed forces of nature, the more he has progressed and the more the universe has progressed with him. Thus, the more complex of our recent discoveries and inventions have been due to the unifying of distinct and separate discoveries in various fields. In other words, progress does not mean contempt of the traditional, neither does it mean the novel or the changing of standards with every succeeding age. Logically understood, progress can only mean, in relation to the universe, the gradual unification of all natures, forces and powers under the kingship of man.

But how is this unification to be effected? How is this progress of the universe to be brought about? It can be brought about effectively only by a faculty which is destined by its very nature to serve the process of the unification of the forces of nature, and that is the human intellect. Man is ordained to the perfection of the universe, and is a very essential

part of its perfection, because he possesses the power
of intellect which nothing below him possesses, and
which must be said to differentiate him from things
more powerful than himself.[19] The intellect is
spiritual, and being spiritual is capable of knowing
all things. Unlike other faculties it is not limited
in its object. The eye is limited to color, the ear
to sound, but the intellect is capable of knowing
not only that which is colored, or audible, or tangible and material, but everything that *is*.[20] And
this is the reason why, according to St. Thomas, the
intellect has a greater affinity for the whole universe
than any other faculty with a more limited object.
Since the intellect can embrace all being, God has
wonderfully subjected all things to it.[21] As the universe contains all things materially, so the intellect,
says a commentator of St. Thomas, contains all
real things intentionally.[22] The physical constitution of man sums up all the orders below him. He
possesses the existence of the stone, the life of the
plant, the sentiency of the animal, but in addition
to these, man has his own peculiar intellectual per-

[19] Homo ordinatur ad perfectionem universi ut essentialis pars ipsius,
cum in homine sit aliquid, quod non continetur virtute nec in elementis,
nec in cœlestibus corporibus, scilicet anima rationalis. De Potentia, q. 5
art. 10.

[20] Quidquid esse potest, intelligi potest. C. G., lib. 2. c. 98.

[21] Naturæ autem intellectuales maiorem habeut affinitatem ad totum
quam aliæ naturæ; nam unaquæque intellectualis substantia est quodammodo omnia, in quantum *totius entis* comprehensiva est suo intellectu;
convenienter igitur alia propter substantias intellectuales providentur
a Deo. C. G., lib. 3. c. 112.

[22] Sicut enim universum omnia continet realiter, sic mens continet
omnia, quæ realia sunt, sed idealiter, quia unaquæque mens est quodammodo omnia, in quantum comprehensiva est totius mentis; qualibet
alia substantia participationem tantum entis habet. Petronius in C. G.,
lib. 3. c. 112.

fection by which he possesses the universe within himself, not materially as it is in the outside world, but spiritually.[23] Thanks to this faculty which is capable of knowing everything that *is*, man can reduce all things to the unity of his own thought.[24] The scattered and disparate forces of nature, uncontrolled waterfalls, coal buried in the bowels of the earth, electricity free in the flash, none of these taken singly or in their native condition makes for scientific progress; neither does the possession of separate and disjointed facts make for knowledge or science unless they have been reduced to the unity of a great principle of thought, like that of causality or finality. The universe is not merely static, like a pyramid of ancient Egypt; rather it is like a pyramid in construction. The world is continually becoming more and more pointed, more and more centred, in just the proportion that man brings it under his control.

Now, this upward tendency of things, evolution in the progress of things, if you will, is being effected by virtue of a double force, one inherent in the things which are perfectible, the other inherent in that which perfects them.[25] An inferior nature can never

[23] To possess a thing not materially but formally, which is the definition of knowledge, is the noblest manner of having or possessing it. In Causis, I, 18.

[24] Cognitio sensitiva — circa multum diffunditur — cognitio rationis — multum ad unum convolvit. De Div. Nom., c. VII, 1. 2. Hoc enim rerum ordo habet, quod quanto aliquid est superius, tanto habet virtutem magis unitam et ad plura se extendentem. I. q. 57 art. 2; 2-2. q. 76 art. 2.

[25] In omnibus naturis ordinatis invenitur, quod ad perfectionem naturæ inferioris duo concurrunt; unum quidem, quod est secundum proprium motum; aliud autem quod est secundum motum superioris naturæ. 2-2. q. 2 art. 3.

attain to the nature of a superior object except by
the action of that superior nature, just as water can
never be heated except by fire, or its equivalent.
Oxygen, hydrogen, phosphates, and all similar elements are constantly moving upward and onward
in the pyramid of creation and entering into the
life of plants, a privilege and a perfection which
would be denied them if plant life did not have
some superior power of assimilating them and making them live its life.   Plants and chemicals enter
into animal life, and have their existence and their
life thus ennobled and perfected, thanks to the peculiarly superior and assimilating power of the animal
organism.   The chemical, plant, and animal king-
doms enter into man, and become one with him,
because of the superior power of the human organism to adopt and perfect and assimilate these lower
natures.   Man, however, has a higher power than
the mere function of food assimilation, inasmuch as
he possesses a soul, and every being assimilates
according to its own nature.   The universe below
him is perfected first because it offers itself to man
in order to be perfected, and secondly because it
is taken up by the intellect which is actively superior to it and capable, therefore, of ennobling and
perfecting and " supernaturalizing " that which is
below.

Let us suppose for a moment that in the universe
there existed no Force or Power superior to man,
capable of perfecting and ennobling him.   If this
were so, then man would be the only creature in the

universe incapable of being further perfected. Oxygen finds its perfection in the plant, the plant in the animal, and the animal in man's organism, and all three are perfected in man's intellect. Man, however, would have no one to whom he could turn in order to be perfected. Such a universe would be irrational and foolish.

Perfection of a lower nature demands two things, the passive power of perfection in that lower nature, and the active power of perfection in a nature above man. Whence would come this perfection if man were supreme, if there is no one above him? Evolution, as you may say, would explain the process. But evolution merely explains the *how* of the process and not the *why*. Evolution, indeed, is one of the possible methods of creation, and every type of evolution which does not presuppose that the greater comes from the less may be regarded as an acceptable working hypothesis. But to deny the existence of a power above man, to deny a perfecting thing antecedent and superior to that which is to be perfected is to presuppose that the greater may come from the less. Evolution then, intelligently understood, does not exclude God any more than a " self-made " man can be said to exclude his mother. The length of time it took for the universe to evolve has, of course, nothing at all to do with the problem of its origin, and those who think it does might equally well suppose that if the handle of a brush were sufficiently long it would paint by itself. The problem is not whether things are going fast or slow. The problem is *why* they go at all.

To return to the point under discussion: If this universe ends with man, then how can man ever be perfected? In a certain sense a purely humanistic religion which denies that God exists makes the chemicals greater than man, for it asserts that they are capable for being perfected, a privilege which is denied to man. It seems clear that no philosophy which stops with mere human values and a spatio-temporal continuum can escape this serious difficulty.

The sacramental philosophy of St. Thomas, on the contrary, maintains the legitimate ideals of contemporary thought by making man the crown of the universe; it avoids the error of making him self-centred and incapable of being perfected by insisting that over and above the imperfect there exists a perfect, over and above the transitory there is the immutable, over and above evolution and progress there is the intelligibility of evolution and progress, and over and above man there exists a God.[26]

Given such a philosophy the things of this universe, even the best of them, immediately take on a new and changed meaning. They are now not ends but means, and means in the sense that they are sacraments; that is to say, material stepping-stones to the realm of the spiritual. The universe thus becomes a scaffolding up which man climbs to the

[26] I. q. 2; 1. q. 85 art. 3 ad. 1; 3. q. 1 art. 5 ad 3. Fulton J. Sheen, "God and Intelligence," p. 218 ff.

heights of the Abiding and the Eternal. Religion, therefore, cannot be wholly concerned with the mere conservation of even the noblest human values; it should seek rather to surmount human values, to make of them instruments of something permanent and lasting. Thus, the world, in the sacramental philosophy of St. Thomas, has a true value, but its real value lies in this, that it leads us on to God, or in other words, it has a value because it is sacramental.

The supreme duty of man is not to conserve the universe; rather his duty is to sacramentalize the universe, which may be effected by sacramentalizing both what he knows and what he does. St. Thomas worked out this idea in detail when treating the ontological character of knowledge. Everything in this world, according to him, has been made according to the archetypal ideas existing in the mind of God. These archetypal ideas existing in the mind of God are spiritual and eternal. Such ideas coming down to matter by reason of His creative act lose their character of spirituality and transcendence and become individual, particular, and finite.[27] But, in order that they may again re-

[27] Manifestum est autem quod a Deo effluit in rebus non solum illud quod ad naturam universalem pertinet, sed etiam ea quæ sunt individuationis principia; est enim causa totius substantiæ rei, et quantum ad materiam, et quantum ad formam; et secundum quod causat, sic et cognoscit, quia scientia ejus est causa rei. 1. q. 57 art. 3. In Verbo autem æterno existiterunt rationes rerum corporalium. 1. q. 56 art. 2. Sic enim scientia Dei se habet ad omnes res creatas sicut scientia artificis se habet ad artificiata. Scientia autem artifices est causa artificatorum, et quod artifex operatur per secum intellectum. 1. q. 12 art. 8. Scientia Dei est causa rerum, secundum quod res sunt in scientia. *Ibid.*,

vive in their qualities of spirituality and transcendence it is necessary that a mind strip them of their material character, disincarnate them, as it were, from all that limits them, and separate them from the particular. This is, of course, the task of the abstracting intellect of man. Standing at the confines of the world of matter and the world of spirit man is particularly fitted for this work. Possessing an affinity for both worlds, he has the power to assimilate matter inasmuch as he has a body, and to abstract the spiritual from it, inasmuch as he has a soul.

But once in the possession of these ideas, man has a double task cut out for himself. First, he must *exteriorize* such ideas, that is, pass them out, communicate them to his fellowmen and to other creatures in order thus to ennoble and spiritualize the world itself. In other words, he must *do* with them, and this makes for the nobility and spirituality of civilization. The more lofty, as a matter of fact, the exteriorization of the ideals of man, the nobler will be our civilization. He will sacramentalize what he does by infusing matter with his own thought, after the fashion of the artist, by readjusting the forces of nature and the energies of the earth in the light of his intellect, so that his fellow-creatures may in their turn be lifted up above themselves as matter has been lifted above itself.

Man, however, must not only exteriorize his own

---

ad 2. Sicut ab illis (divinis) ideis effluunt res ut subsistant in forma et in materia, ita effluunt species in mentibus creatis, quæ sunt cognoscitivæ rerum. De Veritate, q. 15 art. 1; 2d. 16 q. 1 art. 2 ad 2.

ideas, for not possessing a perfect life within himself, he must conserve his forces. His second duty then is to *interiorize* these ideas. Such an act makes for the development of his own spiritual life, and his spiritual life will take on dignity in proportion as he thinks thoughts about the Eternal Thinker. In other words, he must know nothing less than the source of all knowledge, God. The more sublime the interiorization of these ideas, the more sublime his contemplation, the more rich and sublime becomes his spiritual life. And this task belongs to him, not as a citizen of this world, but as a citizen of the world of spirit.

The sacramentalizing process takes adequate account of the fact that man is both material and spiritual, that he has not only a body but also a soul. Sacramentalizing what he does, by spiritualizing the material for the sake of civilization, sacramentalizing what he knows by spiritualizing his interior life, man is thus led to God by the double route of action and thought, power and knowledge, art and science.[28]

The universe is a great sacrament and man is the priest of this sacrament. The mineral hidden in the bowels of the earth has no tongue, the plant has no

[28] 1. q. 15 art. 1. Ideas may be considered either as exemplars, i.e., principles of action, or types, i.e., principles of cognition. The former, in man, belong to the practical intellect; the latter to the speculative. And both of them are one in God. The Second Person of the Blessed Trinity is the source of both and therefore the sources of all art and science, for what is art but participation in the Exemplary Cause, and what is science but participation in the Formal Cause. This is the ultimate reason why there is not and never can be a conflict between art and science.

other language than its flower, the animal has no
speech other than its cry. The gaspings of these
creatures would have fallen dead before the man-
sions of their Eternal Maker, were there not someone to transmute, to ennoble, and to make them
intelligible. If the mineral could speak, assuredly
it would thank God for its existence; if the plants
could speak they would thank God for their life; if
the animals could speak they would thank God for
their sentiency. But man can speak, and he can
not only speak for them, but they can speak in him,
since he sums up all things within himself in virtue
of his spiritual soul. Possessing them within himself by knowledge, he can render thanks for them,
pray for them, praise for them, love for them, plead
for them, rejoice for them, entreat for them; aye
more, like the three youths in the fiery furnace he
can sing in their name a living *Benedicite* to the
Creator.[29]

Such a system of sacramental philosophy admits

[29] As St. Bonaventure puts it in his " Itinerarium mentis in Deum,"
Chap. I. p. 302 — Tria opuscula S. Bonaventuræ, 4th ed., Quarrachi,
1925: " If there be any man who is not enlightened by this sublime
magnificence of created things, he is blind. If there be any man who is
not aroused by the clamor of nature, he is deaf. If there be any one
who, seeing all these works of God, does not praise Him, he is dumb; if
there be any one who, from so many signs, cannot perceive the First
Principle, that man is foolish. Open, therefore, your eyes, incline
your spiritual ears, unloosen your lips and apply your heart (Prov. xxii.
17) so that in every creature you may see, hear, praise, love, worship,
magnify, and honor your God, lest otherwise the whole world should
rise up against you. For on account of such ignorance ' the whole world
shall fight against the unwise '; but to the wise, on the contrary, all this
shall be matter for glory, since they can say with the prophet: ' For
thou hast given me a delight, O Lord, in thy doings, and in the works of
thy Hand I shall rejoice.' "

of "world-loyalty" for which Professor Whitehead is so much concerned, but does not prostitute man by making him the slave of a spatio-temporal continuum, or reduce him to an accident of a mere qualitative physics. There can be no "world-loyalty" unless there is at the same time "loyalty to God." Being "loyal to the universe" is an exaggerated and wholesale form of selfishness and a self-centred universe would be just as cold and chilling as a self-centred individual. The universe and the things that are in it have their function, and their function is to be the servants of man. They await upon his sacramental power; they await to be ennobled in him and by him, and to be brought back to God.

The world then has a value, but a sacramental value — it leads us on to God. And God does not exist to conserve, or to preserve, or to ground our values, otherwise the greater would be the servant of the less. The philosophy of value makes man the centre of religion, God being the preservative of man's interests. The sacramental philosophy makes God the centre of religion and endows the world with a value because it conceives of the world as the instrument of man in the great work of uniting himself to his perfect end. The sacramental philosophy thus adds something to even the best of the philosophies of value, namely, absoluteness. It insists that religion is not concerned primarily with values, but with God, just as art is not so much concerned with the pleasure of man as it is with beauty. The universe, therefore, is not valuable, but sacramental. The valuable looks to man, the sacramental looks to God. Value tends to the relative, the sacramental to the absolute. Values may appeal to God as their Ground and as the hope for their conservation, just as a man may appeal to police protection in time of danger. At bottom, however, it is not so much God in Whom the value-philosopher is interested as it is his own values. To say that he is interested in the preservation of God's values is to say that God has values, which is to misunderstand the very nature of God. God has nothing. He is. God, in the strict sense of the term, has not even a value for man,[30] for to say God has value for man is to distinguish existence from value. God is everything to man, and without God man is nothing. If man had a value for God, then God is not God, for in such a view the ultimate perfection of God would depend on man. The failure of man to worship God would then mean that God would lack the totality of His value, and hence would be deprived of His total perfection. It is quite another thing to say that man may be pleasing to God.

In conclusion, the sacramental philosophy of St. Thomas answers the best ideals of modern thought by bringing man into prominence and making him the king of creation, but it does not suffer from the defect of doing so at the expense of God Himself.

[30] Deus est finis rerum, non sicut aliquid constitutum, aut aliquid effectum a rebus, neque ita quod aliquid ei a rebus acquiratur; sed hoc solo modo, quia ipse rebus acquiritur. C. G. lib. 3. c. 18.

Man is still king of the universe, and God is King of men.   Everything was made for man, and man was made for God.   The universe stands midway between the two as the great sacrament of the natural order, the means by which man elevates himself from a mere animal contentment with things that have value to the very realm where there are no values but only God.

CHAPTER XI

THE PHILOSOPHICAL BASIS OF RELIGION

RELIGION may be studied historically, i.e., in its genesis and development; or psychologically, i.e., in its effect upon the mind of the believer and the reactions following his beliefs; or finally it may be studied metaphysically, i.e., in its rational ground and foundation. Of the three the last is the most important because the most fundamental. Without denying the value of the science of comparative religion, the psychology of religion, and the history of religion, we propose to limit this study to the fundamental reason for religion and primary religious acts.

The philosopher seeking the foundation of religion cannot rest content with certain vague characteristics which refer only to a small part of creation, or to a particular civilization, or to a peculiar mental outlook. If religion is essential it must be rooted in something which quite escapes the psychologist who studies only mind, and the historian who is interested only in persons and events. Only the philosopher who penetrates into the secrets of the universe, not by some narrow abstraction which limits his gaze to strata of earth or motion of stars or whirl of electrons, but who can embrace all in the universality of the science of *being* as *being*, can tell us where the foundations of religion are laid.

Philosophy reminds us that everything in this world, whether inert or living, moral or a-moral, spiritual or temporal, can be said *to be*, to be *true*, and to be *good*. Nothing that is, or was, or can be, can fall under any other classification more ultimate than that of *being, truth,* and *goodness* which the Scholastics have called the transcendentals.[1]

Being

Being is a concept so simple that it cannot be defined for there are no ideas anterior to it. Nothing is known or knowable except in and through being. Even the *possible* and *nothing* are intelligible only through it.[2] One of the great interpreters of the Angelic Doctor, Cajetan, has said that the concept of being is so extensive that it can be applied (with correctives of course) to everything from pure possibility up to God. Man might close his eyes a thousand times and imagine things as small as the dewdrop and as distant as the stars whose light has not yet reached the earth, but he can never escape calling those things *beings*, nor

[1] BEING, De Ente et Essentia. Quod; q. 2 art. 3; De Veritate, q. 1. art 1. C. G. lib. 1. c. 26. TRUE, 1. q. 16 art. 1, 2, 3, 4; C. G. lib. 1. c. 59; De Veritate, q. 1 art. 9; De Veritate, q. 1 art 1; art. 2, 3, 4, in Perih lib. 1. lect. 3. GOOD, De Veritate, p. 21 art. 3, art. 6; 1. q. 16 art. 4; C. G. lib. 1. c. 37; 1 q. 5 art. 1 ad 1; in Eth. Nic. lib. 1. lect. 1 ad 1; 3 d 27 q. 1. art. 4; De Malo q. 1 art. 2; 2 d 34 art 3. Here we neglect the negative attribute of all things, viz., its indivision, in virtue of which a thing is one, and consider only the positive attributes. cf. 1. q. 11 art. 1; 1. q. 6 art. 1 ad 1; De; Pot. q. 9 art. 7; 1 d. 24 q. 1 art. 3.

[2] 1. q. 85 art. 3. q. 1; De Veritate, q. 1.

will he any less escape using that fundamental word in all languages, concerning each one of them: it *is*.

Because of its generality certain ancient philosophers, such as Parmenides, and certain modern philosophers, such as Hegel, have taken it to be purely static or pure indetermination, and have concluded to one or the other forms of pantheism. But such conclusions are travesties on its true notion. Being is not so confined within itself that it cannot get out of itself any more than an equation. In the Scholastic conception, being has a certain referribility to knowledge and to the will — the two great faculties of the soul. Then transcendental property of being loses nothing by these references, for the soul, because of its spirituality, is capable of becoming all things by knowledge — " quodammodo est omnia." It is therefore possible to envisage either in the real state or in the possible state, the concordance or non-concordance of being and the intellect; and the suitableness or non-suitableness of being with the will or the appetite. In the first case the concordance is called the *true*, the non-concordance the *false*. In the second case, the suitableness is called the *good*, and its contrary *evil*.

True [3]

When St. Thomas treats the problem of the object of the intellect, he says indifferently that it

[3] Here we are not concerned with logical or moral, but metaphysical truth.

is truth or being, a statement which betrays his sound realism. There should be no difficulty in understanding true and truth as equivalent to real and reality. We speak of a " true friend," a " veritable saint," etc. What is meant by ascribing truth to a thing? It means that it corresponds to a mental type or ideal. "We call a liquid true wine or real wine, for instance, when it verifies in itself the definition we have formed of the nature of wine. Hence whenever we apply the terms ' true ' or ' truth ' to a thing we shall find that we are considering the thing not absolutely and in itself but in relation to an idea in our minds; we do not say simply that it is true, we say that it is *truly such or such* a thing, i.e., that it is really of a certain nature already conceived by our minds. If the appearance of the thing suggests comparison with some such ideal type or nature, and if the thing is seen on examination not really to verify this nature in itself, we say that it is not really or truly such a thing: e.g., that a certain liquid is not really wine, or is not true wine. When we have no such ideal type to which to refer a thing, when we do not know its nature, cannot classify and name it, we have to suspend our judgment and say that we really do not know what the thing *really* is. Hence, for example, the new rays discovered by Röntgen were called provisionally ' X-Rays,' their real nature being at first unknown. We see then that real or ontological truth is simply reality considered as conformable with an ideal type, with an idea in the mind."[4]   It follows then that if there were no intellect there would be no truth.[5]

Good

Everything is good. This sounds like a paradox, for while it may be admitted that birds and flowers, sunsets and food are good, it seems difficult to admit that even a toothache is good. But this does not contradict the thesis rightly understood. The true meaning of the thesis is not that every being is good in every respect and condition, but only that every being possesses some goodness, i. e., every being is good in so far as it is the object of a natural tendency or desire. Every being inasmuch as it is desirable is good. It is therefore rigorously true to say that every being is good, provided one immediately adds: inasmuch as it is being.[6] This goodness which we predicate of any and every actual being, may be (a) the term of the natural tendency or appetite of that being itself, *bonum sibi*, and thus a cancer even though it be bad for the stomach, considered *in* itself biologically and chemically, has its own tendencies, purposes, laws,

[4] Peter Coffey, "Ontology," 1918, p. 159.

[5] Si intellectus humanus non esset, adhuc res dicerentur veræ in ordine ad intellectum divinum. Sed si uterque intellectus, quod est impossibile, intelligeretur auferri, nullo modo ratio veritatis remaneret. De Veritate, q. 1 art. 2. "Though conceptual truth is caused in our intellects by the object, it is not necessary that the form of the truth should be previously discoverable in the object; just as health is not discoverable in the medicine previous to taking it. For it is the power of the medicine, not its healthiness which causes health; since its agency is not univocal. And in like manner, it is the being of the thing, not its truth which causes conceptual truth." 1–2. 16 art. 1 ad 3.

[6] 1. q. 5 art. 3.

and we cannot deny that its development according to these laws is " good " for its own specific nature. (b) It may be conceivably the term of the appetite of some other being, *bonum alteri,* in the sense that in the general scheme of reality things are helpful to one another, and are intended by their inter-action and coöperation with one another to sub-serve the wider end which is the good of the whole system of reality.[7]

So true is it that everything that is, is true, and is good that it is a commonplace truth of Scholastic metaphysics that being, goodness and truth are convertible terms. *Ens et verum convertuntur; ens et bonum convertuntur.* Goodness and truth add nothing real to being, nor do they contract it, but they formally add a referribility to something else. *Ex parte rei,* they are identical with being. " The true and the good add to the concept of being the relative idea of the perfective." [8]

Stating truths in terms of metaphysics may seem

[7] For a full development of these points, cf. P. Coffey's " Ontology," p. 180 ff, and Mercier's " Metaphysique," p. 231.

[8] De Veritate, q. 21 art. 1. " If, then, the True and the Good are to be considered as they are in themselves, in such manner the True is prior to the Good according to its nature, since it is perfective of something else according to the nature of its form (or species) ; but the Good is not only perfective of something else after the nature of its form, but according to its real entity. Thus the nature of the Good contains within itself more than the nature of the True, and in a manner is constituted by addition to it. Wherefore, the Good pre-supposes the True, but the True presupposes the One; since the nature of the True is perfected in the apprehension of the intellect, and a thing is intelligible, in so far as it is One, according to the Philosopher in the fourth Book of the Metaphysics. Hence, this is the order of these transcendentals, if considered as they are in themselves. After Being comes Unity, then Truth; lastly, after Truth, Goodness." De Veritate, q. 21 art. 3. c. cf. 1. q. 16 art. 4 ad 2.

to some to be equivalent to divorcing them from the practical. Anything that smacks of the intellectual is sometimes termed with ridicule a "dogma" and if there is one thing modern religion will not tolerate it is dogmas; it wants practice and experience. But does not this distaste for a rational presentation of truths seem a little inconsistent? To say we want no dogmas in religion is to assert a dogma, and a dogma that needs a tremendous amount of justification. Two and two equals four is a dogma; two apples plus two apples is experience. The two are not contrary, but one merely the particular application of the other. As a matter of fact the abstract is not true, because the concrete is true, but vice versa. So too in the metaphysical presentation of religion the experience of these truths is not anything different from their essence, but only a difference in application. But how bring these truths down to the level of experience?

There are three fundamental cravings in the human heart, to which all others are resolvable. They are the craving for *being* or life, *truth* and *love*. The first of these, the inclination toward the preservation and the perfection of life is the basis of the others. A human being will sacrifice all other possessions, wealth, pleasures, honors and the like providing that he can cling on to that which he treasures last of all — life. The very tendency to put out our hand before us as we walk in the dark is a proof that we are willing to lose even our members provided we can conserve our existence.

The second fundamental craving is the desire to know and possess truth. The first question a child asks when he comes into this world is the question: Why? Every babe is an incipient philosopher. He tears his toys to pieces to find out what makes the wheels go round, and then later on, when he grows to man's estate he tears apart the wheels of the universe by a mental process to determine why its wheels go round, in other words, to know its causes. Man has an appetite for truth as he has for food, and truth is just as satisfying to the mind, even more so, than food is for the body.

The third fundamental craving is the desire to love and to be loved. From the first day when God said " It is not good for man to be alone," even unto the end, man will hunger and thirst for love. Companions and friends will be sought out to whom he can unpack his heart with words, and above all, life-long friends who will measure up to the test of friendship — one in whose presence he can keep silence.

What makes a man then? A soul which is life, which seeks truth, which seeks love. Being, Truth, and Love. That is man.

But do we carry within ourselves the fulfillment of these appetites? We possess a modicum of life, a modicum of truth, a modicum of love, but do we possess life, truth, and love in their entirety? The richness of our life is borrowed; the children of parents do not always live in the family circle, but obeying the law of nature, leave them who gave them life, to establish their own fireside. Is not our life an approaching death? Does not each tick of the clock bring us nearer the grave; does not the very food we eat burn up our body and hasten the end of our earthly life? "Our hearts like muffled drums are beating funeral marches to the grave." "From hour to hour we ripe and ripe; then from hour to hour we rot and rot." In a word, is not death mingled with life?

And while truth is a condition of our nature, we cannot say that we possess truth in its entirety. Are we not under the necessity of being taught; does not the multitude of religions, political doctrines and social theories prove we are but vaguely and dimly possessing truth? If but our sight were lost in our cradle much of the knowledge of truth would be shut off from us. Are we not always searching after the secrets of life and yet never fully understanding nor comprehending them? In a word — is not truth mingled with error; is not knowledge mingled with falsity? Have not the great geniuses of all times confessed that after years of study they were still ignorant of truth, and that they seemed to stand merely on the shore of truth with its infinite expanse stretching before them? How often too, study in old age corrects the prejudices of youth, and how often those who have come to mock have remained to pray. We do not possess the fulness of truth. Love too is a condition of our nature, and yet who can say that he has never had sorrow? Are not broken friendships, ruined homes, sad hearts eloquent proofs that man does not possess the fullness of love? How often do we not feel that love reaches its satiety; that it loses its bloom and its freshness; that often it turns to hate. And even when it does remain fresh and delicate, it ends and nothing that ends is perfect. A day must come when the last cake is crumbled at life's great feast and the last embrace passed from friend to friend. We do not possess the fullness of love.

Though we are men, though we possess the three conditions by which man is man, we find imperfections in these three conditions. Life is mingled with death, truth with error, love with hate. Our life then is not in creatures, our truth then is not in the spoken word, our love then is not in what we see. Life cannot exist with death, truth with error, love with hate.

But where are we to find Supreme Life, Supreme Truth, Supreme Love? Where find the source of daylight that is in this room? Not under the chair, for there there is light mingled with darkness. Not under the table, for there also there is light mingled with darkness. Where find its source then? I must go outside of this room, out to something which is pure light without any admixture of darkness, namely to the sun. There is the reason for all the light that surrounds me. So too, if I am to find the source of the Life, the Truth and the Love in this world, I must go out beyond this world, out beyond a life which is mingled with its shadow death, out beyond a truth which is mingled with its shadow error, and out beyond a love which is mingled with its shadow hate.   I must go out to that which is Perfect Life, Perfect Truth, and Perfect Love — to God.

> " There is a quest that haunts me
>   In the nights when I am alone;
> The need to ride, where the ways divide
>   The Known from the Unknown.
> I mount what thought is near me,
>   And soon I reach the place,
> The tenuous rim where the Seen grows dim
>   And the Sightless hides its face.
>
> I have ridden the wind,
>   I have ridden the sea,
> I have ridden the moon and stars,
> I have sat my feet in the stirrup seat
>   Of a comet coursing Mars,
> And everywhere thro' the earth and air
>   My thought speeds, lightning shod,
> It comes to a place where checking pace
>   It cries, 'Beyond lies God!'"

Beyond lies God — Perfect Life: *I am the Life;* Perfect Truth: *I am the Truth;* Perfect Love: *God is Love.   Ens, Verum, Bonum* — Life, Truth and Love.

Now we are in a position to understand why Being, Truth, and Love are the transcendental attributes of everything in this world.   As reflections or participations of that which is Perfect, they can exist only in virtue of different kinds of Causality. There is a thing before me.   I may ask: what is it? The answer is: a statue of the Madonna.   In Metaphysics the Madonna, the form, or the model, is called the Formal Cause. Again, I may ask: who made it? The answer is Raphael. In Metaphysics, Raphael would be called the Efficient Cause. Finally, I might ask: why was it made? The answer might be: to glorify the Mother of God. This motive, or intention or end, in Metaphysics is called the Final Cause.[9]

Now the transcendentals are related to these causalities. In other words, everything that is, *is* because God is its Efficient Cause; everything is true, because God is its Formal Cause; everything is good because God is its Final Cause.[10]

Speaking of God as Efficient Cause St. Thomas writes: " It must be said that every being in any way existing is from God. For whatever is found in anything by participation, must be caused in it by that to which it belongs essentially, as iron becomes ignited by fire. Subsisting being must be one; if whiteness were self-subsisting, it would be one since whiteness is multiplied by its recipients. Therefore all beings apart from God are not their own being, but are beings by participation. It must be then that all things which are diversified by the diverse participation of being, so as to be more or less perfect, are caused by one first Being, Who possesses being most completely. Hence Plato said

---

[9] Here we ignore the material cause as we are interested only in Supreme Causalities, and not the matter from which things are made.

[10] 1. q. 44 art. 1, 2, 3, 4; q. 65 art. 2. q. 103 art. 2; C. G. lib. 1. c. 37; lib. 3. c. 17, 18; lib. 4. c. 21. De Veritate, q. 20 art. 4; De Pot. q. 7 art. 1 ad 3.

(Parmen. XXVI) that unity must come before multitude; and Aristotle said (Metap. II, text 4) that whatever is greatest in being and greatest in truth is the cause of all being and every truth just as whatever is the greatest in heat is the cause of all heat.

" Since to be caused does not enter into the essence of being as such, it is possible for us to find a being uncaused. . . . But the reason why an efficient cause is required is not merely because the effect is not necessary, but because the effect might not be if the cause were not." [11]

But God is not only Efficient Cause, in virtue of which things possess existence; He is also Formal Cause in virtue of which things are true. There is an Intelligence to which reality is *essentially* conformed, other than the purely human intellect. Although ontological truth is for us proximately and immediately the conformity of reality with our own conceptions, it is primarily and fundamentally the essential conformity of all reality with the Divine Mind. God has created all things according to the archetypal ideas existing in His Mind, and the essence of everything for that reason is an imitation or reflection of these exemplar ideas. That is why St. Thomas holds there would be truth even though every human mind were annihilated, for there would still be the Divine Mind with which all things are in conformity. [12]

[11] 1 q. 44 art. 1.

[12] De Veritate, q. 1 art. 1 and 2. Sicut enim omnes rationes rerum intelligibiles primo existunt in Deo, et ab eo derivantur in alios intel-

St. Thomas puts this doctrine in these words: "Truth is found in the intellect according as it apprehends a thing as it is; and in things according as they have been conformable to an intellect. This is to the greatest degree found in God. For His own being is not only conformed to His intellect, but it is the very act of His intellect; and His act of understanding is the measure and cause of every other being and of every other intellect, and He Himself is His own existence and act of understanding. Whence it follows not only that Truth is in Him, but He is Truth itself, and the Sovereign and First Truth." [13]

Since God is the Formal Cause of all Truth, because all things are made according to His Exemplar ideas, as the house conforms to archetypal ideas in the mind of the architect, it follows that we see all truth in the Eternal Truth. We can say that we see all bodies in the sun, not because we see them in the solar disc itself, but because we could not see them except by means of the light of the sun. Although there is a proximate ground for truth without taking God into consideration, there is really no ultimate ground for it without Him. As one object may be reflected many times in a mirror, so too, the Divine Truth may be imaged imperfectly in all creatures. That is why there is a unanimous accord among all men in judgments relative to first principles and their legitimate conclusions;

---

lectus ut actu intelligant; sic etiam derivantur in creaturas ut subsistant 1. q. 104 art. 3.

[13] 1. q. 16 art. 5.

all these are ultimately resolvable into the Supreme Truth which is God and by Whom all things are true.[14]

There still remains the question, why things are good, and the answer to this, in its metaphysical and ultimate basis, must be that things are good because God is their Final Cause, and His intention or purpose in making things was the manifestation of His Goodness. " Everything is called good," writes St. Thomas, " from the Divine Goodness, as from the first exemplary effective and final principle of all goodness."

" Nevertheless, everything is called good by reason of the similitude of the Divine Goodness, belonging to it, which is formally its own goodness, whereby it is denominated good. And so of all things there is one Goodness and yet many things which are good."[15]

Everything tends toward its perfection by the very fact that it tends toward its end, because everything is good in the measure of its own achievement. Matter tends toward its perfection through physical laws; living beings tend to theirs by instincts, and man by reason. As the arrow would never speed toward its target unless there was an archer, neither would things tend to their perfection unless there was some Supreme Archer. And in the

[14] Sicut igitur animæ et res aliæ, veræ quidem dicuntur in suis naturis, secundum quod similitudinem illius summæ naturæ habent, quæ est ipsa veritas, quum sit suum intellectum esse; ita id quod per animam cognitum est, verum est, in quantum illius divinæ veritatis quam Deus cognoscit, similitudo quædam existit in ipsa. C. G. lib. 3 c. 47.

[15] 1. q. 6 art. 4.

measure that each tends toward the *good*, it approaches the Divine, for every being resembles God inasmuch as it is good.

God's Will is the Cause of all things, or in other words, since in God, Will and Goodness are identical, God's Goodness is the Cause of all things. God has no need of time for His Life for He is Eternal; He has no need of Space for He is Spiritual; "Since then, the Divine Being is undetermined, and contains in Himself the full perfection of Being, it cannot be that He acts by a necessity of His Nature." [16] If He does act, it is not because of indigence, or need, but because of Perfect Liberality. "He who wills to take a bitter draught, in doing so wills nothing else than health; and this alone moves his will. It is different with one who takes a draught that is pleasant, which anyone may will to do, not only for the sake of health, but also for its own sake. Hence, although God wills things apart from Himself only for the sake of the end, which is His own goodness, it does not follow that anything else moves His Will, except His goodness. So, as He understands things apart from Himself, by understanding His own essence, so He wills things apart from Himself, by willing His own goodness." [17] "God's Will is the Cause of all things. It must needs be therefore that a thing has existence, and is good only inasmuch as it is willed by God." [18] "We love things because goodness in things calls forth our love; but God is not drawn toward things because things

---

[16] I. q. 19 art. 4.   [17] I. q. 19 art. 2.   [18] I. q. 20 art. 2.

possess goodness, but rather they possess goodness
because He willed them." [19]   And since God willed
creatures from all eternity it is true to say that He
loved creatures from all eternity. He did not begin
to love man when man was made, as He did not begin to know man when man was made. He knew and
loved man when man existed only as an idea in
His Mind from all eternity.[20] God's love is eternal
and infinite. Our love is temporal and finite. Our
love is like the estuary of a stream which flows
strongly and abundantly as long as it is confined
within narrow banks, but becomes feeble and
shallow when its banks widen. The more we love,
the less we love; i.e., the greater the extension of our
affection, the lesser the intensity. As the circumference of our love widens it becomes farther and
farther away from the centre of its flame. But
this is not true of God. Though all enjoy sunlight,
yet one does not receive less of it than the other.
Though God loves all, He loves each one infinitely,
and even though thousands sit down on the green
grass for the banquet, each one rises " with his fill."

Being, Truth, and Love — three names for God
Who is the Efficient, Formal and Final Cause of
this universe. These three: Power, Law and Goodness are found written across the face of this universe; Power, because God is the Omnipotence that
acts; *Potentia ut exequens;* Law because God is

[19] *Ibid.*, C. G., lib. 1. c. 91; De Veritate, q. 27 art. 1. C. G. lib. 3,
c. 150.

[20] Deus ab æterno dilexit creaturas in propiis naturis et volent eas
esse, non autem tunc. 1. q. 20 art. 2 ad. 2; 3 d 32 q. 3. C. G. lib.
4 c. 23.

the Wisdom that directs: *Sapientia ut dirigens;* Goodness because God is the Will that orders: *Voluntas ut imperans. Ex Ipso,* because *from Him* all things have received their being; *Per Ipsum,* because *through Him,* all things have been ordered according to law; *In Ipso* because *to Him* all things tend and strive as their ultimate end.[21]

Reason then can know God through the visible things of the earth, and the conclusion of reason is not just the *idea of God,* but God, and God is not an abstract mathematical entity, not a temporal-spatial quality, but the Perfect Being, Truth, and Love of Which all earthly existence, and earthly truth and earthly love is but a dim far-off echo and feeble reflection. And if we would transpose these philosophical terms to the concrete and still know what God is in the realm of the human experience, we need but sound the depths of the human heart. If we receive but a two-billionth part of the light and heat that streams from the sun, may it not be that we receive an equally small fraction of that which is Perfect Life, Perfect Truth and Perfect Love? If human life at its best is a joy, then what must be Perfect Life! If a feeble truth which we but dimly grasp can so possess our minds as to give us a peace which no earthly treasure can give, then what must be Perfect Truth! If a human heart in its purest quest for love can so thrill and exalt and cast us into an ecstasy, then what must be the Heart of Hearts! *If the spark is so bright, what must be the Flame!*

[21] St. Thomas In Rom. iii, 16.

And here, if we be permitted to go a step further and make use of revelation, the meaning of Being, Truth and Goodness becomes even more clear. Revelation and faith, be it understood, do not mean doing violence to our reason. Faith no more destroys reason than a telescope destroys the vision. Faith is a new kind of daylight. We have the same eyes at night as we have in the day and yet we cannot see things during the night. And why? Because we lack the light of the sun. So too, two men may have the same minds, but one cannot see truths which the other can see; two look on bread, the one sees bread, the other Emmanuel. "Two men looked out through prison bars, the one saw mud, the other stars." And faith does not mean, as it does in the minds of some modern theologians, a leap in the dark, an hypothesis, a chance, a wish or a will to believe; faith is the assent of the intellect to a truth on the authority of God revealing.

Now, if we make use of this new kind of daylight, what new illumination is brought to a natural knowledge of God? Certainly this, if nothing else, namely an answer to the question the Greeks used to ask: If there is only one God, how is He happy; and what does He think about? The answer is the Trinity, which so expands the rational knowledge of God as to reveal that Being, Truth and Love; Power, Wisdom, and Goodness; are really God the Father, God the Son and God the Holy Ghost.[22]

[22] Ex creaturis, ex quibus cognitionem accipimus, possumus per

God the Father: the Power and Efficient Cause; God the Son: Truth and Formal Cause; God the Holy Ghost: Goodness and Final Cause.

"To the Father is appropriated Power which is chiefly shown in creation, and therefore it is attributed to Him to be the Creator. To the Son is appropriated Wisdom, through which the intellectual agent acts; and therefore it is said: *Through Whom all things were made.* And to the Holy Ghost is appropriated goodness, to which belong both government which brings things to their proper end, and the giving of life — for life consists in a certain interior movement; and the First Mover is the end and goodness." [23]

But how are there three Persons in God? God thinks; He thinks a thought. But thoughts are not born to die and die to be reborn in the mind of God. In God there is one Thought which reaches to the abyss of all things that are known or can be known. That Thought is a Word as my own thoughts are words: "In the beginning was the Word and the Word was with God." And the Word is called a Son because generated, not physically, but spiritually as my own mind generates such thoughts as justice, fortitude, prudence. The principle of generation is called the Father; the term of generation is called the Son. And thus the

---

certitudinem devenire in cognitionem essentialium attributorum, non autem in cognitionem personalium proprietatum . . . Ex his manifestatis personarum per essentialia attributa apropriatio nominatur. 1. q. 39 art. 7.

[23] 1. q. 34 art. 8 ad 4. (error)

1q. 45, art 6, ad 2 .

Father in the ecstasy of the first and real paternity can say: " Thou Art My Son ; this day have I begotten Thee " — this day of the agelessness of eternity, this day without beginning or end ; this day without morning or night, the Father without any priority in time communicates to His Son all the nobility and majesty of His Being, as an earthly father in time may communicate to his earthly son all the nobility and majesty of his character.

Every being loves its own perfection. The perfection of the eye is color, and the eye loves color ; the perfection of the mind is truth, and the mind loves truth. Love is not something in me, or in you ; it is something between us in which two hearts beat as one. The Father loves the Son Whom He has eternally engendered ; the Son loves the Father Who engendered Him, and love between them because it is infinite, does not express itself by cries or canticles, or embraces, but only by that which is ineffable, the like of which we have nothing in this world, save a sigh. And that is a poor, earthly reason why that mysterious bond of Love between Father and Son is called the Holy Spirit.

Just as water, ice and steam are all manifestations of the same substance ; just as the length, breadth, and thickness of a cathedral do not make three cathedrals, but one ; just as carbon, diamond and graphite are manifestations of one and the same nature ; just as the color, perfume and form of a rose do not make three roses, but one ; just as the soul, the intellect and the will do not make three lives, but one; just as $1 \times 1 \times 1 = 1$ and not 3, so in a much more mysterious way there are three Persons in the Blessed Trinity and yet only one God.[24]

This is but the feeblest exposition of the mystery of the Trinity, but it may serve as a suggestion of the continuity of philosophy and theology. It is not our purpose to go into the field of Revelation, but merely to suggest it as the crown of philosophy. The important element in the demonstration thus far is that God as Power, Wisdom and Goodness is the cause of this world and everything in it from material to the spiritual.

Since God is to be defined either as Pure Being (*Actus Purus*), Truth and Goodness, in the natural order, or as Father, Son and Holy Ghost in the supernatural order, it follows in virtue of the three-fold causality that there will be a three fold link binding man to God thus constituting the essence of religion.[25] First, we must *know* God (Truth); secondly, we must *love* God (Goodness); thirdly, we must *serve* God (Being), and in these three words, " Know, Love, and Serve," is contained all human wisdom in the natural order, the end of every student's quest, and the goal of every inquir-

[24] Cum increata Trinitas distinguatur secundum processionem verbi a dicente et amoris ab utroque, in creatura naturali, in qua invenitur processio verbi secundum intellectum, et processio amoris secundum voluntatem potest dici imago Trinitatis increatæ secundum quamdam repræsentationem speciei. In aliis creaturis, non invenitur principium verbi, et verbum et amor. 1. q. 13 art. 4.

[25] Religio proprie importat ordinem ad Deum; ipse enim est, cui principaliter alligari debemus tamquam indeficienti principio. 2-2. q. 81 art. 1.

ing mind. And the child in a foreign mission who from the simple examples of a foreign missionary has learned that life means to know, love, and serve God, knows more than our learned philosophers for whom God is a mental projection or a "nisus of the spatio-temporal continuum."

KNOW GOD

The human mind is on the quest of causes, and can find no repose short of Him Who is First Cause. There are some philosophers like Spencer, who have said that the First Cause is Unknowable, but Spencer really has told us more about it than many Scholastics have told us about God. The hunger and thirst for truth is as deep-seated as human nature; the very restlessness the mind experiences under an unsolved problem proves that error, half truths and ignorance are radically unsatisfying.

St. Augustine has very well expressed the craving which drives the intellect to know its God. " I asked the earth," he writes, " and it answered me, 'I am not He'; and whatsoever are in it confessed the same. I asked the sea and the deeps, and the living creeping things, and they answered, 'We are not thy God, seek above us.' I asked the moving air; and the whole air with its inhabitants answered, 'Anaximenes was deceived. I am not God.' I asked the heavens, sun, moon and stars; 'nor' (say they) 'are we the God whom thou seekest.' And I replied unto all things which encompass the door of my flesh: 'Ye have told me of my God, that ye are not He; tell me something of Him.' And they cried out with a loud voice, 'He made us.' My questioning them, was my thoughts on them: and their form of beauty gave the answer. And I turned myself unto myself, and said to myself: 'Who art Thou'? and I answered: 'A man.' And behold, in me there present themselves to me, soul and body, one without, the other within. By which of these ought I to seek my God? I had sought Him in the body from earth to heaven, so far as I could send messengers, the beams of mine eyes. But the better is the inner, for to it, as presiding and judging, all the bodily messengers reported the answers of heaven and earth, and all things therein, who said, 'We are not God, but He made us.' These things did my inner man know by the ministry of the outer: I, the inner, knew them; I, the mind, through the sense of my body. I asked the whole frame of the world about my God; and it answered me, 'I am not He, but He made me.' " [26]

The mind must know, but it never knows anything fully until it knows God, and the least knowledge of God is worth more than the knowledge of all created things. If we knew what the sun was we would not need to know what its ray is; if we knew the ocean we would know the chemistry of a drop of water; if we knew the circle, we would know what the smallest arc is; and in knowing God we know all things.

[26] " Confessions," Bk. 10.

If we do not know God, then we know nothing, for we know nothing in its ground, its cause or the reason of its being. Education does not mean the knowledge of facts such as might be gathered in a five-foot shelf, or condensed in an "Ask Me Another." Education means a knowledge of the relation between facts, and a relation between facts implies an intellect capable of searching the why and the wherefore of things. As a man could not lay claim to being a geometrician if he were ignorant of the fundamental principles of Euclid, neither could a man lay claim to being a philosopher, or even a man, if he were ignorant of the basic principles of life, of truth, and of happiness. A mind may not go to the sources of knowledge because of a myopic interest in transitory things, just as a man may shorten his vision by putting his hand to his eyes, but such a condition is not normal. Every search for truth, every scientific enquiry, every piece of historical research, every painstaking microscopic study of a biological field, every search for new stars and distant planets, is really a search for God, for every quest for knowledge is a quest for Truth.[27] In the psychological order the knowledge of finite trifles may be the goal, but in the ontological order it is God Who is first sought. Every being endowed with an intellect knows God implicitly

[27] Res intellectu carentes tendunt in Deum sicut in finem per viam assimilationis, ita substantiæ intellectuales per viam cognitionis . . . Intellectus humanus magis desiderat et amat et delectatur in cognitione divinorum, quamvis modicum quidem de illis percipere possit, quam in perfecta cognitione quam habet de rebus infimis. Est igitur ultimus finis hominis intelligere quoque modo Deum. C. G. lib. 3 c. 25.

in everything it knows, for nothing is knowable except by a similitude of the First Truth Who is God.[28]

LOVE GOD

Man must not only know God, but he must also love God. Knowledge and love are correlative. There is no love for the unknown, but there is greater love where there is greater positive knowledge. That is why a perfect proportion should exist between knowing and loving, as there is in the Trinity where Son and Spirit are equal. On a lower level, morality, for the same reason, can never be divorced from dogma, nor vice versa. Religion can never be just mere morality, as it can never be just speculation.

Love is a movement, a unitive adaptation, a complacency or an alliance with that which constitutes the perfection of a thing. Love, according to this definition, applies not only to man but to all creatures.[29] This complacency of one thing for another is manifested first of all in the chemical order, in which each element in virtue of the property of valence, is capable of combining with or replacing other elements. In beings endowed with life this urge is instinct, in which love is affective; in man it

[28] Omnia cognoscentia cognoscunt Deum implicite in quolibet cognito . . . nihil est cognoscibile nisi per similitudinem prinæ veritatis. De Veritate, q. 22 art. 2 ad 1. This does not mean God is the first object known by the intellect. 1. q. 83.

[29] Primus enim motus voluntatis, et cuiuslibet appetitivæ virtutis est amor . . . et propter hoc omnes alii motus appetitivi præsupponunt amorem, quasi primam radicem. 1. p. 20 art. 1.

is rational because of reason, not instinct or blind law gives it its direction. But since its direction is derived from reason, it follows that since reason can know what is Perfect, man must therefore love the Perfect and tend to it with his whole body and soul. In practice this does not always work out, because man has free will, and he may choose, if he so desires, to follow the shadow instead of the substance. The acorn which is not endowed with liberty is not free to remain only a sapling, but man can so distort his growth as to remain always either an intellectual pigmy or an irresolute moron.

But even in loving that which is below the Perfect, man testifies to the great truth, that he never loves but that he loves the good, even though it be evil in the guise of good. In seeking good, in its varied forms, he is consequently seeking God under a veil, for nothing in the world escapes or can escape loving God, by the mere fact it loves the good.[30] There are really two laws of gravitation, one referring to the material world, the other to the spiritual. Just as all material bodies are drawn to the centre of the earth because they are of the earth earthly, so all spiritual realities, such as the souls of men are drawn to their centre, Who is God.

Loving God in the natural order, and in the sense in which we have taken the world, is not and never can be arbitrary. Everything loves God in seeking the end for which it was created.[31] "Whatever

[30] 1–2. q. 1 art. 8.
[31] Unumquodque autem tendens in suam perfectionem tendit in divinam similitudinem. C. G. lib. 3 c. 21.

brings us into personal relations with wider worlds, with larger and more enduring life, gives us a sense of freedom and joy; for we are prisoners of love; and are driven to make a ceaseless appeal to it to enlarge the confining walls; to constitute us, if so it may be, dwellers in a boundless universe, where truth and beauty and goodness are infinite; where what uplifts and deifies is eternal, where ceasing to be the slaves of animal tendencies, we are made citizens of a spiritual kingdom and have divine leisure to live for and in the soul. Now, more than anything else, religion is able to realize for us these ideals; to diffuse itself through our whole being; to level the hills and fill the valleys, to bridge the chasms and throw assuring light into the abysses of doubt and desire; to make us know and feel that God is near, and that God is love." [32]

Creatures not only love God, but they love God more than themselves, as any man must necessarily value the perfect whole rather than the part. St. Thomas adds that if a creature really loved itself more than God, this would argue that natural love was perverse, for it would equivalently assert that it could not be perfected by charity.[33] And lov-

[32] John L. Spalding, "The Victory of Love," "Religion, Agnosticism, Education," p. 237.

[33] Quia igitur bonum universale est ipse Deus et sub hoc bono, continetur etiam angelus, et homo et omnis creatura, quia omnis creatura naturaliter secundum id quod est Dei est, sequitur, quod naturali dilectione etiam angelus, et homo plus, et principalius diligat Deum, quam seipsum. Alioquin, si naturaliter plus seipsum diligeret, quam Deum, sequeretur, quod naturalis dilectio esset perversa, et quod non perficeretur per caritatem, sed destrueretur. 1. q. 60 art. 5; De Malo q. 16 art. 4 ad 15; 1–2 q. 99 art. 1 ad 2; 3 d. 30 q. 4.

ing God, above all things else, does not mean loving creatures less; it means only loving God more. *It does not require much time to make us saints; it requires only much love.*

This almost seems as if His wish that we should love Him argues some want on His part. God can receive no perfection from man's love but, since man alone of all the creatures of earth can be perfected only by Divine Goodness, it follows that nowhere can the Divine Goodness be so well exercised as upon man. One has a great need and a great capacity to receive love, and the other has a great abundance and a great inclination to give it. Nothing is quite so apropos of indigence as liberal affluence, and nothing quite so agreeable to liberal affluence as a necessitating indigence, and the greater the affluence, the greater the inclination. "We can hardly conceive of God creating, if He did not set a value upon His own creation. Yet we could not bring ourselves to believe that God set any great value upon a few millions of round orbs, or on their velocity, or on their fidelity to their orbits, or to their eccentricities, or to the mere vastness of siderial space, or to the various structure of matter, or to the threads of metal in the bowels of the mountains, or to the vivifying force of the solar ray, or the gigantic play of the ubiquitous electricity, or to the trees, or the clear lakes, or to the sylvan dells, to the outlines on the seacoast, or to the gorgeousness of sunsets, or to the pomp of storms, or to anything whatever of that sort. Even we creatures should feel that we were lowering Him in our estimation, if we thought that He set a value upon, or took pains with, or had an interest in, such things as these. Yet we are told that He does distinctly set a value on the hearts of men. Man is the end of the material world, but God alone is the end of man. Physical philosophers can love strata of the rock, or the distribution of plants, or peculiar fauna, or the habits of earthquakes, or the oscillation of stars, or the physical geography of the sea, or the delicacies of chemistry, more than they love the hearts of men, or the inmates of a hospital. But God cannot do so. All His own material creation is worthless to Him in comparison with one peasant's heart, or with one child's first serious prayer. He has given away, with the indifference of indeterminable wealth, all the rest of His creation; but hearts He has kept for Himself, and will not even share them, much less surrender them." [34]

SERVE GOD

Man must not alone know God because by nature he must know Truth; man must not alone love God because he cannot help but desire goodness; man must also serve God, for knowledge and love result in action. The service of God is based on the fact that God is the Cause of all being in the world. " Behold heaven and earth have a being, and they cry out that they were made; for they do change and vary. Whereas whatsoever hath not been made,

[34] F. M. Faber, "Creator and Creature," p. 109.

and yet is, hath nothing in it now that was not before; and this is to be changed and to vary. They also cry out that they did not make themselves; but they say, 'For this reason we are, because we are made; we were not therefore, before we were made, that so we might give being to ourselves.' Now this evidence of them that speak, is the evidence of the thing itself. Thou, therefore, O Lord, Who art beautiful didst make them, for they are beautiful; Who art good, for they are good, Who art, for they also are; yet they are neither so beautiful, so good, nor are they in such wise as Thou, their Creator, art; in comparison with Whom they are neither beautiful, nor good, nor are they at all." [35]

We owe God, because we are His; all that we have and are is His since He is our Author and Giver. Since God owns our whole being, He owns all its faculties, and therefore all that we can acquire by their exercise. If a genius invents some labor-saving device the government, recognizing his rights, will give him patent rights entitling him to all returns on his invention. By making everyone who makes use of it pay royalty the government testifies to a strict right on the part of its creator. Now God is Our Creator and we are His "invention." Creating us, not out of raw material, but by the Omnipotence of His Will, we are wholly dependent on Him. To say that He is entitled to royalties is merely to say that justice should be done to whom justice is due. The earnings of prop-

[35] St. Augustine, "Confessions," Bk. 11, chap. 4.

erty are the proprietor's. The rose belongs to the gardner, and in a deeper sense the lives of all who live belong to the Life of all living. God was not Lord until there were creatures subject to Him,[36] but when He did create He necessarily created beings dependent on Him, as the sun when it shines necessarily has rays which are dependent on it.

Service of God means simply giving honor to whom honor is due, and is based on the truth that God is Efficient Cause of all being, for without Him was made nothing that was made.[37] This recognition of God as the Principle whence all proceeds and the consequent recognition of a debt in justice to Him, is according to St. Thomas the very essence of religion.[38]

To serve God does not mean to be a slave, but rather to be free. If a flower is more noble in serving man by beautifying his sickroom than it is in the field, why should not man be more noble in serving God Who is above him, than by merely serving his fellow-creatures?

Service of God is not founded on Divine indigence any more than royalties are founded on the

---

[36] Unde Deus non fuit Dominus, antequam haberet creaturam sibi subjectam. 1. q. 13 art. 7 ad 6.

[37] Eodem actu homo servit Deo, et colit ipsum; nam cultus respicit Dei excellentiam, cui reverentia debetur; servitus autem respicit subjectionem hominis, qui ex sua conditione obligatur ad exhibendam reverentiam Deo. 2-2 q. 81 art. 3 ad 2.

[38] Dominum convenit Deo secundum propriam et singularem quamdam rationem; quia scilicet ipse omnia fecit; et quia summum in omnibus rebus obtinet principatum; et ideo specialis ratio servitutis ei debetur; et talis servitus nomine latriæ designatur apud Græcos; et ideo ad religionem proprie pertinet. 2-2. q. 81 art. 1. ad 3; C. G. lib. 3 c. 120.

indigence of an author. God is not enriched by our service, but we are enriched. God is the inseparable end of man, and so much so that if man does not attain to God he misses his own completion. Just as learning is inseparable from knowledge, and is not added to it like frosting to a cake, so too, God is inseparable from the happiness of man. To serve God is to rule — *cui servire, regnare est*. To lose God is to lose oneself, for God is not something extrinsic to us and to our being, as a shining copper is unrelated to a child who takes medicine, but something much bound up with us as heat is bound up with fire. And the reason for all human misery is serving anything less than the Perfect for Whom we were made. A bone that is out of joint pains for the simple reason that it is not where it ought to be. A compass pointing south, if it were sensitive would be in pain, for it would not be tending toward its due direction. So, too, a soul that deliberately turns away from the Being, the Truth, and the Love which constitute the plenitude of his participated being, Truth and Love, is " out of joint," in pain, and suffers. It is matter that enslaves, because matter has a monotony about it — it always acts in a determined, routine and involuntary fashion. God, on the contrary, Who is Pure Spirit and Pure Act, is free from such determinations, and in becoming one with Him we enjoy the glorious liberty of the children of God.

There are, of course, many imperfections in the philosophical outlook on religion and one of these is the coldness of the obligation of service. But this is due to the fact that the outlook is purely philosophical, whereas religion is historical. *De facto,* there is not only the relation of *sovereignty* by which we are creatures; there is also the relation of *paternity* by which we are children, but this belongs to the supernatural order. According to reason and nature we are merely *creatures* of God, but according to grace and revelation we are *children.* God then is not merely Lord, but Father. The *creature* is simply a fabric of the skill of God, related to Him as the texture to the hand that weaves it, indebted to Him for its existence, but only a *thing* in the outfit of the world. But in the supernatural order, man is a *son* and partakes of the nature of God — *consortes divinæ naturæ* — and related to Him as a child whom the parents cannot hinder from being like themselves. Corresponding to these two titles of Sovereign and Father there are two corresponding orders of duty. (1) We pay our debt to the Sovereign Lord by an act of religion. (2) We render duties to our Father by sentiments of piety. Of the two the latter is more excellent. The service of God must not be a purely subjective and spiritual one, but must also be objective and liturgical. It is the whole man who is dependent on God, hence a service rendered by the soul which is interior, and a service by the body which is exterior.[39] The fallacy of a purely subjective worship

[39] Utruque debet applicari ad colendum Deum, ut scilicet anima colat interiori cultu, et corpus exteriori. 1–2 q. 101 art. 2; 2–2 q. 93 art. 3; 2–2 q. 81 art. 7.

of God is that it ignores the objectivity of man, the realness of his environment and the presence of his body. Man as a composite being of body and spirit stands at the confines of the world of pure matter and pure spirit, and his service of God must betray this double relationship.

The universe necessarily tends to the end for which it was created, but this finality never becomes articulate until man is reached. Rocks and rivers, planets and plants, flowers and forests, all are dependent for their being, their form, their end on God, and hence all are bound to Him by a threefold relation. The necessity of religion, then, is not merely a psychological one, namely an outlet for emotions or a symbol for the world's values. Its roots lie deeper than the surface scratchings of the human heart. Dependence is its root, and knowledge, love and service its stalk. Since not only man, but all creation is dependent on God,[40] it follows that things have need of religion in the broad sense of the term, namely, an acknowledgment of dependence. They do in their own mute way acknowledge their indebtedness to God by obeying the laws of nature, or instinct. But this is not enough. Smiling valleys won by a conqueror do not thrill him as much as a *Vive* in his honor. Speech is the supreme service, and dumb gaspings of irrational

[40] Deus sit finis rerum, non autem sicut aliquid constitutum, aut aliquid effectum a rebus, neque ita quod aliquid ei a rebus acquiratur, sed hoc solo modo quia ipse rebus acquiritur. C. G. lib. 3 c. 18 . . . Si igitur res omnes in Deum sicut in ultimum finem tendunt ut ipsius bonitatem consequantur, sequitur quod ultimus rerum finis sit Deo assimilari. C. G. lib. 3 c. 19.

creatures need the complement of an intellect. Man supplies the want, first of all because he combines within himself the existence of the chemical, the life of the plant and the consciousness of the animal, and secondly, because endowed with a spiritual soul he can assimilate the world spiritually by an act of knowledge. When man knows and loves and serves, all creation summed up in him knows and loves and serves. The dumb are given a tongue and the senseless a power of speech, for he who is the priest, pontiff and king of nature speaks, prays, and thanks in their name.

Man, therefore, has tremendous responsibilities, namely, the task of articulating the speechless dependence of all lower creation on the Creator. Failure in this task of sacramentalizing the universe is in a certain sense the failure of the universe. As the universe comes more and more under the domination of man, the realization of his religious obligations should become increasingly more clear. What are the marvelous inventions of our day and the apparent discovery of the key to great Nature's chest, but the secrets of God whispered to men? The more we get out of the universe the more thankful we should be. But the contrary seems to be the case. Intoxicated with success, and unmindful that the universe is a usufruct and not a pawn, man forgets the true Giver of good gifts and shouts out a conflict of religion and science. How could there be a conflict when God commanded man to be a scientist the day

He charged him to rule over the earth and sub-
due it?

In the supernatural order this duty of man to
worship God not only in his name, but in the name
of lower creation, becomes as clear and objective
as the stones on a road. It was not man alone,
but all creation that groaned for a Redeemer. But
if this be so, why not Pantheism instead of an Incarnation, in order that all creation and not man
alone might return to God? Because man is a
microcosmos, and physically and intellectually
sums up the universe; in becoming man, then, God
became all things by extension. It was through
man the universe became disordered and thistles
grew; it must be through man that the universe
must be reordered and grace abound. Notice how
well this is borne out in the words of the Word In-
carnate: "Preach the Gospel to every creature."
He did not say: "Preach the Gospel to every man,"
but "every creature," because every creature needs
to be readjusted to God, its ultimate end. Religion,
then, is something more than a "unified complex of
psychical values," or an "attitude of friendliness
to the universe." Religion, historically and philosophically, has always implied some dependence of
man on God, even to the point of sacrifice of what
man has or what man is. To go from religion to
God is to assert absolute independence of God, and
as unintelligible as to proceed from biology to life,
or physics to matter, or sociology to men. The science of biology cannot exist without life, but life
can exist with biology. The relation between man

and God, it has been pointed out, is that of a science to its object, namely, a relation of dependence. Religion without God is as meaningless as water without hydrogen and oxygen. Religion without God, Christianity without Christ — these are the vacuous non-entities which anemic thinking has foisted upon a non-thinking world. Man's relation to God is now considered in the same light as a man's attitude toward the League of Nations, whereas man's attitude toward certain scientific hypotheses is regarded in the same light as his attitude toward the multiplication table. We may empty religion of God, but we may not empty our cosmology of the quantum theory!

We have no need today of a new idea of God, any more than we need a new idea of a triangle. There is a limit to adaptiveness, especially when it reaches a point where entities are dissolved into environments. Ultimately there are only two possible adjustments: one is to adjust our lives to truth, the other is to adjust truth to our lives. " If we do not live as we think, we soon begin to think as we live." May it not be true that the desire for a new idea of God and religion is founded rather on a desire to accommodate these doctrines to the way men live, rather than by sound logic and right reason? If men want ghosts, they get ghosts; if men want to be Godless they are given "mental projection"; if men want to be irresponsible, they are made the " off-spring of the matrix Space-Time." Just suppose that men, in numerous moments of intellectual perversion, would so add two and two

as to make five. Would it be necessary to revamp
our mathematics and give to the world a "new idea
of the multiplication table," and ignore as antiquated the poor befogged individuals who still lived
in the Middle Ages of a two-and-two-makes-four
existence? To answer that a thing may be absurd
in the speculative order, but not in the concrete,
is not to escape the issue; for the concrete is absurd
only because the abstract was absurd before it. It
is not the sun which is to be adjusted to the lens of
the telescope, but the lens to the sun. After all,
a healthy philosophical examination of conscience
might reveal the astounding truth that the idea
of God needs no more toning up than the multiplication table, but that man stands in greater need
of God than children in need of sunshine. It has always been the great fault of man to see only the mote
in the eye of someone else, but never the beam in
his own. The day philosophy returns to its high
heritage as the science of Wisdom and not utility,
that day man will make a great discovery — he
will discover God and in finding Him will find
himself.[41]

[41] In conclusion, it is worth remembering that this is just a philosophical study; philosophy is a study while religion is a commerce.
Philosophy teaches us to contemplate God, while religion leads us to
Him. Philosophy must always fall short of answering all the problems
of religion, for religion is also an historical fact. Natural theology,
or better, Metaphysics, must always conclude humbly, i.e., with an
acknowledgment of its own insufficiency. This we do in the light of two
objections urged by many of our contemporaries. First of these is the
problem of evil. There is evil in this world, the unjust prosper and the
just suffer. How account for it? The second is the difficulty of God
the Creator being so remote from the world, and not in it more
intimately.

Really these two difficulties prove Christianity and the very answers

Sooner or later philosophy must return to its Father's house, which is Wisdom and Truth, and realize that as all fires mount to the sun, and all waters flow into the sea, so too all men must return to God, for Whom they were made and in Whom they find their rest, their peace, their perfection: their *rest,* for "Our hearts are disquieted until they rest in Thee, O Lord"; their *peace,* for peace is the tranquillity of order, and order is never tranquil unless man loves God; their *perfection:* for in Him is found the plentitude of the human heart's quest for Being, Truth and Love. A godless universe cannot exist for it cannot bear the sorrow of not knowing its Cause and its Author; nor can a Godless humanity exist for it cannot bear the burden of its own heart.

---

to them are the perfection of the philosophical outlook on religion. Original sin is the answer to the first difficulty, and the Incarnation the answer to the second. In the universe as constituted Christ is its order, its harmony and its end. As the universe would be irrational if it stopped with a rose, so it would be irrational if it stopped with man. "For without Him was made nothing that was made." In a future work, *Deo volente,* we hope to show how Christ is the perfection of the universe, and that as all things were made for man, so man for Christ and Christ for God.

INDEX

A

Abstraction, 200, 313–314;
 three degrees of, 235 ff.
Acts of religion, 342–356.
Aesthetics, 265–267.
Alexander, S., 14–19, 256–257, 285–286, 295.
Als-Ob, 184, 211–216.
Ames, E. S., 43, 55, 282.
Arminianism, 117.
Atheism, 288–290.
Aubrey, Edwin, 46.
Augustine, St., 342–343, 349–350.

B

Beauty, 265–267.
Being, 204 ff., 261, 321;
 relation between things and human intellect, 261–270;
 relation between man and God, 271 ff.
Belloc, Hilaire, 276.
Benedicite, 316.
Bergson, H., 294.
Berthelot, M., 14.
Bonaventure, St., 316.
Bosanquet, B., 44.
Boutroux, E., 229.
Brightman, E. S., 66–67, 301.
Bruhl-Levi, 139.

C

Carr, H. W., 4, 224.
Causality, 206;
 efficient, 331–332;
 formal, 333;
 final, 334.
Chesterton, G. K., 252.
Creation, 277 ff.
Croce, B., 39, 283.

D

Denifle, 103.
Descartes,
 origin of philosophy, 129–130;